Furthermore!

By Andrew M. Greeley from Tom Doherty Associates

All About Women
Angel Fire
Angel Light
A Christmas Wedding
Contract with an Angel
Faithful Attraction
The Final Planet
Furthermore! Memories of a Parish Priest
God Game
Irish Eyes
Irish Gold
Irish Lace
Irish Love★
Irish Mist
Irish Whiskey
A Midwinter's Tale
Sacred Visions (editor with Michael Cassutt)
Star Bright!
Summer at the Lake
White Smoke
Younger than Springtime

★Forthcoming

Furthermore!

Memories of a Parish Priest

ANDREW M. GREELEY

A TOM DOHERTY ASSOCIATES BOOK

NEW YORK

FURTHERMORE! MEMORIES OF A PARISH PRIEST

Copyright © 1999 by Andrew M. Greeley Enterprises, Ltd.

All rights reserved, including the right to reproduce this book, or portions thereof, in any form.

This book is printed on acid-free paper.

Book design by Diane Hobbing of Snap-Haus Graphics

A Forge Book
Published by Tom Doherty Associates, LLC
175 Fifth Avenue
New York, NY 10010

www.tor.com

Forge® is a registered trademark of Tom Doherty Associates, LLC.

Library of Congress Cataloging-in-Publication Data

Greeley, Andrew M.
    Furthermore! : memories of a parish priest / Andrew M. Greeley.
      p. cm.
    "A Tom Doherty Associates book."
    ISBN 0-312-86964-9 (hc)
    ISBN 0-312-87608-4 (pbk)
    1. Greeley, Andrew M. 2. Catholic Church—United States—Clergy
Biography. I. Title.
BX4705.G6185A3 1999
282'.092—dc21   99-38399
[B]   CIP

First Hardcover Edition: November 1999
First Trade Paperback Edition: December 2000

Printed in the United States of America

0 9 8 7 6 5 4 3 2 1

For two of my mentors in the priesthood,
Jack Egan and Bill Quinn, and one of my current
sociological mentors, Mike Hout.

Contents

I

What Has Gone Before[1]

[1]As they used to say in the Saturday afternoon serials in the movies when we were growing up.

Introduction

I began the penultimate revision of this second volume of my memoirs, an updating of *Confessions of a Parish Priest*, in the week I celebrated my seventieth birthday, a fitting time to review the trajectories of my life and to try to evaluate what I have done with the gift of life, the gift of faith, and the gift of priesthood. Life is a gift which demands gratitude, even if it ends totally at death, a gift which demands gratitude even if there is no giver. Life is a gift for which one is accountable, even if there is no accountant.

I believe in a Giver who is, of all things, not an Accountant, but a Lover; a Lover, as Robert Barron has recently observed, who is as caught in the need to love me just as a mother is caught in the need to love her child, a Lover who, according to Irish Dominican poet Paul Murray, would die of sadness if I should cease to exist.

So I revise this book of memories with the obligation of gratitude firmly in my mind. The book is not about who I am but about what has happened to me in my life, especially in the fifteen years since I published the first volume of memoirs. If you want to know who I am, then read my novels. Necessarily, as I shall point out later, a storyteller reveals himself intimately and personally in his stories. The seanachie is well aware that he is notably less than perfect and that his imperfect self will be disclosed in his stories, sometimes painfully. He understands that there is no choice but to do so for if he wants to tell his stories he has to run the risk of self-disclosure. She cares whether people will like her, but not so badly that she is willing to shut up. If her stories provide grist for the mills of those who already hate her, then she is troubled, but not so troubled as to remain silent.

I therefore commend my stories to those who want to know what I'm really like. This book is an account, much more reserved (because not in fictional form) than my stories, of what my seventy years has been like.

The other day I was making a call to my office in Chicago from a public phone in the Tucson Marriott in the shadow of the University of Arizona. We had just ended a meeting about a project to study the religion of Latino Americans in which the National Opinion Research

Center (God and benefactors willing) and scholars from UCLA (in Tucson also known as the Hated Bruins) will cooperate. Perhaps with the thought of my seventieth birthday at hand, I found myself asking what in the world I was doing here. What unexpected processes brought me from being a quiet and studious boy growing up during the Great Depression on the West Side of Chicago who wanted nothing more than to be a priest to the person I am today.

For a moment, as I walked out into the clear light of a Tucson afternoon, I felt just a bit disoriented. Yes, what was I doing at the University of Arizona, which would shortly press an honorary degree into my hands? What was I doing as a visiting professor at the University of Cologne? What was I doing as a senior fellow at University College Dublin? I didn't belong in any of these places, did I? What had happened to my life when all I wanted during the thirties and forties and the first half of the fifties was to be a parish priest in Chicago?

The disorientation passed and was replaced by surprise and wonder— and gratitude to Lady Wisdom who paid no attention to my own plans and waylaid me down the path of Her own plans.

The continuity in this strange and often crazy journey is priesthood. I always wanted to be a priest. My core identity is priest. I will always be a priest. I will, with the grace of God, never leave the priesthood. I will not go even if they try to throw me out, something which "they" have never tried to do and are most unlikely to try now.

I wanted only to be a parish priest as a boy in St. Angela parish in the 1930s. I will not give up that definition no matter how much some of my nastier colleagues rail against it. I still like parish work and I still do it on weekends. I still like teenagers, even though at my age in life that indicates either special gifts of nature and grace or weirdness. However, as a profile in the *New York Times Magazine* said many years ago, my parish is in my mailbox and more recently in my E-mail. The challenge for me is to explain how I made the journey from being a parish priest in the more traditional form to being the kind of parish priest I am now, and in particular the kind I have become in the last fifteen years since the publication of *Confessions of a Parish Priest*.

Sometimes I'm not altogether sure of that myself, as baffled as I was when the question surfaced in my mind in the Tucson Marriott.

I am, however, surprised, and pleasantly so. I do things that I did not imagine I would ever do, that I had no strong motivation (or so I thought) to do. I'm a priest who is a mix of storyteller, research scholar, university teacher, and journalist.

How good am I at these activities? It is not for me to judge. People whose opinions I value—readers, colleagues, students—seem to think that I do a good enough job at each of them. Others react with fury to any and all of my roles and all my work in whatever role and would destroy me if they could. Such anger baffles me. I don't quite understand why I'm worth such outrage. Perhaps if I knew myself better I would.

Before I began writing this book (at the suggestion of Monsignor Bill Quinn) I gritted my teeth and read (for the first time) its predecessor. I have never been able to read any of my books all the way through after they've been published. A few passages here and there perhaps but never a whole book. The passages seem all right or at least good enough, but I don't want to go on. I am especially reluctant to read my prayer journals (more about them later); after a page of one of them, I close the book with a loud bang.

Like a lot of other things about myself, I don't understand this reaction. It certainly does not result from shame or embarrassment over what I have written. Sometimes I think that I don't want to face the self-revelation of the person who wrote them, especially in the prayer journals and the novels. That the journals have been well reviewed doesn't enter into the calculation.

I feel about all my writing that it is bad enough that one reveals oneself in books, especially in novels or poems, without having to face the revelation oneself.

Sometimes when I pick up a novel and read a passage I am astonished that I wrote it and cannot recall the frame of imagination I was in when I produced those words. It is not that such a passage is badly written. I'm not ashamed of the passages at all (even the erotic ones, the extent of which is greatly exaggerated). They are always smoothly, sometimes imaginatively, and on occasion, beautifully written. I just don't want to read any more.

Odd. Maybe the reason is that I find it hard to identify myself with the writer, as if someone else wrote the words. I never particularly wanted to be a writer and now find it hard to identify as a writer, much less with my own writings. Perhaps that is the reason I write so easily.

So I especially did not want to read *Confessions of a Parish Priest*, even though the reviews were favorable (save naturally for those written by priests) and the book had earned out its advance (a rare enough phenomenon in the publishing industry). I most certainly did not want to identify with the self-portrait in the book. Yet if I were to follow Bill Quinn's suggestion, read it I must.

The book surprised me in a number of ways. It was better written than I had expected it to be, thanks largely to the wonderful editorial work of Patricia Solomon. It was an interesting portrait of the American Church and one of its priests during the years of turbulence that marked the second half of this bloody and chaotic century. The author, I thought, had covered his tracks well. No, that's not fair. He had rather been perhaps more candid than he should have been.

But I had a hard time seeing myself in that author. There seemed to be an enormous emotional difference between him and me.

The author was far more defensive than he needed to be. *Confessions* was written at the end of a very bad time in my life, a bad time that had begun with the death of Cardinal Meyer twenty years before, a time when I found myself pushed to the fringes of both the Church and the academic world. Moreover, my novels, astonishingly more successful than I had expected, had stirred up firestorms of criticism, mostly from those who had not read them or had read them with closed minds about what they would find. Anyone who was convinced in their heart of hearts that the stories were "steamy" before the fact would certainly find steam, even though the steam would turn out to be minimal.

I had felt for most of those two decades, especially after 1972, that I was under attack from all sides and that I had to answer the charges. I was right, I think, about the attacks, but wrong about the need to defend myself.

Moreover, I was hurting when I wrote the book, hurting perhaps more than I realized at the time. Many of the things which were being said about me were untrue; some of them in fact were deliberate lies. Anyone who is constantly under such assault is bound to be hurt, especially at first when he strains for understanding. The notion that one ought to be utterly indifferent to such assaults is naive (perhaps deliberately) about the nature of human nature.

I will not claim fifteen years later that I am immune to the pain of attack or from the propensity to react defensively. But I take the attacks much less seriously than I used to because I can now see them in context, which I was less able to do even ten years ago. Pain and defensiveness do not crowd my worldview anymore. I can still become angry when someone tells a bare-faced lie about me, but the anger goes away because I have learned that these assaults are not typical and should not be taken seriously.

I understand that to be on the margins of the academic world and on the margins of the Church is a grace, a blessing, great good fortune. The "stranger" who is not constrained by rigid structures may be a wonderful inkblot for the sick or the troubled. He is also blessed with freedom. I understand that those who like my work far outnumber those who don't like it, that I have more friends than enemies, and that support is everywhere.

All of these things were true fifteen years ago and I might well have expressed them verbally then. But I wouldn't have known in those dark days how important they were and how they should have shaped my worldview and my perception of my own identity. I don't claim a complete transformation, but I do claim a change which has notably altered the structure of my perceptions during the last decade.

Grace. Pure grace.

My friend (and publisher) Irving Louis Horowitz, who has produced a powerful autobiographical fragment about the early years of his life, remarked to me that it takes a great deal of narcissism to write a memoir because the work presumes that people will want to know more about you and there is no reason to think that's true of many people. Moreover, he added, you won't tell the whole truth in your story. You will tell the truth as you see it perhaps, but that is another matter.

Fair point, Irving. Still the need to tell one's story in one's own way comes, it would seem, from the nature of human nature. So I tell it again (with an emphasis on the last fifteen years) with what I hope is a somewhat (modestly, moderately) changed perspective. I write as an attempt to understand my life (thus far) and myself. If this exercise is useful to anyone in their search for understanding or if they find it interesting, fine. If not, well, they're under no obligation to read it, are they?

As I strive for a focus in this book of retractions, I realize that I have spent half my life in what historian Stephen Avila has called the "Confident Catholic Church" (the untroubled American Catholicism of the 1950s and before the Second Vatican Council) and half my life in what I call the "Confusing Catholic Church." The Second Vatican Council met at the midpoint of my life, as presently calculated. I am one of a diminishing number of Catholic clergy who remember what it was like to be a priest (for ten years) before the council and have lived through the thirty-five years after it. I grew up on the West Side of Chicago during the Great Depression and the World War II. I went off to the major seminary at the beginning of the postwar world, and spent ten years as a parish priest in one of the first college-educated Catholic parishes in Chicago. After six of those years Cardinal Meyer sent me to the University of Chicago to obtain a doctorate in sociology so I could serve the Archdiocese as a research sociologist, a role I've never played. Then, just before he died, he assigned me to full-time work as a scholar and a writer—with parish work on weekends (work I never want to give up).

The "Confident" Church was the Church of the first two decades after the end of the war. Mass attendance and vocation rates were at an all-time high. New parishes and new primary and secondary schools were popping up in new suburbs. Traditional (St. Vincent de Paul Society) and new (Cana, CFM) Catholic organizations were flourishing. Catholic social service groups, hospitals, and universities were flourishing. Catholics either had large families or stopped receiving Communion. Young Catholics struggled, with considerable success, to sustain premarital chastity. Catholics contributed 2.2 percent of their income to the Church, about the same proportion as did other Americans. They were proud to have their sons and daughters become priests and nuns. Catholic divorce rates were low. No one would have dreamed of questioning (out loud) the teachings of the pope, the cardinal, or the pastor (unless race was the issue). It was unthinkable that a priest would want to leave the priesthood. The Church was, in other words, efficient, strong, and, well, confident.

Then in a very few years the whole house of cards collapsed—it must have been a house of cards to have collapsed so quickly. Priests and nuns have left their ministry and married, often to each other. Vocations to the priesthood and the religious life have dried up. Church attendance has declined sharply. Contributions have declined even more. Young Catholics live together before marriage and still receive the Eucharist. Catholics defy the teachings of the Church on birth control. Untrained lay staff introduce new tyrannies into many parishes. Traditional devotions have been abandoned. Gregorian chant has disappeared. Theologians boldly disagree with the teaching authority of the Church. No one seems to believe in mortal sin anymore. Priests do crazy things, like the one who tore a rosary apart and threw it to the floor in front of a pulpit and announced, "You don't have to say that anymore." (As if people ever had to say it!) The Church, it seems, is falling apart.

For reasons that I will outline later in this book, I think the Confusing Church is much better than the Confident Church.

For the last thirty-five years I have engaged in three tasks which are about the two Churches from my perspective as one who stands with a foot, so to speak, in each of them: as a sociologist I have done research on the changes from the Confident Church to the Confusing Church and reported these changes. As a journalist I have commented forcefully, if truth be told, and at some length on the changes. I have written novels to illuminate the continuities between the two Churches.

Clearly, any one of the three main tasks enumerated above—sociology, commentary, storytelling—is enough to get someone into considerable trouble. All three of them are enough to lead people to condemn one, perhaps correctly, as a public nuisance.

My position as a public nuisance becomes clear when I note that in my exercise of these three vocations (which no one forced upon me) I have reported the following: the Catholic laity (nine out of ten), supported by their lower clergy, now deny the right of Church authorities to regulate their sexual lives. Much of the loss in the transition from Confident to Confusing Catholicism is not the result of the Vatican Council but of the birth control encyclical of 1968. Despite the present confusion, the defection rate among non-Latino Catholics has not changed in this century (11 percent of those who were raised Catholic are no longer Catholic). However, the defection rate of Latino Catholics is over 25 percent and no one seems to be doing anything about it. Most men who leave the priesthood do so not because they want to marry but because they don't like the work. For those who are happy being priests, celibacy is a difficult but not insupportable burden. Two-thirds of the priests in a recent study say that the priesthood is *better* than they expected it would be. Catholic schools are a superb educational bargain and an important capital investment for the Church. There is virtually no decline in belief by Catholics in the major tenets of their faith. Their problems with the leadership are almost entirely in the areas of sex, gender, and authority. The most destructive of the changes from the Confident Church to the Confusing Church are the results of these three dimensions of Catholic teaching and attitude (which for conservative Catholics and for many leaders, up to and including the pope, seem to be the only ones that matter). Catholic laity in six nations by overwhelming numbers want more democratic Church structures (election of bishops, more power to the local churches) and the ordination of married men and women. Moreover, the United States is not the most radical country on these issues. Ireland and Spain are tied for first place on the radicalism scale, Germany is third, and the United States is fourth. Conservative Catholics are no more than 5 percent of the Catholic population.

Obviously someone who reports these findings, even with high quality data to back them up, is in deep trouble, not only with the Catholic right (*The Wanderer, Crisis*) but, surprisingly, also with the Catholic left (*National Catholic Reporter, Commonweal, America*). Who does he think he is?

Sometimes I wonder myself.

To make matters worse, I have engaged in two crusades: one against the destruction of the Chicago Archdiocese by Cardinal Cody, who was what the clinicians call a "borderline personality," and the other against the Church's long-time cover-up of the abuses of children by pedophile priests.

Dermot Coyne in the Nuala Anne stories has dialogues with an "Adversary," a part of himself who is highly critical of what he says and does. I have an Adversary too. He will turn up occasionally in this book.

Adversary: Why get into such fights, into which, again, no one invited you?

Good question.

Adversary: Why don't you just shut up?

Good question.

Adversary: Why don't you just go away and stop being a public nuisance?

Wonderful question!

Adversary: All right, just don't blame me for all the trouble you get into.

To compound the effrontery, in some of my novels there are priests who are less than perfect and in all of them erotic love is portrayed as a sacrament of the love between God and us. It would be bad enough to write such novels if no one read them, but alas, lots of people do.

To establish that this peculiar personality trait (character defect, perhaps) is not limited to my relations with the Church. I have done similar things in my university role. I have engaged in a long-run battle with most of the sociological profession on the issue of "secularization"—the alleged decline of religion. I have tried to outline a new theory of religion as story before it's anything else and after it's everything else. I have studied the incidence, prevalence, and correlates of mystical and psychic experience (though not their metaphysical reality which is a question beyond sociology). I was the first one to report on the religious revival in Russia. I have argued that Catholic schools are more successful in dealing with minority children than public schools. I have insisted that European ethnic background is still an important predictor of attitudes and behavior in our society.

Adversary: Didn't you have enough trouble with the Church? Why did you have to take on the sociological profession too?

Excellent question.

A woman whom I've known since she was a teenager in my first year in parish work, at whose marriage I officiated, and whose children I baptized broke off her friendship with me because of the novels in particular but more generally because I was always making trouble. She was tired of having to defend me, she said. Why don't you just stop all these foolish things and enjoy life as you are entitled to?

Adversary: Brilliant question! Now, how did you answer it?

How did I answer it?

Adversary: My very question.

The way I usually answer when people tell me how much they have to defend me: Don't!

Adversary: Not a very good answer, huh?

I do miss her, however.

Do I enjoy stirring up trouble? No, not really. Then why do I do it? I don't do it deliberately. I am always surprised when the trouble comes. Consider my novels for example. I began to write them because I thought that popular fiction might play a role in our times like stained-glass windows did in the Middle Ages. I expected neither the uproar nor the success which greeted the novels. I wasn't trying to be a gadfly (a word I despise) or to create controversy. Naively, and with almost simpleminded innocence, I thought it would be obvious they were all stories about God's love—as tens of thousands of readers perceive them. I was utterly surprised by the fury they stirred up. I still am.

Adversary: You were a friggin' eejid if you believed that shite!

Yeah, but I did.

Adversary: Don't you have a character problem that drives you into such ventures?

Perhaps. At a minimum, there is something a bit unusual about me.

Adversary: To put it mildly.

That observation comes only with the wisdom of hindsight. Naïf that I was (and, much to be feared, still am) I never thought that the combination of these three activities would make me unpopular with many on both the right and the left of American Catholicism. Nonetheless, as I look back on my childhood and young adulthood, I can see a pattern of engaging, with almost complete innocence, in similar follies. I always knew the answers in grammar school, leading my classmates to describe me as a "walking encyclopedia." In high school I would, for example, turn in a history exam of a hundred questions after nine minutes. In graduate school I would give the professor a term paper in the third week of the quarter and pass my comprehensives after six months on the campus. As a staff member at the National Opinion Research Center it was bad enough in the judgment of many in the university community that I was a practicing Catholic priest. To make matters worse, I would publish articles in the *New York Times Magazine*, in which most faculty members would have given their eyeteeth to appear. As a novelist I've had ten books on the *Times* best-seller list.

Too much, as the Irish would say, altogether.

Adversary: So you're surprised that a lot of people don't like you and that you're a marginal man both in the University and the Archdiocese? You gotta be kidding!

In retrospect I ought not be surprised, but I am.

I am not apologizing for any of these activities or any combination thereof, but I do find myself wondering whatever possessed me to try them all. Moreover, whatever possessed me to think that there were no costs in these disparate projects? As one of my colleagues at the National Opinion Research Center remarked to me, "You like to do things with flair, but you don't like the reactions your flair stirs up."

Fair enough.

I guess.

Though it escapes me why flair, such as it may be, upsets people.

Adversary: Sure, that's a dumb thing to say!

Priests claim that I have never had an unpublished thought. Now, after my novels, they claim that I never had an unpublished dirty thought. They also ask me why I didn't concentrate my energies on doing one thing "really well." They also piously tell me that it is a shame that I have discredited my sociology by writing fiction. It doesn't help much when I say that I think I do my four major tasks (weekend parish work being the fourth) better than most people.

That answer merely restates the problem, doesn't it? Maybe as the late University of Chicago sociologist Morris Janowitz (with whom I was reconciled before his death) remarked that I was nothing more than a loudmouth Irish priest. Write "smart-ass" before "loudmouth" if you want.

From the perspective of seventy years, how do I judge these madcap adventures?

To my surprise I think maybe the battle against "secularization" is being won at least within the sub-profession of the sociology of religion—with the help of such brilliant allies as Mike Hout, Rod Stark, Roger Finke, Larry Iannaccone, Philip Gorski, Wolfgang Jagozinski, and Jose Casanova. The rest of the sociological profession, however, is not persuaded. Nor are the Washington bureaucrats who fund research. What difference could religion possibly make in adolescent behavior regarding sex, drugs, and alcohol? Right? Perhaps the battle over Catholic schools is closer to being won than it has been in the last thirty years, though perhaps it would have been won anyhow. Most everyone admits that Paul VI's birth control encyclical was counterproductive.

Adversary: You win some and you lose some and sometimes by losing you win, right?

The rest? Failures, I'm afraid. The worst may be the pedophile mess. Most priests and most bishops simply don't get it. The latter now at least want to avoid shelling out tens of millions of dollars for the settlement of suits. Very few really seem to know—or care—about the suffering of the victims and their families. Whoever told me that their suffering was my problem?

Why did I bother with these other ventures? To repeat myself perhaps,

I really don't know. Would I do them all again, even if I knew the outcomes? Oh, yes, as Blackie Ryan would say.

Adversary: God help you if you don't say that. And anyway, whoever appointed you to monitor and comment on the change from the Confident Church to the Confusing Church?

Patently no one. Why should I then be surprised when no one seems to listen?

Adversary: More of your shite. You know very well that a lot of people listen, that's why you are always in trouble.

A couple of years ago I analyzed data from two new studies of the American priesthood. In a report in the Jesuit magazine *America*, I observed that most priests were very happy in their work. You'd think priests would applaud the finding, wouldn't you? The next newsletter of the Association of Chicago Priests (which harasses me whenever it can) presented twelve articles by priests attacking me for the report. One even insisted that his personal experiences were as valid as my data.

For his personal life, sure. As an accurate reflection of the American priesthood, hardly.

Offended? No. I'm used to such reactions. Disappointed? Sure! But so what else is new?

Adversary: You're mistaken altogether if you think that the priests in Chicago are going to accept you. But weren't you knowing that when you first set a word on paper.

The question remains, however: Why have I engaged in all these behaviors which were losers from day one? Why do I say that I would do them all again? What's wrong with me? Some of my friends compare me with Don Quixote. Maybe I do tilt with windmills. But why?

The best answer I can come up with is that I might joust with windmills in an imitation (perhaps misguided) of my father's integrity, at least as I perceived it. It is too late to stop, of course. Not that I would even if it were not too late.

Adversary: Your old fella was quite a fella. You could do worse than imitate him.

What about the novels? Were those failures?

Oh, no, as Blackie would not say. They have been enormous successes, not because millions of people have read them but because they have strengthened the faith and hope and love of the tens of thousands of people who have written to me. They are the most priestly thing I have ever done.

So on with the story. You make sense of it, gentle reader, if you can.

Adversary: I'll be around, gentle reader, to make sure he doesn't get away with anything!

Reunions

The St. Angela neighborhood looked crisp and clean under the spotless blue sky and golden warm autumn sunlight. It seemed not to have changed, save for the big white stone Gothic church and the sculptured lawn, both of which appeared only twelve years after our graduation. If the old gravel playing fields (which wreaked havoc on the young knees of the parish children) had still been there, it would have been easy to convince us that the year was 1942 instead of 1992. We hesitated in front of the church, not sure that we would recognize anyone or be recognized. Then the smiles and laughter began and we knew everyone and it was 1942 and we had just graduated from grammar school.

We were older of course and so was the neighborhood, but, it seemed, not that much older. The community was still made up of respectable, hardworking middle-class men and women who keep their yards clean and their window frames painted. Kids still played on the sidewalk. Teenagers ambled down the streets in Sunday clothes. The skin pigmentation was different but on that Sunday it didn't seem to make any difference.

Priests that we were, Larry McNamara (bishop of Grand Island, Nebraska, now) and I immediately began to work the crowd. What else do priests do when they face a crowd in back of a church, even if they haven't seen some of the faces in five decades?

From that moment on the day was magic, sacramental as I would later say. We drifted into the church. I might have shouted one of my favorite lines, "OK, let's do Mass and get it over with!" Larry said the Mass and preached (told a story) and later at the dinner I told a story. We toured the school which was as cheerful and as pin-neat as it had been a half century ago. Then, in the still glowing sunlight, we adjourned to the Carlton Hotel in Oak Park (a favorite haunt of many in years gone by, but not of this seminarian) for drinks and dinner and conversation. Rita Murphy and Marilyn James, the organizers of the event (at the instigation of a certain priest who figured women are much better at these things than men—and at most everything else as far as that goes), had calculated nicely how much we could afford to pay (not everyone had been successful in fifty years) and still have a good meal. The latter, efficient and charming banker that she is, kept careful and precise records and would not let us exceed our budget. The food was delicious and the conversation was brilliant. Laughter filled the room all the time. Every moment was precious. We wanted the day to go on forever. We were all sad when it was time to go. For a few hours on a beautiful autumn Sunday we had been young again.

Class reunions, dubiously organized and diffidently attended, are often like that, though, alas, not always. Proudly we claimed that our golden jubilee was the best ever. It didn't matter whether it was or not. Sufficient that we thought it was and would always think so.

As I reflected the next day on this astonishing Sunday afternoon, both delightful and deeply moving, I came to understand that it was a sacrament, a hint, a mystery, a promise, a sign. If we could recapture our youth, however briefly, then it was not gone completely and could perhaps be recaptured again and permanently in the world to come. No one, except this specialist in reflection, would think that explicitly (at least as far as I know); but the nice thing about sacraments of grace is that you don't have to reflect consciously on them to be influenced by them. The Spirit (Lady Wisdom, Whoever) lurked there with us during that reunion, doubtless enjoying it as much as we did, just as She had enjoyed the graduation a half century before and enjoys all human joy.

We had all aged, some more gracefully than others. Yet we were almost all recognizable and some seemed not to have changed at all. Some of the women were attractive and a few very attractive indeed. (One of the graceful things about growing older is that you realize how many different kinds of good looks there are in the other gender!) Most of us seemed to have done pretty well with our lives, some of us very well, all of us much better than we had expected a half century before as the gloom of the Great Depression had changed into the horror of war. Pearl Harbor, Bataan, Wake Island, and Corregidor were names from the last six months of our lives. If the war went on for many years most of the boys would have to fight in it and most of the girls would have to pray for us. And after the war . . . what then? Depression kids that we were, our expectations were limited. Never in our wildest dreams could we have expected a half century of prosperity—and by the standards of the Great Depression even recessions are times of prosperity. For us, life, no matter how many heartaches and pain, would be filled with surprises. Many of us, like me, sat in the church during our golden jubilee Eucharist and shook our heads in astonishment. We were virtually the last of the Depression generation. We would never be able to explain to our children, our nieces and nephews, and to their children how grim, how chill, how, well, depressing those years were. Or the excitement when we discovered a decade after our graduation that the Great Depression had not and probably would not return.[2] Then our expectations exploded and we never looked back—save in our nightmares and our times of trouble and doubt.

We are the last to stride the gap between two totally different times in our nation's experiences—depression and prosperity (as we would have called it). Growing up in the Great Depression was not a good experience, but to emerge from it into a world of surprise was a wonderful experience indeed. Somehow—and through no particular merit of our own—we had made it. And "it" was almost incomprehensibly better than we thought possible. I wonder if, on the average, those who came after us could have found their lives so surprising.

We all had experienced both Churches, the Confident one and the Confusing one. My classmates seemed quite untroubled by the change. Like me, they liked the new Church better than the old. For all the angst in the Church as institution, for all the conflict between Rome and the theologians, for all the defections and unease among the clergy and the religious, my generation of laity was not at all confused.

Mixed in, then, with the joys of recaptured youth on our golden anniversary was bewilderment at the unexpected trajectories of our lives. Today, there cannot be neighborhoods like St. Angela was in the 1930s and 1940s, if only because the universality of auto ownership has broadened the horizons of those over sixteen beyond anything we could imagine in the middle 1940s. Ridgeland Avenue, Central Avenue, North Avenue, and Chicago Avenue—these were our boundaries. Except for a few tentative explorations beyond these boundaries and an occasional El ride to the Loop, the neighborhood was our world. Young men and women still courted by "walking out" as the Irish would say. On serious dates they would ride public transportation to distant theaters like the Marlboro (a classic movie palace of the art deco era) at Madison and Crawford (Pulaski Road to those who weren't Irish). Usually we would go to the Ambassador at Division Street and Monitor Avenue where,

[2]The attempts to re-create its atmosphere in various books and miniseries never seem able to capture the restraints it put on our hopes, our expectations, our ambitions. The people that try to describe it simply weren't there when the national unemployment rate was over 25 percent and there were no jobs for young men and women coming out of college, none at all. Since there has never been a time like that in the ensuing half century, there is nothing to which it can be compared in the experience of those who were born after 1935. Comparisons of the various blips in the economy to the "hard times" of the 1930s are simply absurd.

for twenty-five cents, we could watch three films, a newsreel, a cartoon and endless previews and receive free dishes to boot.[3]

By the time my classmates had graduated from high school in 1946, all this was already fading away. If we are the last to remember what it was like to grow up in the Depression, so we are the last to remember what neighborhoods were like when most people did not have cars. It was not a bad life. We did not feel unfairly constrained because we were unaware that there might be other possibilities. Indeed, despite the Depression, we knew that we were living better than our grandparents had and infinitely better than had our great-grandparents in the Old Country. I'm probably the only one from St. Angela, '42, to lament the passing of such communities which in many ways had more in common with the villages from which our ancestors had come than with the neighborhoods of today. I'm certainly the only one in the class to write novels about that kind of neighborhood;[4] and while I lament their passing (and sometimes grow angry at my fellow priests who babble about community and don't see the possibility of community within their own parishes), I would not want to return to them. The more freedom of choice humans enjoy the better, even if freedom often means loneliness and alienation.

I joke that the wisdom of the ancient Arab proverb that a man should choose his wife and his horse from the tent across the road was abrogated by the custom of sending kids away to college (and thus creating the jams at O'Hare at Thanksgiving and Christmas). Kids these days even marry spouses from Boston and New York and Minneapolis and Macon, Georgia! Yet these couples in exogamous marriages seem eventually to settle down in neighborhoods which, while not as constrained as was St. Angela, nonetheless exist because of a hunger for a "place" to which to belong and for the support that such places offer. I am angry at those theologians who don't seem to realize that this American experience of creating and re-creating and then re-creating yet again the peasant communes of Europe is worthy of serious reflection because it tells us much about the nature of human nature (and confirms some of the basic tenets of Catholic social philosophy).

So in October of 1992 we celebrated our recovered youth and the

---

[3]The theater later acquired the name "Rockne" and then, in an almost sacrilegious abuse of the legend of the Notre Dame coach, became a skin-flick house, and then, in a marvelous manifestation of divine humor, a Black Baptist church!

[4]Two of my novels, *A Midwinter's Tale* and *Younger than Springtime*, explicitly try to re-create that era.

surprises of our lives and our memories of growing up in a neighborhood which by present standards was extraordinarily supportive (and constraining) even if it did not seem so unusual to us then.

I was impressed at the reunion and in the recovered friendships that I described in *Confessions* and by how well my classmates had survived both as Americans and as Catholics. I don't mean merely that some of the women were still disturbingly attractive. Rather, many of the class of '42 had made the transition from depression to prosperity and from the Counter-Reformation to the Ecumenical Age with graceful ease. They knew who they were and where they came from and neither an elegant suburban home nor Mass in English shook them. They surely enjoyed the suburban home and also enjoyed the new Church (and deplored the present pope's attempts to restore the old one). Their faith had not been weakened by either (often modest and sometimes substantial) affluence or a Church in turmoil. Quite the contrary, both developments seemed to have strengthened their religious commitments, as had their responses to life's troubles and tragedies. On the average their faith meant more to them now rather than less.

I often reflect that they have survived the twin changes, from depression to prosperity and from Counter-Reformation to Ecumenical Age, better than have many priests of our generation. They seem happier and more alive and more Catholic than do many of my clerical contemporaries. My suspicion is that religious experience is more frequent and more meaningful for lay Catholics than it is for many clerical Catholics. In today's Church the clergy ought to look to the laity for spiritual inspiration instead of vice versa.

One night at a mini-reunion dinner some of them began to tell horror stories about their experiences with priests, mostly on the subject of sex—like that of a young mother with a new baby living in a strange city, asking a priest for permission to practice rhythm, a permission for which she did not have to ask and perhaps should not have asked.[5] He excoriated her lack of generosity and gave her permission for three months, "but no more!"

What a fool! Small wonder that the Church has lost its credibility on sex, especially on married sex.

Why did you stay in the Church? I finally asked them.

"It's our Church," one of them replied. "As much as it is theirs. Why should we let them force us out?"

So they stayed in the Church and grew in faith and are happy in their

---

[5]But it was 1953.

religion not because of priests but despite them. Try as we might we have not been able to drive the laity out.

What did I discover about myself at our golden reunion and from the old friends who have become new friends?

At the reunion and at our mini-reunions each year, I play almost automatically the part of the grinning, genial leprechaun, oozing (mostly authentic) Gaelic charm, a mask that has become an ineradicable part of my identity and reveals much more than it hides. (Every public presentation of the self—any self—hides something.) At the October 1992 event I wondered if my classmates from fifty years ago would be astonished by a persona that they had never seen when we were kids (though the leprechaun was always lurking). If they were surprised, they didn't let on. Rather, they told me how much they liked my novels about the old days and the old neighborhood. Hey, when the people you went to school with read your stories and like them, you can't be all bad, can you?

But later some admitted that they were surprised and delighted.

One woman (still totally gorgeous and married to a man with a Phi Beta Kappa key) said, "We thought of you as a cute little boy with beautiful blue eyes who was very smart, very quiet, and was going to be a priest."

It was a view of myself I did not have in those days. I would have rather said that I was a shy outcast. Two sides of the same coin maybe and the first side burnished gently by time. And *cute!* Granted that word has multiple meanings when spoken by a woman, but I would not have thought that any of the meanings applied to me. God may have been wise. If I had known that, I might have stopped being shy and then what?

Well, then I'd still be a priest and maybe with more confidence and more joyous memories.

And another (equally lovely) one said, "I knew you liked me and I kind of liked you. Well, maybe liked you a lot. But you were going to be a priest and I wasn't going to tell you how much I liked you."

Yeah.

I still would have been a priest and my shyness would still have melted into Celtic charm (a much more pleasant and revealing mask behind which to hide). Yet my life would have been perhaps marginally different. And better.

It dawned on me that I had misread the data from my grammar school years. I grant that time had modified their images of me and that they perhaps didn't recollect them precisely as they were, but I had still completely misread the evidence. My classmates had genuinely liked me and I didn't think they had. They liked me as much as I had liked them. Such a misunderstanding was no great tragedy for them or for me. But it was a lesson that I did not (and probably still do not) see myself as others see me and that their view of the matter is often much more benign than my own. I have not quite absorbed this insight yet and probably never will. But unlike most people, I was given the grace of discovering it while I was still alive and thus modifying my life accordingly. It is unfortunate to be unloved. But it is also a loss to be loved and not realize it. Finally it is a great blessing to realize that you were loved while it's not too late to do anything about it.

Perhaps it is that way with God. She may love us more than we realize, more than we feel we deserve, and more, we might think, than She ought to love us.

So the rediscovery of my friends from the past has been a rich experience, a disconcerting, disturbing, and unsettling experience. It has forced me to pause to realize that I have not known very well who I really am. I don't know quite yet what to do about this discovery, but it is certainly changing the direction of my spiritual growth and of my life.

If you don't think people like you and then discover that they do, you'd damn well better change your life—and thank God for the insight.

And maybe be less defensive—and also perhaps less offensive!

The second reunion was the all-alumni reunion at Christ the King in the autumn of 1994, an even more magical event, if that were possible.

I must have been reluctant to attend (I was about to leave on a trip to Ireland for work on the International Social Survey Program) because I had convinced myself that the Mass was at 5:30. Luckily I left my apartment early so I would have plenty of time in case the Saturday afternoon traffic was worse than I thought it would be. When I parked at 4:55 next to where the basketball courts used to be, the parking lots around the CK were already filled. I wandered into church at 4:57 for the Mass which was in fact scheduled for 5:00.

"I thought you weren't coming," Pat Dowd Coffee exclaimed as she hugged me.

"I said I'd be here," I replied, still not getting it.

I got it only when, vestments donned, we swept out of the sacristy at 5:02.

Well, some mistakes are not Freudian.

There were fourteen hundred people jammed into the church, and the building, now forty years old but so modern as to seem almost brandnew, was saturated by strong emotions—nostalgia, happiness, surprise, delight. Only at wedding Masses (and by no means all of them) have I encountered such a palpable curtain of joy—and usually with a lot less than fourteen hundred people crammed into the church. In the old days we all knew, even the kids, that CK was a special parish. Our gratitude to the school and the neighborhood was always strong. However, when all the gratitude and all the powerful memories were jammed together at one time with so many people, the chemistry and the electricity in the building was breathtaking.

We had created what the French sociologist Émile Durkheim had called "effervescence" in a collective ritual ("representation collective"), an energy which seemed to have coalesced apart from us and to have a life of its own. The effervescence continued for the next several hours, at least until, overwhelmed by emotion, I finally had to leave.

As I explained in *Confession*, my ten years in CK, my first assignment, were an enormously important formative experience in my life. St. Angela and CK together shaped much of what I am. The latter is still *my* neighborhood even though I now say Mass there only one weekend a month. I would return tomorrow if I could. And in my dreams I often do, dreams from which I awake convinced that they were real. It has become the site of many of my novels, a place to be admired and celebrated so much that it has become a character in the stories (especially in *Lord of the Dance, St. Valentine's Night*, and *Fall from Grace*). It is the home of the Ryan clan who infest many of the novels. Indeed, at the reunion Mass I imagined the good bishop sitting in the sanctuary and beaming as his eyes blinked rapidly behind this thick, rimless glasses and muttering over and over to himself, "Remarkable!"

Yet I had always imagined that my work there was a failure. For all the energy and effort I put into it (with the heedless zeal of the newly ordained), I had few results to show for it. Most of my projects had not worked; most of the young people to whom I tried to offer possibilities of a richer and more generous life had rejected my message, eventually with hatred in their voices. The older people in the parish hardly knew me because the pastor had effectively barred interaction between his young priests and them: we could not visit them, we could not stand in back of the church after Mass to talk to them, we could not even preach at the last two Masses which more than half of them attended. But, it seemed, that not knowing me, they still disliked me. Some were offended because I didn't show proper gratitude at being accepted by people whose social station was above my own (it wasn't). Others thought I was a "radical," though they would have been hard put to say in what respect. Some resented the fact that a priest with the oils of Ordination scarcely dry on his hands would give such smooth (glib, I would say) and "intellectual" sermons. How come he knows so much? Still others were convinced that I was trying to accomplish racial integration in the parish,[6] mostly because I would on occasion read at Mass passages from *The New York Times* which described the depraved character of a certain minority group. Only after I read the passage would I tell them that the article was from the 1850s and the minority group was Irish.[7] Finally, many of them resented the fact that I had written books, though they had of course not read them. They were convinced that the books were about them (which they were more or less) and that they were unfavorable (which they certainly were not),[8] though in fact they were about the religious possibilities of the (then) emergent college-educated Catholic professional class. Later some of them denounced me to Cardinal Cody when I bought my summer house at Grand Beach on the grounds that I was going to use it as an interracial retreat house. (Hadn't busloads of blacks poured into the house?)

When I left the parish, I figured that just about everyone except some of the teenagers were delighted to see me go.

As it turned out, I couldn't have been more wrong. It was not that the complainers in the penultimate paragraph did not exist. They surely did. And they made a lot of noise. But they were only small minorities. Most of the people in the parish were as sad to see me leave as I was to leave. As the years went on and I would encounter them in many different places and they would praise my ten years at CK, I began to believe that they represented the authentic reaction of most of the people in the parish. I wondered why they had not said so when I was still there.[9] I

----

[6]Beverly, the neighborhood in which CK is located, is now integrated and for the most part stably integrated. I deserve none of the credit for this, nor do any of the community organizations with which I worked. Neither do any of the pastors who tried to placate the local racists, who were only a minority of the parish. All of the credit must go to the late Mayor Daley ("Da Mare," as opposed to his son "Rich," who spent some of his time as a teenager hanging around CK). Da Mare insisted that if you worked for the great city of Chicago, you had to live in the great city of Chicago, effectively stopping white flight from the southwest corner of the city. He fought it all the way to the Supreme Court and won.

[7]Judge Tom Donovan, God be good to him, was sitting in the first row one of the times I pulled that trick. He laughed through the rest of the Mass. But a lot of people didn't. Neither, as far as that goes, did the monsignor.

[8]Just as G. K. Chesterton's book *Orthodoxy* was banned in tsarist Russia because it was thought to be about the Orthodox Church and was certainly unfavorable to it. Why else write about the Church unless to attack it?

[9]One learns after a few years of controversy that one's friends are more likely to be silent than one's enemies.

had come to realize that my earlier evaluation of my CK years was mistaken. However, I had not realized just how much love there had been—and still was—till the day of the all-alumni reunion.

Absence indeed makes the heart grow fonder. Nostalgia does indeed coat our memories of the past with a gilded patina. We tend to forget the bad times and remember the good. I'm sure the crowd at the all-alumni reunion was looking at me and their memories of me through rose-colored glasses. Moreover, many of the priests who succeeded Jack Hotchkin and me were dolts; one could not help but look good in comparison with them. Even allowing for that, however, I wondered if they thought I was someone else. The procession down the aisle at the beginning of Mass was like the triumphant return of a hero—people waving at me, shaking hands, hugging me, and broad smiles everywhere. I had a hard time for the first few minutes of the Eucharist fighting back tears. At homily time I told two brief stories about characters from homilies in the old days—Lemuel X. Quicksilver, an anthropologist from Mars who parked his flying saucer next to my window and discussed Beverly people with me, and Maximilian the Mad Monk who lived in (the now defunct) bell tower and played the Angelus every day. Both had been banned by the monsignor on the complaint of a single adult—though I resisted the temptation to say that. Then I told my "St. Brigid goes to heaven and hell" story which was rewarded with a tremendous ovation. My emotions were just barely under control for the rest of the Eucharist.

The commentator was my old nemesis Phil Doran, one of the best teens I ever knew. We had developed a "Philly-Greels" act which went very well because we both love to argue, usually in fun, occasionally for real. On the latter occasions, Phil was sometimes right. So at the end of the Mass we did the routine again as Phil awarded me a diploma from CK grammar school, *honors causa*, so I could legitimately attend the party afterward. I thought the rules required that I have the last word in the exchange—I *always* had the last word in the old days. But this time I thought better of it and shut up.

One of the results of this reunion was that I began to say Mass again at CK on one Sunday a month. It was always an exciting Sunday morning for me. Presiding at the Eucharist in my first parish forty-four years after I first came there is not exactly going home again, but it is still a powerful emotional experience.

At the reunion Mass, Phil Doran had challenged me to renew our old rivalry on the basketball courts, a prospect about which we both laughed. Later in 1997 when Phil asked me to contribute to the construction of a "family center" at CK (a gym actually and thirty years too late) and I did so, he warned that they would inaugurate the gym with a one-on-one between the two of us. I responded (not seriously) that we should not wait but have a best-of-twenty free-throw contest *now*. Threats and predictions were exchanged at my monthly visits to CK. As Christmas (and my seventieth birthday approached) we found ourselves in the gym of the Walsh Brothers (also teenagers from my CK days) construction company shooting free throws.

The outcome?

We tied at nine for twenty, a better shooting average than that of Dennis Rodman be it noted. I claimed moral victory because of Phil's thirteen-year advantage in youthfulness! Actually I should have won because I had two shots left after Phil had finished his turn but I blew them both! At my seventieth birthday Mass I asked him and his wife Mary I (short for Irene) to represent the CK years in bringing up the bread and wine. I would have done the same thing even if he had beaten me!

And after the birthday Mass I did stand in the back of the church and talked to everyone as they poured out and hastened to the tented parking lot. I trust that in his place in the world-to-come, the monsignor was not too upset. I talked to hundreds of (now) fellow alumni and remembered most of their names and many of the stories they recounted. I toured the school building (unchanged like that of St. Angela) and the room where all the mad high club dances had taken place, and talked with some of my closest friends from yesteryear, a couple from whom I am still alienated despite my perhaps clumsy efforts at reconciliation.

I even ate some Italian sausages and the famous rainbow cones from a legendary ice cream store. Finally, I could stand the emotional overload no longer and fled CK, with a new set of memories that provided a very different prism from the one I had been using. I had much to think about on the American Airlines flight to Manchester.

Just as I had misconstrued the St. Angela experience, I had misconstrued the CK experience. I had exaggerated the amount of dislike and hatred and underestimated the amount of affection and love.

I must ask myself why. Doubtless the resigned priest-psychologists who have made a cottage industry out of psychoanalyzing me (in violation, I think, of the ethical norms of their profession) will have a field day with these admissions. I was unloved at home, they will say, and tried to earn love by hard work.

Well, maybe. But I think not. I work hard because my father worked hard and because he and my mother said that hard work was good (and they were right). But success in my work was never a condition for love.

When a kid appears at grammar school for the first time and leaves behind his home, where everyone loves him, for a good part of the day, he encounters with dismay the horrible truth that in the real world not everyone will love him and that many will resent and dislike him. Normally the kid wants to please everyone so he does his best to persuade all his classmates to like him. Normally this means that you don't know the answers to every question (and sometimes correct the teacher), you're not a "walking encyclopedia," you don't stroll out of history tests after the first twenty minutes, you don't write books or columns ("never had an unpublished thought"), you don't criticize your fellow priests for bad preaching and for failure to respond to the pedophilia problem, you don't write best-selling novels.[10]

If you do any of these things and, indeed, through the years do all of them, you are bound to stir up animosity. There will be people who resent you, dislike you, and hate you. There *are* enemies out there.[11]

Why do the things that stir up enmity? Why know the answers in school when no one else does? Why write books and columns? Why criticize fellow priests?

Because I was raised to believe that if something needs to be done and no one else is doing it and you can do it, then you should. It is not a worldview that I would walk away from even if I could.

There are also friends and lovers and far more of them than there are enemies. I knew the first truth in the last sentence, but until recently in my life I didn't fully appreciate the second truth, though I suppose the evidence was there. I had begun to discover it before the two reunions but they confirmed it dramatically. God hit me over the head with Her cosmic baseball bat, as She did Redmond Peter Kane in my novel *Patience of a Saint*. I don't think I've adjusted yet to the powerful impact of the bat.

Why so long? Why so much influence by enemies? Why are the occasional nasty attacks on my fiction not canceled out by the tremendous positive mail from readers?

I'm not sure what the answer is. You're too sensitive to criticism, some priests tell me, too thin-skinned—as though they would not be, as though no one is bothered by criticism, and as though anyone (them-

---

[10]It's all right if you write novels so long as no one reads them.

[11]Bob Hoyt, sometime editor of the *National Catholic Reporter*, and a lot of other Catholic "liberals" claim that I have an "enemies' list." Dymina Renshaw of the Sexual Dysfunction Clinic at Loyola replied to me, after I had questioned how she could comment on a book of mine she had not read, that she really didn't belong on my enemies' list. (She did belong on a list of irresponsible and unethical academics, however.) I don't have such a list and never did. I suppose I could assemble one if I had to. But Mr. Hoyt is not nearly important enough to make the list.

selves included) has thick skin. I would rather say that someone with the permeable boundaries that I described in *Confessions* would be more open to sensing resentment and hatred and more likely to think that such reactions are widespread, especially in the absence of visible support from friends.

Still it is a stupid and perhaps childish reaction.

Adversary: Every bit that? And didn't all those people at CK and St. Angela act like you're some frigging prophet?

It should not, I admit, have required Lady Wisdom's bat or the Adversary's irreverence to knock that crazy perspective out of my head. Moreover, even if there were a lot more enemies out there than there really are,[12] my ultimate worth as a person is based on my relationship with the Transcendent (aka Lady Wisdom) and in that relationship there is only love, freely given and never withdrawn, no matter what I do or don't do. The true self is that relationship and not certain talents or even a collection of talents or certain things that one has made or done. The best any of us can do is be aware some of the time of that truth. And that love.

The two reunions, then, were a turning point in my life, though perhaps they were turning points because I was already at a turning point. They symbolize what was happening to me. In an earlier time, they would not perhaps have meant nearly so much as they do now.

In any case, the truth is that there is much more love for me than I had realized (indeed much more love for each of us than we realize). That is very happy news. Even good news. I am certainly not running away from it.

---

[12]There are, however, some enemies and they are grimly determined. Later in this book I'll discuss a few of them.

Religion as Poetry

The setting was an international symposium that the late Jim Coleman had organized on "Social Theory and the Third Millennium." I flew from Tucson to Chicago to be a commentator for a paper on "Social Theory and Fundamentalism." I thought the title of the symposium was a little grandiloquent, but you do favors for your friends. The paper by Professor Thomas Luckmann of Basel was a rehash of the standard European stuff about the decline of religion, though Luckmann did not mean that religion was declining but only the influence of religion on society. (As Rodney Stark has argued, the latter position usually is a cover for the former.) No fundamentalist religion, Luckmann observed, could possibly lead to a major social movement in the West.

This set me up for a response which had been lurking in my head for years, "I have two words to say: Solidarity and the Civil Rights Movement." In the discussion, one of my local bêtes noires said simply, "Of course, Father Greeley is right."

Of course. Naturally. Jim Coleman caught my attention and rolled his eyes.

You can't tell the story of those two revolutionary movements without telling the story of the religion which animated them. Attempts to prove that religion is fading simply cannot cope with the power of religious stories. Religion is story before it is anything else and after it is everything else—that is my theory of religion and now one of the driving energies in my life.

The pages of this chapter are more than just intellectual biography. Struggling with and developing my sociological model of religion has had a profound and positive effect on my life, my spirituality, my prayers, my orientation toward God, my relationships with others, my understanding of the meaning of my life and the meaning of my self, my relationship to the institutional Church, and my faith. I said in *Confessions* that St. Angela and Christ the King were the major influences in the development of my priesthood. Now I must add a third major influence: my theory of religion as story or as narrative poetry has had a major impact on my priestly development. Its effect on me has been so strong that it would be more than worth the effort even if no one ever reads

Religion as Poetry, the book in which I tried to explain this approach to religion over which I have labored for at least a quarter century. The theory has become a tool for me to understand what is essential about Catholicism as it struggles in the transition between the Confident Church and the Confusing Church.

This theory has also led me to write stories and to tell stories instead of give homilies at the Eucharist. It also opened me up for the influence on my life of reunions and reconciliations. It became not only a theory about grace but a theory which was grace.

I can't remember when I first became interested in religious stories and symbols (which always contain a story). It seems like a concern that's always been there and has had a powerful impact on my life.

When I was in eighth grade I was impressed by Lloyd Douglas's novel *The Robe* because it demonstrated to me that fiction could be used to talk about religion.[13] In the seminary I was interested in religious symbolism because I sensed there was something important there. But in the hyper-cognitive atmosphere of the seminary no one took symbolism seriously. It was nice but the really important teachings were all contained in the documents of the various councils.

Only in graduate school at the University did I begin to realize that religion *was* symbol. As I related in *Confessions*, a lecture by Clifford Geertz in an afternoon class in which he was substituting for another faculty member (I don't remember who the other teacher was) opened my eyes. The lecture later appeared in his famous article "Religion as a Culture System." Religion, he argued, is a set of symbols which purport uniquely to explain the meaning of life and death.

I knew by then that the Greek word *"symbolon"* was translated into Latin as "sacrament" and that it meant a revelation of God, a hint at a deeper hidden truth. Suddenly everything clicked. Religion was story (a narrative symbol) before it was anything else. Our religion was first story and only afterward creed and catechisms. The latter were important but

---

[13]In a snide, snotty, snobbish review of *Confessions* in *Commonweal* (where else?), John Deedy ridiculed this influence and hinted that it revealed my lack of literary taste. Hey, I was only thirteen! Doubtless Mr. Deedy would have been happier if I had said that I had discovered the religious value of story from reading Graham Greene or Sigrid Undset. Then he could have said that I was no Graham Greene or no Sigrid Undset. In fact, I read both those authors before I was sixteen. Since then I've always admired Greene, though I could contain my enthusiasm for Ms. Undset. Neither Mr. Deedy nor anyone else has ever said that I'm no Shusaku Endo, who is in fact the greatest Catholic novelist of the present century, mostly because *Commonweal* types have never heard of him.

they were not where religion began. For most of human history, religion was story and nothing else. We learned about religion from our parents through stories (especially Christmas and Easter) before we ever learned about it in school.

This explained why the important religious truths among the ordinary faithful were not always on the importance list of the theologians and the catechists. There were in fact two different religions, not opposed necessarily but of different shape and form. In most sociology we study propositional and devotional religion. Yet if religion was story first, we ought to be studying (also) story religion. For the last thirty years I've been trying to work out that insight. The result is a theoretical "model" of religion, which is probably still crude and preliminary, but at least has strong explanatory power.

Religious traditions usually have two components. The first is the formal tradition or the high tradition or the official tradition or the propositional tradition. It is articulated by scholars and religious leaders, either together (sometimes the same people) or separately (and on occasion in opposition). This tradition is organized systematically and logically and presented in prose propositions which are often supported by philosophical argument. The propositions tell the devout member of the tradition what one must believe, how one must behave, what rituals one must follow, which leaders one must obey. It is assembled from the writings of the ancients, the teachings of the wise, and the decisions of the leaders. It is supported by a claim to sacred authority, whether the Bible or the Koran or the Talmud or the pope. While the propositions may sometimes change and will almost always be added to, the assumption is that they are always the same truth in slightly different wording.

Perhaps the most elaborate detailed example of the high tradition today is the new *Catechism of the Catholic Church*, which requires eight hundred pages to describe a tradition whose key truth is that God IS love—a truth which *you* could easily miss as you read the *Catechism*.

Some, perhaps many, members of the tradition take this codified statement of their faith to be a paradigm for how they must live if they wish salvation. In fact, however, most of them also are deeply influenced by another component of the tradition, one composed from stories, metaphors, rituals, popular devotions, and often traces of magic and superstition. For want of a better name I call this component the popular tradition.

Neither component is necessarily better than the other. Both need each other. Without the high tradition, the popular tradition becomes not a stately rain forest but a dangerous jungle in which magic and superstition convert it into folk religion. Folk religion in its turn all too easily degenerates into idolatry and crosses the line which separates the tradition from paganism.

Without the popular tradition, however, the high tradition becomes abstract and has little appeal to the total human personality. It becomes an arena in which scholars and leaders play their own self-important games with little regard for the problems and possibilities of ordinary people. Even if the *Catechism of the Catholic Church* were not poorly written, even if it did not misuse scripture texts, even if it were not only marginally influenced by the Second Vatican Council, even if were not an attempt to restore the rigidities of the preconciliar Church, it would still be too long and too dull, a useful reference book on occasion perhaps, but also a wonderful cure for insomnia.

I do not intend to disparage the high tradition. It is absolutely necessary because we are reflective creatures and must reflect critically on our experiential religion. Perhaps the expressions of the high tradition could be less opaque and more flexible—and hence more accessible to ordinary people. Certainly the claim that the Catholic high tradition never changes will not stand up to even cursory examination. As Judge John Noonan wrote in a brilliant article in the Jesuit journal *Theological Studies*, the Church has in recent years (the last century) changed its stand on slavery, Protestant churches, religious freedom, and marriage (the addition of the so-called Privilege of the Faith) just as at the end of the Middle Ages it changed its teaching on usury. He might also have said that in practice it has changed its position on coeducation which Pius XI condemned as against the "natural law" about the same time he denounced birth control as against the "natural law."[14] No amount of verbal gymnastics by conservative Catholics can cover up these changes. The dictum that the "Catholic Church does not change" simply cannot stand up in the face of the data. The proper questions are why does it change, what is the process that leads up to change, and how is change accounted for after the fact. A promising explanation is that the official Church, with the passage of time, understands better the nature of human nature (the violation of personal dignity in slavery, for example, or the harmlessness of young men and women going to school together) and is forced by its own most fundamental principles to modify its position.

---

[14]I do think there is a natural law: slavery is wrong, exploitation of women is wrong, racial prejudice is wrong, abuse of children is wrong, genocide is wrong. I fail to see how any ethical system which does not agree that the rights violated by these actions are "written on the human heart" can claim an absolute prohibition against them.

If we were seraphs (like the angels in my stories), we might need no more than the high tradition. But since we are humans with senses and imaginations, we will invariably develop a popular tradition too. Just as it behooves the popular tradition to listen to the high tradition, so it behooves the high tradition to be aware of what's going on in the popular tradition.

The two obviously overlap and in many cases do not fall into conflict. Thus someone may accept all the theology in the Nicene Creed and still run off to the local monastery to have Masses said for a special intention or pray to St. Anthony (patron of lost causes)[15] and badger one's pastor to reinstall votive candles (against the wishes of the parish liturgists, needless to say). An interesting question, however, is what will happen when the two of them are in apparent conflict.

For the last twenty-five years I have been wrestling with the development of a theoretical approach to the sociology of religion. By theory I mean what Robert K. Merton calls "a theory of the middle range," that is one from which a person can draw testable hypotheses. This concern about testable theory led me, especially during the last ten years, to become more aware of the importance of the popular tradition, which it seems to me shapes most people's religious lives. Children are Catholics long before they have their first catechism class because Catholic images have already filled their imaginations. These images will remain with them for the rest of their lives, no matter what final decision they may make about religious affiliation. Adult Catholics may dip into the high tradition when they have a question or feel guilty or become interested in intellectual religion, but the images of childhood and adolescence, modified a bit and subjected to some criticism, still shape their religious lives and keep them in the Church.

I was also convinced from the beginning of my attempts to develop a theory that it was time to return to the concerns of Weber and Durkheim about religion as predictor variable (an antecedent variable, perhaps even a causal one; a variable that explains variance in other behaviors and attitudes). According to Weber, there was a special affinity between the Protestant ethic and the spirit of capitalism. According to Durkheim the strong social structure of Catholic communalism held down Catholic suicide rates. More recently sociolo-

[15]My colleague and friend Robert Orsi of the University of Indiana has written a wonderful study of devotion to St. Jude (*Thank You Saint Jude*) who is also the patron of lost causes. It's a fine companion book to his earlier sympathetic study of the Italian religious street festival in his *The Madonna of 115th Street*.

gists have turned away from these two fathers of sociology to study the decline of religion as predicted by Freud and Marx. Religion thus becomes a dependent variable, something to be explained instead of something to explain. The dominant theory is one of "secularizations"— religion isn't as important as it used to be. Peter Berger, for example, has argued that once there is religious competition the "sacred canopy," the "plausibility structure," of religion collapses. Most recently, however, a new theory of religion has emerged, an "economic" or "competitive" model. Such men as Rodney Stark, Stephen Warner, and Laurence Iannaccone have contended that, far from diminishing the importance of religion, competition enhances it because religious leaders are forced to work much harder (and I would add because in a pluralistic society religion may easily become an essential component of one's personal identity). The model fits almost perfectly the United States on the one hand and Britain and the Scandinavian countries on the other. However, I fail to see how the model fits Ireland or even Poland for that matter. But more important to me is the fact that it is still an attempt to explain religion, and I am interested in religion explaining other attitudes and behaviors. I do not reject research on religion as a dependent variable and do not propose my approach as a substitute for it, though I think the secularization "theory" in any and all of its many forms is ridiculous. It explains very little variance in the data, especially when, as I did in 1992, one is able to examine religion in eighteen countries. If the secularization theory persists, the reason is not that it provides testable hypotheses that are sustained (or as a cautious sociologist would put it, null hypotheses that must be rejected), but rather that it is a secular dogma to which many social scientists are totally committed. Recently, an editor of a major journal automatically found reasons to reject (and referees who would agree) any article that did not show religion declining and to accept any article that purported to show it in decline, no matter how poor the data or the analysis was. I suspect that he didn't even realize what he was doing.

Nonetheless, if religion is, in the definition of Clifford Geertz, a set of symbols which explain the ultimate meaning of life, then surely it should have some impact (as Weber and Durkheim well knew) on the rest of human life. From John Shea I learned the notion that religion is narrative, story. From Mircea Eliade I learned the religious importance of the most fundamental human symbols—light, dark, food, drink, sex, sky, earth, trees, sun, moon, birth, death. (Both Eliade and Geertz were teachers of mine in graduate school.) From William James I learned about religious experience and studied such experiences, major and minor, in our various surveys. From David Tracy (a friend and a colleague and the top Catholic theologian in the world)[16] I learned about the different imaginations: analogical (which tends to be Catholic) and dialectical (which tends to be Protestant). The propensity of the former is to see God lurking everywhere in the world while the latter is to see God absent from the world. The first worries about a godforsaken world, the latter about a God too closely identified with the world (and hence the subject of idolatry). Neither is inherently better than the other, both have valid defenses, both need each other for correction. But both also have different tendencies—thus Catholics have angels and saints and souls in purgatory and statues and stained-glass windows and holy water and elaborate vestments and rituals and, above all, Mary the Mother of Jesus, while Protestants tend to lack such imagery and to consider it close to idolatry.[17]

In 1989 I published an article in the summer issue of the *American Sociological Review* which explored the possibility that the differences that Weber and Durkheim both found between Protestant individualism and Catholic communalism might be superstructure. Perhaps, I suggested, the substructures which separated the two religions were different images of God, world, and life. I tested some seventy-five hypotheses against data from two separate multinational data sets and found that almost three-quarters of them were sustained. Tracy could be harmonized with Weber and Durkheim and tested successfully by the methods of contemporary empirical social sciences.

These two different imaginations affect both the high and popular

[16]And also the Andrew Thomas and Grace McNichols Greeley Professor at the University of Chicago. I have been known to harass David, one of the nicest human beings I've ever met, at the Quadrangle Club as to whether he has earned his money this week. He is from New York, which ought not to be held against anyone because they have no choice about where they were born, but he has become a Chicago Bulls fan and even attends the Bulls–Knicks games and cheers for the Bulls, which is an impressive virtue in my judgment.

[17]I presided some years ago over a mixed wedding ceremony in which the bride was not Catholic. Her parents had no objection to a religiously mixed marriage and were apparently not all that devout in their religious practice, but they could not abide the ceremony in a Catholic church because of all the statues. They would have especially not liked it in Old St. Patrick's Church in Chicago because that marvelous church in one of the best parishes in the nation has more saints (not all of them Irish) per cubic foot than any church in the world. I suspect that such deeply rooted imaginative and emotional differences will persist long after the theologians and the bureaucrats work out all of their problems. There should be no obligation for Protestants to accept our popular devotions, but they should listen to our explanations and not damn us as idolaters or Mariolaters.

traditions. Mary the Mother of Jesus certainly has an important place in official Catholic theology, but she is also the central image in popular Catholicism. Sometimes the two different versions of Mary—one high, one popular—seem to have little in common.[18] Because Catholicism emphasizes religious metaphors (often without realizing it), one would expect that the Catholic popular tradition would be much more elaborate than the Protestant or Islamic popular traditions and even somewhat more elaborate than the Jewish popular tradition.

With all these skeins in hand I began to fashion my theory. Religion was story before it was anything else and after it was everything else. It begins in experiences which renew hope, is encoded in images which are symbols, is shared with others in stories which recall parallel experiences of their own (hence a community), and is often enacted in rituals. The theory then is experience–image–story–community–ritual, with each of the points in the theory influencing all the others. Thus my initial hope-renewal experience is already shaped by the symbols and the stories and the ritual that my community (heritage, tradition) has passed on to me.

Religion,[19] I assume, is the result of two incurable diseases from which humankind suffers, life from which we die and hope which hints that there might be more meaning to life than a termination in death. Humankind in the form in which we now know it is the only being of which we are aware that is conscious of its own mortality and is capable of hoping that death is not the final act in human life.

Thus religion becomes possible when a being is conscious of the inevitability of its own death and becomes inevitable when the being has experiences which suggest that death does not have the final word. We know nothing about the consciousness of mortality among *Homo habilis* and *Homo erectus*. But our immediate predecessors in the human family tree, *Homo neanderthalensis*, had not only developed sufficient consciousness of death but also hope in immortality, if we are to judge by their

[18]And sometimes Mary slips over the line and becomes a pagan goddess, and not a pleasant one either as Michael Carroll from the University of Western Ontario has pointed out in his brilliant book *Madonnas that Maim*. Our Lady of Guadeloupe began her career as a transformed pagan goddess at Guadeloupe in Spain (where her image was imprinted on a rock instead of a peon's coat) before she migrated to Mexico. However, in my judgment she is well over on the Christian side of the line in her manifestations in Mexico and the United States. (Where is Jesus in the picture? one asks Mexican Americans. She's pregnant, they respond.)

[19]In the next several pages I rely heavily on my book *Religion as Poetry*.

burial sites. Whether there was religion before them we cannot say. But there seems little doubt that religion existed among them.

Should there exist a species whose members know they must die and yet, for reasons of genetic hardwiring or soft-wiring or cultural conditioning, have no experiences of hope, then that species would not create for itself a religion—and would probably not survive for long. There are few if any evolutionary advantages in despair.

The issue here is not whether every human hopes, much less whether, as Lionel Tiger suggested some years ago, there is a gene which creates hope even though the situation is hopeless. To explain religion, it is not necessary that every human have experiences which renew hope, nor is it necessary to contend that every human has a religion of some sort. It is enough merely to say that most humans have experiences which renew their hope and that therefore humankind has religion.

Hope, however, is not certainty. Certainty precludes religion just as despair does. Should there exist somewhere in the cosmos (or in other cosmoses) a mortal being which has absolute certainty that it will be victorious over death, that being will not need religion either. Hope and therefore religion exist only in conditions of uncertainty, of possibility, of relative degrees of probability. Hope and hence religion emerge only when the data are inconclusive. Mortality, uncertainty, possibility—these are the triangle of factors out of which religion comes.

It is not necessary for the purposes of my model that the content of hope be specific. Hope can remain vague. It need not specify a God or an explicit conviction of personal survival. Hope may involve nothing more than an uncertain sense that things will get better or that tomorrow will be different, even when today is the last day of one's life.[20]

Hope therefore permeates the human condition and not merely the last day of life, though some of the research on dying and death suggests that it increases in intensity as life approaches its end.[21] Nonetheless, because the data are inconclusive and the outcome uncertain, hope wavers. Religion exists to confirm and reinforce and renew hope through

[20]Hope is often dismissed by hardheaded unbelievers as "wish fulfillment," a will to believe that there are grounds for hope when in fact there are none. But the fact that we would be much happier if there were grounds for hope neither proves that such grounds exist nor that they do not exist. The data remain inconclusive.

[21]Can Hope be completely extirpated from human consciousness by those who believe that there are absolutely no reasons for hope? Perhaps. Once again, however, I am not making a case for the universality of hope, only its commonality.

its crises, major and minor, daily and life cycle. More precisely religion grows out of those experiences, major and minor, in which hope is confirmed, reinforced, and renewed. Therefore religion arises and continues because of the human propensity to experiences which renew hope.

By way of illustration: I am walking through the chaos of O'Hare International Airport a week before Christmas. The weather is terrible, flights are delayed, the crowds are irritable and impatient. No one is smiling, I least of all. I reflect that many of these Christmas travelers are moving about the planet because of an obligation that they cannot resist and that their tense, hasty visits are likely to be unsatisfactory both to them and those whom they are visiting. Humankind, I continued to reflect, is adept at folly. It turns arduous family festivals into situations in which it can punish those it loves. Old Qoheleth (Ecclesiastes) was right: all is vanity. This mob scene at O'Hare, a search for love, is, to quote him again, nothing more than chasing after the wind. As is the whole human enterprise. Why bother about anything, why bother about Christmas, *especially* why bother about Christmas?

Then coming out of the American Airlines gates, in the midst of a particularly frantic troop of descendants of *Homo habilis*, I see a lovely young mother with a tiny infant in her arms. She is so proud of her child (blue means little boy, doesn't it, I ask myself), so determined to protect him, so overwhelmed by his wonder, that she seems oblivious to the crowds, the noise, the electricity of tension and frustrations in the airport. She is unable to restrain a radiant smile at him and the miracle that he is. I pause to revel in this snapshot of beauty and goodness. She notices my admiration, and assuming motherlike that it is for her son, she smiles at me, as though I have joined her in admiration for her sleeping babe.

She disappears with the crowd and I go through the security checkpoint, a Christmas carol in my head, a smile on my lips, and a sense that Qoheleth had it only half right at best and that neither Christmas nor life is merely an exercise in chasing after the wind.[22]

Some immediate comments before I analyze what has happened:
1. The smiling-mother-with-tiny-boy-child phenomenon is interpreted in the very act of experiencing it. Indeed, an interpretation is waiting

---

[22]By choosing an "ordinary" religious experience, I wish to exclude but not slight the importance of mystical and shamanistic experiences. I am not persuaded as some scholars (Ginzberg, for example) that shamanism accounts for the origin of religions. The shaman or the mystic obviously has every reason to believe. But I fail to see how he could sell his faith to others unless they also had lesser but sufficient religious experiences.

even before the experience because I carry around in my preconscious a Madonna model[23] waiting to be activated, especially at Christmas. My Madonna image is a sensor scanning for a corresponding reality.

2. While there is a preconscious interpretation waiting for the experience, the initial effect on me is unreflective. I do not argue about anything from it, not at least until later. Rather I am absorbed by it, possessed by it, transformed (however temporarily) by it in the experience itself.

3. The experience itself is purely secular. It is not formally religious. It does not occur in church. It is a commonplace, utterly ordinary event. The statistical chances of encountering a young mother with a baby at O'Hare at Christmas are probably close to 100 percent. I am indeed disposed for this renewal of hope by my own religious heritage and its repertory of vivid symbols, especially Christmas symbols. But Catholic Christianity has no monopoly either on mother goddesses or on wonder at the miracle of new life.

4. Because of the secularity of the experience, I need not be detained by the question of the sacred versus the profane which so concerns anthropologists. Every object, event, and person in life is potentially an occasion of hope renewal and hence potentially sacred. The secular or the profane—words which for my purposes mean the same thing— becomes sacred when it occasions a hope-renewal experience. Some realities may be more sacred than others in that they are especially disposed to occasion grace-renewal experiences. On the other hand for all its beauty and all its solemnity, the reality (like *San Pietro in Vaticano*), which seems especially designed to hint at something or someone beyond itself, may leave me cold, unimpressed, and if anything less hopeful.

5. In the course of far too many ventures to O'Hare, I might have encountered hundreds of thousands of mothers with newborn children. The same woman with the same child might have earned no more than a passing glance any other day of my life. They occasioned a hope-renewal experience, that is a "religious" experience, that day though they might not have done so on any other day.

6. I experience the woman-and-child event as purely gratuitous (one might almost say "graceful"). It is a result of, as its seems, an improbable concatenation of contingent circumstances. She didn't have to be there. I didn't have to notice her. She didn't have to smile at me. It

[23]Formed from, among other things, paintings, sculptures, songs, festivals, devotions, liturgical celebrations, hymns, and stories—to bring all the other elements of my theory into play.

all "just happened." It was a "surprise." If I had reflected on the meaning of that surprise and the joy it has restored to my being as I was emptying the coins from my pockets into the tray at the checkpoint, I might have realized that I had spontaneously reacted to it with an emotion which contained the feeling that in a world in which such a surprise is possible, there are still some reasons for celebrating Christmas.

7. I have deliberately chosen a small and low-key, though delightful, religious experience to emphasize that there is a gradient in hope-renewal experiences, from the very small to the very large about which William James wrote in his *Varieties*.

8. In response to the sociological voice, which I have carried from many seminars into my head and hear and respond to often in this book, that insists "you don't have to be religious to have that kind of experience," I reply that such is precisely my point. Of course you don't. The experience is not so much the result of religion (though a specific interpretation may be the result of one's heritage) as the cause of it.

In addition to the "sociological voice" which complains in my ear that it never has had such an experience (which I doubt) or that the experience is not religious (though the way I define religion it is),[24] there is also a "theological voice" which insists with grim determination that I am paying no attention to the doctrinal content of religion or, as Andrew Sullivan did in a review of an earlier version of this theory in *The New Republic*, that without a cognitive system of belief there can be no religion. The voice continues to argue this position even though I have insisted that my theory does not exclude reflective religion but rather concentrates on examining the poetry which precedes reflection while of course admitting that—as in my case with the Madonna at O'Hare— previous reflections shaped my Madonna "sensor" which was operative at O'Hare and shape all my hope-renewal experiences.

The theological voice wants doctrines, creeds, and moral obligations, more recently obligations toward social activism and "concern for the poor." I reject none of these. I merely insist that experiences which renew hope are prior to and richer than propositional and ethical religion and provide the raw power for the latter.

Moreover, for most of human history there was little if any doctrinal and philosophical reflection on religious experience. Doctrinal convictions and devotional habits become necessary for a religious culture at a certain point in its development, but if they are to be of any use they

[24]The sociological voice equates religion with institution and with God and generally, perhaps for very good reason in its own life story, doesn't like either.

must build on experiences which renew hope. Otherwise those who propagate them may well become either bishops or full professors, but no one other than their colleagues will be listening to them.

Symbolic language, Fawcett tells us, attempts to "reach out to grasp that which is not immediately known. Symbols do not denote things which are already understood, but attempt to . . . grasp the reality of things, the real nature of life, the stuff of existence itself . . . by taking images derived from the world of sense experience and using them to speak of that which transcends them."

But what about the doctrine of the Immaculate Conception of Mary, says the theologian, or (if s/he be of the left) Our Lady of Guadeloupe as patroness of the poor and the oppressed.

I might, if I've had it with the theologian, say something like "Gimme a break!" Or I might reply that one should revel in the illumination the symbol provides before trying to reduce it to prose.

What of the God symbol? Voltaire argued that humans create God in their own image and likeness. My theory would rephrase his epigram somewhat: humans create God in image and likeness of the goodness they encounter in their grace (or hope-renewal) experiences. Since the moments of grace (like my encounter with the young mother at O'Hare) seem like pure gift, one begins to postulate a giver. God is therefore the agent to whom humans assign responsibility for their experiences of hope renewal; God is the author of grace. The symbol of God—a metaphor suggesting that someone is the giver—for most people is the central and primary religious symbol, the one in which all the metaphors are combined and into which all are projected. If I learn what your image of God is I may have a good indicator of what your religion is because your God symbol tells me the story of what you feel life is about, far more powerfully in fact than do your doctrinal convictions about God.[25]

If you claim that you do not believe in God, which is your privilege of course, then I must probe further to find out what image ties together all your ultimate metaphors for what life means.[26] But I find it difficult to believe that you do not have memories of experiences which become

---

[25]Sociology, to repeat myself perhaps, has nothing to say about whether there is a reality which corresponds to the God image. It must be content to note that for large numbers of people the God image does serve as a privileged symbol of the collection of metaphors which explain their lives to them. As I often note facetiously, the National Opinion Research Center interviewers have tried repeatedly to interview Her, and She's never been home to us.

[26]Gods come in many shapes and kinds and some are notably less gracious than others. Indeed, it is precisely the graciousness of your God which provides me with a good hint of other stories in your life.

permanent metaphors that explain to you (still on the pre-propositional level of the personality) what life means and that these experiences and metaphors are not bound together by some privileged metaphor (and the experience it reflects).

Finally, I must insist that such terms as "only a symbol" or "only poetry" or "only a story" are obsolete. If we were Cartesian ghosts in a machine or if we were disembodied angelic spirits,[27] pure ideas, devoid of emotional and imaginative resonance, would be the more satisfactory means of explaining reality and, should there be one, Reality. Even for the ghost and the angel, God talk would still necessarily be metaphorical if prosaic. However, for humans, images which appeal to the senses as well as the mind are necessarily the most powerful and effective form of religious language, although as a reflecting being, a human must reflect on her images and experiences, if only to re-present them to herself and "harden" them in her personality by lifting them from the imagination and "freezing" them in the propositional memory.

The experience which the symbol implies is shared with others in stories that are reflective, either in careful propositional narration (plot) or in carefully thought out expansion of poetic imagery. Humans need both experience and reflection, both poetry and prose, both fiction and nonfiction.

Thus the fairy tale about Cinderella might make one recall times in childhood when it seemed that parents were discriminating unfairly in favor of other siblings. The most common plot of all, "boy meets girl, boy loves girl, boy loses girl, boy finds girl again,"[28] appeals to the universal human experience of finding love, losing it, and (maybe) finding it again.

The storyteller is bent on doing more, however. Not only does she want to enthrall the listener by leading him into the world of the story and "hooking" him on it by stirring up in his imagination a recollection of a previous experience, she also wants to provide for the listener a touch of illumination (sometimes a very small touch) which offers the possibility of a return to the world beyond the story with an awareness

---

[27] I leave open here the issue of whether angels, should they be, are necessarily incorporeal. For the first thousand years of Christianity, theologians believed that angels had bodies, if ethereal ones, because only God was pure spirit. The medieval theologian John Duns Scotus also argued that angels were embodied. I address this problem at some length in my novel *Angel Fire*, which is about the angel Gabriella (Gabriel in the tradition is often being depicted as a womanly angel). Social scientists who are not Marxists will perhaps not be offended to learn that Gabriella is a high-status angel, a seraph in fact.

[28] Or a similar plot in which the gender of the protagonist is changed.

of (perhaps only slightly) expanded possibilities for his own life. Maybe it is possible, for example, to find that girl again, even if you have been married to her for a quarter of a century.

Thus:

"Did you hear the story about the Yuppie who made a lot more money when he acquired a mistress as well as a wife?"

"How come?"

"After work his wife thought he was with his mistress and his mistress thought he was with his wife and actually he was in his office getting more work done!"

The listener is intrigued by the odd premise. There might, after all, be something to be said for having both a wife and a lover. But how could anyone, even a Yuppie, turn such a situation into a profit? The explanation makes fun of the success-crazed culture of the young urban professional, calls to mind the experience of being caught between work and family, and warns the listener of how badly such an obsession can pervert the joys and pleasures of human relationships.

Or:

"I had a fascinating experience at O'Hare this morning."

"Yeah?"

"I was really discouraged and pessimistic about Christmas and everything else."

"So what else is new? Why should you be different?"

"Then something happened."

"Yeah? What?"

"I met a Madonna."

I could have streamlined the story and merely said, "A funny thing happened to me at O'Hare this morning: I met a Madonna." The effect would presumably have been the same. In either case, I probably would not have had to explain what happened. My listener would recall similar experiences of hope in life renewed by a new mother and a new child. He would know exactly what I meant without another word being said.

Moreover, stories illumine and renew not only the listener but the teller. When I tell the Yuppie story, I remind myself of the folly of work obsession; and when I tell the Madonna of O'Hare International story, I renew in myself the afterglow, as it were, of that religious experience.

Similarly: "And the prince and Snow White lived happily ever after."

Or: "Michael Collins said to the British general, 'I'm not seven minutes late. You're seven centuries late.' "

Or: "Abraham Lincoln freed the slaves, won the war, and then they killed him on Good Friday."

Or: "Upon hearing that General Ulysses S. Grant was drunk, the president asked what kind of whiskey he drank so he could send some of it to his other generals."

Or: "Our father was a wandering Aramaean whom the Lord called into Egypt."

Or: "He went before us with a pillar of cloud by day and a pillar of fire by night."

Or: "A child is born to us in Bethlehem."

Or: "Jesus who was dead is alive."

Huge volumes of psychology or history or sociology or theology could not tell the stories so well—though the volumes are necessary too.

No one has ever denied the fascination of stories, nor their ability to make a point. But until recently both preachers and professors, critics and columnists, literalists and lecturers, have thought it essential to turn the stories into nonfiction as quickly as they can, either to explain the "point" of the story or to protect the unwary from thinking that the story has said all that needs to be said.

More recently, however, scholars from a wide variety of disciplines have come to believe that the story *is* the truth and that the exegesis of the story, however necessary it may be, invariably deprives the story not only of its wonder and its fascination but also of some of the resonance and nuances that lurk in the periphery and the penumbra of the tale.

We tell stories, it is now understood, to explain ourselves and our lives, first of all to ourselves and then to others. Storytelling is humankind's primary meaning bestowing activity. Without stories nothing makes sense.

This notion is extremely difficult to explain to the products of the American educational enterprise, (perhaps especially) including the products of Ph.D.-granting institutions. Is not truth contained in the precise and measured sentences of the professional scientists? Are not clear and concise ideas the stepping-stones to truth? Do not the messy and imprecise components of narrative—plot, character, atmosphere—risk inaccuracy, misunderstanding, self-deception?

But many of science's most fruitful terms are metaphors which tell stories—black holes, great attractors, big bangs, double helixes, survival of the fittest, $E = MC^2$. Is not the closest thing to a paradigm sociology has—the social mobility model—a story (and a very interesting one at that)?

There is a time, in other words, for precision and a time for narrative. The story provides the big picture; precision is necessary for the details. In the case of the social mobility model, the precision comes after the first story (children of rich parents have a greater chance of success than do the children of poor parents) and before the second story—or perhaps as the second story evolves (in the United States a college education levels the playing field).

The French philosopher Paul Ricoeur has applied the same model to religious stories—critical analysis of the story intervenes between the "first naiveté" ("Remember, O most gracious Virgin Mary . . .) and the "second naiveté" ("This morning at O'Hare I met a Madonna"/"A mother's smile reminded me of the life-giving love of the Ultimate").

Understanding, then, does not proceed from the general to the particular, from the abstract to the concrete, from the theoretical to the practical. Rather it proceeds from the particular to the particular, from story to story—with intermittent forays to the general and the abstract.

Here then is the core of my theory, its very essence: religion *is* story, story before it is anything else, story after it is everything else, story born from experience, coded in symbol, and reinforced in the self and shared with others to explain life and death, death and life. Religious stories— while they must be subjected to analysis and criticism because humans are analyzing and criticizing beings—are elemental religion, religion pure and simple, religion raw and primordial.

The important question is not whether the story is true (though in some religious heritages, including the three Religions of the Book, that is a legitimate question) but whether it is True,[29] that is, what explanation it offers for the meaning of human life and whether that explanation corresponds to one's own experiences of hope renewal. Nor does it suffice to dismiss something as "only a story." There is no such thing as a story that is only a story.

In its nuances and resonance, its shadings and allusions, its suggestions and its hints, its density and its ambiguities, its many levels and its multiplicity of messages, the story appeals to and discloses the total human person, soul and body, intelligence and senses, reason and intuition, reasoning and instinct—or whatever other metaphor you may wish to use to divide up the seeming duality of human knowing.

Precisely because of its multifaceted possibilities and the richness of potential interpretations, a story may have unrecognized depths that are recognized only with time. Paul Ricoeur writes of the "meaning in front of the text" of a story, that meaning we may legitimately find in the

[29]The difficulty that inhabitants of the world of prosaic nonfiction have in grasping the distinction between literal and historical truth on the one hand and existential and religious Truth on the other was driven home to me when in the usual disclaimer at the beginning of one of my novels I wrote, "The story is nonetheless True." An officious copy editor corrected the last word to read "true" and thus provided grist for the mills of reviewers who wanted to claim (falsely) that the story was autobiographical. I should have known better.

story although the one who first told it and those who have repeated it through time have not been aware that such meaning lurks in the story. Thus when I say that the Madonna story reflects the mother love of God I am finding in the story a possibility that actually lurks there, but which I would not have recognized without knowledge of the history of religion and anthropology that was not available at earlier stages of the story's life.

For the social scientist who wants to study religion—not necessarily religious institutions—there is no escape from a study of religious stories, from the poetry of religion which antedates its prose. While I believe in a catholicity of disciplinary boundaries, I cannot see at the present stage of our understanding of religion how an enterprise which ignores the narrative dimensions of religion can define itself as sociology of religion.

In the language of the 1992 election campaign, "It's the STORY, stupid!"

After a quarter century working with this theory and many different data sets, I finally felt I had enough to put it all together in a book I have called *Religion as Poetry*. I summarize the book by saying it makes three points:

1. Religion does matter in modern society.
2. Religious imagery is the most powerful religious predictor variable currently available to us.
3. Catholics are different and usually in ways that one would not expect unless one was making predictions on the basis of my theory. Thus Catholics are more likely to oppose racism, to support environmental reforms, to sympathize with AIDS victims and condemned criminals, and support civil liberties. The differences can be accounted for by different Catholic religious images.

I am now working on a second book which will develop my theory of religion as narrative into a broader theory combining my narrative theory with socialization theory and rational choice theory—the last of which I have learned from Gary Becker, Rodney Stark, and Laurence Iannaconne. Narrative theory tells what religion is, socialization theory how it gets passed on, and rational choice theory why most people tend to remain in the religion of their origins, a phenomenon which most American sociologists do not seem to have noticed.

I hardly expected either secular sociologists or Catholic theologians to welcome *Religion as Poetry*. Too many cherished stereotypes are knocked down. In truth, I didn't expect the book to have much effect at all. In terms of its short-term impact—and its long-term impact too—my quarter century of theorizing and research, I figured, would turn out to have been a waste of time. It is not easy to make such a judgment about one's master work, but I think it's an accurate judgment. Do you expect your work will have much influence, I am asked on occasion. Hardly any, is my response as far as my sociology is concerned. The fiction may enjoy somewhat more influence.[30] However, questions about the impact of one's work are ultimately irrelevant. If one worries about that, one won't do anything at all, much less anything that is risky and perhaps a tiny bit original. One does one's best; if one is ignored, that is a problem over which one has little control. I can at least translate the theory into stories and run around both the sociologists and the theologians.

Actually, *Religion as Poetry* did rather better than I had expected. All three relevant sociological journals gave it favorable reviews as did two Irish theological journals. It sold through a couple of printings and is now available in paperback, a sure sign of success in the scholarly publishing business.

Of American Catholic journals only the Jesuit *America* noted its existence. Their review was written by a graduate student at Yale Divinity School (Jesuit no doubt) who knew no sociology and complained about the graphs and tables (sociology is apparently not permitted its own tools). You win some and you lose some.

Yet now I find that as my career winds down, my struggle with those who think that religion is no longer important may have had some impact. The scholars who are devastating the "secularists"—Rodney Stark and his allies, Jose Casanova, Philip Gorski—are citing my work, especially a book I wrote thirty-five years ago called *Unsecular Man* which argued, long before survey data appeared to sustain the argument, that religion was no more unimportant than it ever was.

You lose some and you win some!

Adversary: Seems to me you've won most of them. And the ones you didn't win, wasn't it better for you that you didn't win?

---

[30]Which is just the opposite of the usual Catholic liberal cliché: too bad such a good sociologist wastes his time on potboiler (or trashy) fiction.

II

Windmills

In the next five chapters I recount some of my charges against windmills during the transition from the Confident Church to the Confusing Church. One could make a pretty good case in support of the proposition that I am a Quixote. Why try to write a study of papal elections? Why take on Cardinal Cody? Why become involved in the pedophile mess? Why defend the rights of the laity against neo-authoritarian parish staff? Why worry about Catholic schools? I don't know. Maybe the question is why not.

Adversary: Admit it, boyo: You've had a hell of a good time.

Filling in the Blanks

I must fill in the blanks about the Cardinal Cody years in Chicago and the succession after him.[31] I discussed these matters partially in my *Making of the Popes 1978* and the first volume of this memoir. However, for various reasons I was not able to tell the whole story. Now I can write about most of what I had to leave out in the past. It is important for the historical record that this story be told.

By the early 1970s. Rome knew it had made a mistake in appointing Cardinal Cody to Chicago. Several unsuccessful attempts were made by Archbishop Benelli, the de facto chief of staff to Pope Paul VI, to persuade the cardinal to accept a "promotion" to Rome. Then in the middle seventies, Rome decided to act more directly. Benelli established a "commission" composed of himself, Archbishop Bernardin of Cincinnati, Cardinal Baggio of the Congregation of Bishops, and Archbishop Jadot, the apostolic delegate to the United States. The charges against Cardinal Cody were that he was guilty of "unusual behavior," dubious financial manipulations, and stirring up the hatred of the people. Various Chicago priests were asked to submit evidence for Jadot's dossier, including Father James Roache who was the cardinal's press secretary. A group of Chicago priests—Monsignor James Hardiman (Cardinal Stritch's secretary), Father William Goedert (a seminary rector), and Father Leo Mahon (for many years the head of the Archdiocese's fabled mission in Panama)—were invited by Jadot to present their views at the Vatican. In 1976 they met with Cardinal Baggio in Rome. They had the impression that Baggio had heard all the things they reported. At the end of the conversation he promised action "within two months."

It hardly needs to be said that the Vatican never even thinks of moving against a cardinal unless the evidence is overwhelming. Cardinal Cody was afflicted with what a psychiatrist would call "a borderline personality disorder." A less obscure label would have been a "psychopathic paranoid." He was also, if not exactly an alcoholic, given to binge drinking

[31]Documentation for this account will be found in my archives at the Chicago Historical Society in a document called "The Unmaking of the Cardinal."

in strange places—like hotel rooms in a southwestern Chicago suburb, the Athens Hilton, and the Royal Hawaiian. It was widely known in Chicago that the mayor had to intervene frequently with the Chicago police to quash drunken driving arrests.

Just as Paul VI needed two years to make up his mind about birth control after his commission had recommended a change, it took two years for him to make up his mind about Cardinal Cody. In the summer of 1978, Joseph Bernardin was appointed coadjutor archbishop of Chicago with right to succession. The papers he received made it clear that he would have full power in the Archdiocese. Cardinal Baggio was dispatched to Chicago to impose this arrangement on Cardinal Cody. The pope called Baggio at Fiumicino airport just before he boarded the plane to add a qualification: Cardinal Cody must consent to the new arrangement. Paul VI could never get over the trauma of his removal from the Vatican as a younger man because of the conspiracies of his curial enemies.

Obviously this change in plans cut the ground out from under the work of the commission Benelli had established and put Bernardin's assignment to Chicago in grave doubt. Nonetheless, Baggio flew to Chicago, hoping that the argument that the change was the wish of the Holy Father would be effective. Neither the pope nor Baggio knew their man. In a noisy shouting match at the cardinal's villa on the grounds of the seminary in Mundelein, Cody flatly refused to accept the change and threatened a public conflict. Neither Baggio nor the pope realized what every priest in Chicago knew: one should let Cardinal Cody rant and rave and continue to stand up to him. Invariably he would back down.

Baggio returned to Rome to report failure to the pope. Shortly after his return the pope died. His successor, John Paul II, knew that he had to act on the Chicago problem. The papers were in his room the night he died of an embolism. Archbishop Bernardin continued in limbo: he had been appointed to Chicago but was unable to act on that appointment.

John Paul II did not want to remove Cardinal Cody before his visit to the city in 1979. Cardinal Cody gave the pope a large financial gift—according to some sources, a million dollars. Nonetheless, the pope knew that something must be done. On Ash Wednesday of 1980, both Cody and Bernardin were in the Vatican Palace. The scenario was that the pope would tell Cody that he was finished as archbishop of Chicago and then meet with Bernardin and tell him that his appointment would be announced immediately.

However, Cody stonewalled John Paul II the same way he had stonewalled Cardinal Baggio. He threatened public scandal. Like Paul VI, John Paul II backed off, taking the calculated risk that no further scandal would occur in Chicago before the ailing cardinal died. It turned out to be a bad bet. He offered Archbishop Bernardin the Archdiocese of Washington, an offer which Bernardin gracefully declined.

The following summer a lay employee of the Archdiocese contacted the United States Attorney for the Northern District of Illinois with charges of vast misuse of funds for the cardinal's personal benefit. A grand jury was empaneled. The *Chicago Sun-Times* began its own investigation.

Now I come to my own involvement in the Cody endgame, a surrealistic nightmare that became one of the worst experiences of my life. That autumn a reporter from the Notre Dame alumni magazine begged me to grant him an interview. In one of the worst decisions I ever made in all my life, I finally agreed. He came to Tucson during my term at the University of Arizona and spent an enormous amount of time with me for what was to be a three-thousand-word article. At one point he asked me whether he could read the manuscripts of my novels. I told him that they were at my archives in Rosary College.

I would later learn that Rosary had been negligent (to put it mildly) in its care of my confidential material. Contrary to their promise, my archives had never been catalogued and no effort had been made to protect them or keep them confidential. The nun in charge permitted the Notre Dame writer to go through all my material and make copies of whatever he wanted to copy.

I had been keeping a diary of my interviews and observations in preparation for a book on the next papal election. In them I mentioned in passing the possibility of a newspaper exposé of Cardinal Cody to deliver Chicago from his psychotic tyranny. Since everyone presumed that Archbishop Bernardin would succeed Cody, I reflected that he would have great influence at the next conclave. Nothing much came of that idea. A reporter visited Chicago—three years before the grand jury investigation—and found that no one was talking.

The Notre Dame journalist removed all of these files and the tapes from which they had been transcribed. His story was no longer to be about me, but about the "Plot to Get Cody!"

There were a number of "plots" to get Cody, if one wants to use that word: the one presided over by Archbishop Benelli and Archbishop Jadot, the investigation undertaken by the United States Attorney, the investigation of the *Chicago Sun-Times*. Somehow or other the journalist conflated my remarks in the diary with these other three "plots" in a story that was a hundred pages long. The first I knew about it was when Archbishop Bernardin called me in July to ask what was happening. I felt like I had been run over by the Amtrak at the gates of Grand Beach.

I persuaded Father Hesburg of Notre Dame to tell the journalist that he had no right to take the tapes and documents and order him to return them to Rosary. Indeed, Hesburg told him that they just didn't do things like that at Notre Dame. He did return the tapes and the documents, but only after he had made copies of them all. He continued to write his story, on Notre Dame time. I had made my third mistake, trusting Notre Dame to enforce Hesburg's orders.

I did not realize as the summer went on that the journalist was trying to peddle his story to Chicago journals in exchange for a job and that Eugene Kennedy, whom I thought of as a close friend, was not only urging him to do so but setting up interviews for him with editors all along Michigan Avenue. Fourth major mistake—trusting Kennedy to act like a friend.

We had been friends, close friends, I had thought, for a long time. I had trusted him completely. I had dedicated my book *The Friendship Game* to him. At the request of the Maryknoll order we had toured their center houses in Asia in 1967 to explain what the Vatican Council was about. We spent much time together in subsequent years. He once rented a house in Grand Beach down the street from me so we could be near one another. We drifted apart after he left the priesthood and married a former Maryknoll nun, despite my constant efforts to keep in touch with him. (Reasons always came up at the last minute that would force him to cancel dinner.) I do not understand what happened between us. He betrayed me without warning and without any attempt to straighten out the problems in our friendship. In some very real sense he broke my heart—as well as stuck a knife in my back. When I first discovered the extent of the animosity toward me (from sworn depositions of the Notre Dame journalist in his libel suit against me which Kennedy had brokered), I was shattered.

I now come to a part of the story that I have never put on the public record before, although Kennedy has told everyone who will listen, even to the present, how I had endangered Cardinal Bernardin's career. His story is often vague and allusive and confuses time sequences and details and changes to fit the one to whom he is telling it. I don't like to have to record what really happened because both in the first volume of these memoirs and in this book I do not want to name names. I don't know how many people believe Kennedy's story. Most who do will probably go on believing it. Nonetheless, it is now time to tell the truth.

Much of the story can be found in the Notre Dame journalist's deposition in the suit he later filed against me. The entire text of the dep-

osition can be found on the net at http://www.usao.edu/~facshaferi/
winters.html.[32]

In September, on doctor's orders, I went off for a month's rest in
Corfu, quite unaware of the tinderbox I had left behind. Only when I
had settled in on the island (a delightful place for a rest, by the way) did
the box explode. Someone leaked a partial version of the journalist's
article to a weekly paper called *The Chicago Lawyer*. There were in those
days only two long-distance lines into Corfu. I spent much of the day
trying to communicate with Chicago to dampen the fires as best as I
could. It was too late.

However, as I insisted then and as I insist again, most of the "exposé"
had already been published in my book *The Making of the Popes* and my
alleged plot—now three years old—had nothing to do with the inves-
tigations of Cardinal Cody currently under way. It was, I fear, too subtle
a point.

The story made no difference to me personally. They had, after
all, spelled my name right. I was not ashamed of my opposition to
our psychopathic cardinal. However, I was devastated by the possibility that the incident would destroy the career of a man who was
not only the best leader the American Church had, but also a close
personal friend. I didn't see how he could be blamed for my reflections in the diary. But apparently he was. The new apostolic delegate,
Pio Laghi, told him that he had "blotted his copy book" and would
not be archbishop of Chicago. Whether that was Laghi's opinion or
the pope's is not clear.

Who did leak the story to *The Chicago Lawyer*? Ingrid Shafer, who had
been a private investigator before she became an academic, did a detailed
examination of all the events of the story and concluded that Eugene
Kennedy probably had provided the newspaper with a partial text of the
article, most likely indirectly. Anyone who is interested in her reasoning
can find her paper on her Web site (http://www.usao.edu/~facshaferi/
SALIERI.HTML). I find her argument persuasive. If Kennedy was willing to risk harm to Bernardin's career by promoting the article with
Chicago editors, he would certainly not hesitate to see that it was published some other way.

I would learn later from his book *Cardinal Bernardin and the Struggle
for the American Church* that at the very time he was promoting the article,

---

[32]When I first read this deposition I was rocked to the depths of my personality. For days I was sick because of the betrayal by men I thought were my
friends. Now I find it kind of funny, like cheap fiction. The journalist not only
hung himself but a lot of other folks.

he was also acting (or at least claiming to act) as an adviser to the archbishop.

While I was reeling from *The Chicago Lawyer* article, another Amtrak train ran over me. I received a message from Bernardin, through a strange indirect route, but one that sounded like him. It said that the Vatican would not object to my writing unless I wrote anything more about the Cody situation. But if I did, I would be punished severely. Moreover, I was told that this was a message from the highest authority (Vaticanese for the pope). I asked the messenger whether the highest authority realized that a threat like that would almost guarantee that I would write on the forbidden subject. The response was that the point had been made, but the message was still the same.

I tried to get through to Bernardin several times, but the telephone lines on Corfu blocked my efforts. So I sent him a letter warning him never, never to threaten me again. The letter apparently persuaded him that I was around the bend, as well it might have. The message, as plausible as it sounded, had, according to Professor Shafer's research, come from Kennedy, as seemed clear to me from reading his subsequent book. My friendship with Joe Bernardin would be in ruins for years. Even when it was renewed, I don't think the cardinal ever really trusted me fully.

Fifth major mistake: I did not try to talk to the archbishop when I returned from Corfu.

Kennedy was not finished, however.[34] He urged the Notre Dame reporter to sue me for saying that he did not have my permission to remove my diaries and that he had not told the truth to Father Hesburg about keeping copies of my documents. Moreover, he provided the young man with his own lawyer to pursue the suit. Eventually, I was persuaded to settle for a trivial sum (paid eagerly by my insurance company) but the suit caused me considerable mental anguish. Kennedy apparently didn't care that journalists don't sue and that the reporter's career was dead as soon as it became known in the profession that he had filed a libel suit.

The *Sun-Times* backed off its investigation, apparently because Catholics on the staff had persuaded its editor Jim Hoge that they would revolt if he did not kill the story. Rumors on LaSalle Street had it that a Catholic judge stalled the grand jury investigation until the cardinal died in the early winter of 1982. In the summer of 1982 Joseph Bernardin became archbishop of Chicago. He had suffered from the apparent wreck

[34]Documentation for this part of the story is in the depositions (in my archives) from the trial Kennedy brokered.

of his career. The young reporter's reputation in his own profession was in ruins. I was haunted by the nightmare of 1981 for years.

Eugene never gives up. In his book on Cardinal Bernardin, he blames me for embarrassing the cardinal (and almost costing him the appointment to Chicago). He tells the story to any journalist who will listen to him. His analyses seem credible both because we were close friends for many years and because of his professional qualifications as a psychologist. However, he violates both the norms of friendship and the norms of the profession in such psychobabble.

I was not the one responsible for the cardinal's embarrassment. Rather, the responsible parties were the nun at Rosary, the man who removed my confidential files, and Eugene who conspired to get them published, while all the time pretending to be the cardinal's adviser and friend. However close he may have been to the late cardinal, Kennedy's friendship did not preclude him from engaging in activity which would embarrass the cardinal. It was obviously more important to embarrass me than to protect the cardinal.

In his book *Cardinal Bernardin and the Struggle for the American Church*, he informs his readers that my warning in the paperback edition of *Confessions of a Parish Priest* about the serious pedophile problems in the Chicago Archdiocese was merely an attempt to get the cardinal's attention and that Bernardin had better things to do than to worry about such matters. It turns out that my warnings were unfortunately prophetic. Subsequently, a priest reported to me that Eugene had been telling people that I was obsessed with pedophilia because I had been sexually abused by my father.

I hope he did not say that. But if he did, I will reply in the language of Nuala Anne McGrail in my novels: if he really said that he is a lying, frigging gobshite!

Cardinal Bernardin and the Struggle for the American Church was not about Joe Bernardin. As the cardinal himself would later say, it was about me—I'm mentioned far more often than the cardinal. My advisers persuaded me not to respond to the book because a response would only give him the publicity he wanted. Instead I wrote a memo for my archives. I sent copies to Dick Phelan, my lawyer; June Rosner, my able media maven (and Jewish mother); and to the cardinal. Two days later Chicago columnist Irv Kupcinet called me and asked if I had written such a memo. I said I had. Did Eugene tell you about it, I asked. Kup, an old friend from way back, laughed in a fashion which suggested that was exactly what happened. I checked with Dick and June before I called the cardinal. They knew nothing about the leak. So I called the cardinal.

"Did you show my memo to Eugene?"

"I did . . . The book is about me and I wanted to know whether there was falsehood in it. Actually, there is more in it about you than about me. I asked him to change it, but he did not do so."

"My memo said 'confidential!' "

"I didn't think that meant I couldn't ask him about it."

"You showed it to him."

Silence.

"Yes, I did."

End of conversation.

A few days later there was an item in Kup's column in the *Chicago Sun-Times* about the memo. The publicity did not help the book which shortly was remaindered and sank without a trace. Yet I was appalled by how many Catholic reviewers were willing to believe everything he said about me, though he offered no proof, no documentation—other than his own word—for what he wrote about me.

I will not burden the reader with a refutation of the book. If anyone in years to come cares about the subject, my memo is at the Chicago Historical Society. But I will cite one paragraph from my memo to illustrate the technique of the book: Eugene authoritatively describes something I have done and then interprets my behavior with the professional skills of a psychologist:

> *On page 57 he says that I "was deeply disappointed not to be elected by his fellow clergymen as a member of the first board of the Association of Chicago Priests, or to any role in the National Federation whose aims he had encouraged." I didn't run for the Association of Chicago Priests. I didn't run for the Federation of Priests Councils. I was not active in the formation of either. I had no reason to think I was going to be elected to the board and would not have accepted nomination to the board if it were offered. So I certainly was not disappointed by not being elected. And here we come to the first example of his projection of his own emotions into mine. How would he know that I was disappointed unless I had told him, and he doesn't claim that.*

I count at least twenty similar segments in the book. He alleges something false about me and then, without a shred of evidence other than his say-so, explains my motives.

Three times he quotes the late Dan Herr, president of the Thomas More Association, a major figure in Catholic publishing, and a very close friend of mine. I asked Dan for a letter for my archives on the subject of those quotes. He replied:

> *Several months ago when I was first informed of Kennedy's infamous book and the three quotations attributed to me, I wrote him a vehement letter. But after due consideration I decided not to send it— the book was sure to be a dud and the best revenge against a publicity-hound is to ignore him.*
>
> *Because of our very long friendship I was not concerned that you would take his charges seriously, particularly because you would know better than anyone how distorted his portrait of you was.*
>
> *Although I thought the phoniness of the quotations was obvious, I made no attempt to deny them to you or to other friends. Now, at your request, I do so deny their veracity for the archives.*

Dan and the other advisers who told me to ignore the book were doubtless correct. Yet Eugene continues to tell his crazy stories about me to any reporter who seems willing to listen. For example, to one reporter he apparently accused me of "self-plagiarism," complete with an exact page reference to where I do it. How can one plagiarize oneself, how to pretend that something you wrote, you didn't write yourself but stole from someone else, that someone being yourself? I looked up the page the reporter gave me. Sure enough it was the first page of a chapter in my book on ethnicity which, as I noted on that page, came from a technical article I had written in a professional journal, the exact reference to which was in my note!

Priests who know about the ruins of our friendship tell me that Eugene is a collector. They point out that he collects celebrity friends. Paul D'Arcy, a fellow member of the Maryknoll order, was the first of them (of whom I am aware). He was quickly discarded. I was the next. Perhaps I fell from grace when *The Cardinal Sins* sold three million copies and his book *Father's Day* (published at the same time) sold fifteen thousand. It was a long time before I realized that I had fallen from grace. After that came Jacqueline Onassis, Norman Mailer, Saul Bellow, and Cardinal Bernardin—and many prominent Chicago media types. Some of the collected dropped away. Others declined admission to Eugene's museum, most notably the Daley family. I presume that Cardinal George will be his next target. It is all faintly ludicrous, a search for reflected celebrity status which is both patent and sad.[35]

[35]While as I was revising this chapter, at a dinner a number of Chicago priests, who apparently did not remember Kennedy's book (or more likely had never

Have I learned anything from the extraordinary and devastating assault orchestrated through the years by Gene Kennedy? I'm not sure. One of Professor Shafer's sources describes me as too trusting. I suppose I still am. That is not necessarily bad. I have learned that I can survive such an ingenious and devious campaign of destruction. I have learned how fragile anyone whose name appears in public can be when attacked by someone determined to embarrass him. I have learned that one can never count on most of one's friends in such crises. My ordeal was minor when compared to that of many other people. Yet, let those who think it was trivial and hardly worth mentioning beware that something like such a betrayal of friendship ever happen to them.

Adversary: Now that you've got that stuff off your chest, would you ever forget about him and listen to me!

Will I admit the possibility of reconciliation with Gene, especially since on the rare occasions we meet he fawns over me with characteristic flattery? Sure, I'm a Christian. I believe in reconciliation. I also believe in cutting the cards. I need some evidence that he has given up his attacks on me. I continue to wonder why a man of such great talent would waste so much time on a venture which was bound to be unproductive and which had at best modest chance at success.

---

read it), complained about Eugene's using Cardinal Bernardin's death to show case himself. "It's supposed to be about Joe, but the focus is always on Kennedy himself."

Pedophile Problems

Of all my tilts with windmills, the most unpleasant was my involvement as a critic of the Church's response to the charges against priests of sexual abuse. I don't like to think about it now. Even less do I like to write about it. I don't regret that I spoke out on the abuse of women and children by priests. Someone had to. Most priests either denied the problem or covered it up. But the evil of sexual abuse is so ugly and the institutional Church's response so pathetically inadequate that my stomach tightens up whenever I force myself to contemplate such abuse. There is nothing that I've done or said which has made me more of an outcast in the priesthood. It has won me the status of a permanent outsider. Still I must record the story because it has been an important, if unwanted, dimension of my life.

In the Confident Church few cases of sexual abuse ever became public. Priests got away with it and the Church got away with covering up. The Confusing Church men are caught and the Church has lost much of its power to cover up. Many of the laity will no longer remain silent when their children are abused by priests. Lawyers no longer seek settlements which continue the conspiracy of silence. The criminal justice system will no longer wink at priest abusers. Almost by themselves these changes makes the Confusing Church better than the Confident Church.

In 1989 HBO presented a film called *Judgment* about the Lafayette, Louisiana, pedophile case. It was, I thought, a fair and honest presentation of the story. Children were abused by a deeply troubled priest, he was transferred to several other parishes where he abused more children, the parents were devastated, the Diocese tried to cover up and was caught, the parents sued, the priest went to jail. Compared to subsequent media coverage of the Church's pedophile problem, *Judgment* was a model of restraint and objectivity.

The then vicar for priests of the Archdiocese of Chicago attacked the film on the grounds that it was diabolical "because it is going to destroy the faith the average person has in their minister or priest." He showed rather little confidence in the maturity of the laity, and in fact, the subsequent explosion of pedophile charges did not destroy the faith of the laity in their clergy. According to a survey done by the *Boston Globe* of the reaction of Massachusetts Catholics to the famous Father Porter Case, the laity were quite capable of distinguishing between one priest or a few priests and all priests. Many laity in the survey would be a little more wary of priests—a wise attitude. However, the alleged "loss of faith" became part of the "ostrich head in the sand" attitude toward pedophilia which is still characteristic of the clerical reaction to the pedophile problem.

The other argument against the exposure of pedophila was that priests would be embarrassed by the suspicion the laity might have for them personally. They were concerned about themselves and their public image, not about the victims and their families. I have never been able to comprehend the blindness of my fellow priests to the suffering of a victim of child abuse and the victim's family. Compassion disappears when it is necessary to rally round one of one's own. Just like cops, priests cover up and deny (even to themselves) when one of their own is attacked.

The vicar for priests then went on to say that it couldn't happen in Chicago because the Archdiocese of Chicago had guidelines which prevented it. A few years later twenty-three Chicago priests were removed by the cardinal on the recommendation of the commission he had established and two priests had been sentenced to jail. It *did* happen in Chicago. As far as I am aware, the vicar for clergy[36] (now an auxiliary

---

[36]When I go on these crusades of mine—against Cardinal Cody, against the pedophilia cover-up, and now against the violation of the rights of the laity by those clergy and quasi-clergy who deny them the sacraments—I must always be careful that I am concerned primarily about the freedom of the laypeople and not motivated by a general anger at clerical culture (and the priests who are possessed by it) or a specific anger at certain people. It is not an easy task. Many Catholic zealots, particularly of the social action or "peace and justice" variety, turn me off because their zeal is so patently motivated by anger and resentment rooted in personality problems and not in concern for the poor or the suffering. Anger is an appropriate response to injustice, so long as it does not exist primarily as an emotional release for the angry person. The best I can say about myself is that on the average my mixed motives were more pure than impure. Anyone who denies their motives are mixed is not to be trusted. I must say that in all three of my "crusades," I have not enjoyed the fight. In the pedophile problem, I hated every moment of it. Yet I was one of the few priests free to speak so, my father's son that I am, I could not maintain my self-respect or sense of personal integrity unless I spoke up.

The vicar for priests and I have had strong personality conflicts since our days in the seminary (he is two years older than I am). We get along all right on the personal level—we recently exchanged notes in which I praised him for an eulogy he had given for one of my classmates—but on the level of ideology (which in this case is another form of personality) I have always seen him as a "company man," one for whom loyalty to superiors, to the institutional Church,

bishop and vicar general of the Archdiocese—the Peter Principle does not apply in the Church) has never admitted on the public record that he was mistaken or apologized for the sexual abuse of children. But there is no reason why he should be different from other priests and bishops. Most of them refuse to apologize or even see the need of an apology.

Cardinal Bernardin was an exception to this refusal. He apologized on the record and repeatedly. Unlike most bishops and priests he understood that your appeal increases if you admit you have made a mistake and promise you will do all you can to see that it never happens again.

I was furious about the vicar's comments and wrote a column for the *Chicago Sun-Times* in which I said that the really diabolical people were the clergy who covered up for pedophiles and then reassigned them to new parishes where they found new victims. Since I was free to speak up, I figured I had to. I don't regret the decision. My efforts might have been an utter waste of time, but I had to try, even if I knew I was going to fail. I thought the horror of sexual abuse and the terrible harm done to the priesthood would both make priests and bishops listen. I couldn't have been more wrong.

I also called for an outside agency to investigate charges, past and present, against priests in the Archdiocese. Later the cardinal would set up two such commissions, one to investigate files for past charges and another to consider new charges. In both cases the majority of the members were lay and not beholden to the Church.[37] I believe that I was the first one to suggest on the record review by outside agencies—so that

---

and to the priesthood were nearly ultimate values. I'm sure he has seen me as a loose cannon devoid of such loyalty. I wish he'd apologize on the record for the pedophile mess.

[37]The second commission, which currently reviews all charges, is made up of three priests and six laity, five of whom are women, one a victim of sexual abuse. It is the first time since Brigid of Kildare that women have had authority on the assignments of priests. It will take time for this commission to establish the credibility that will eliminate the suspicion caused by past mistakes. However, it has acted promptly on a number of occasions to exercise its mandate of protecting children. For the most part Chicago priests have bitterly opposed the commission because it takes away the last shreds of clerical immunity. They also continue to be sympathetic to the priests who were removed by the cardinal's first commission. Priests are willing to admit that there is a problem of pedophilia, but are unable to accept the charges against any specific one of their clerical brothers. Only three-tenths of one percent of the priests in the *Los Angeles Times* study thought that pedophilia was a serious problem for the American Church. Most were satisfied that while once it had been a problem, the new procedures had eliminated it as a problem. Such blindness staggers the mind.

priests would not be sitting in judgment on fellow priests. I claim no credit, however, for the cardinal's two commissions because the idea was pure common sense.

However, I am unaware of any other diocese in the country (with the exception of Seattle) in which a priest or a group of priests is not responsible for the final recommendation to the bishop. It doesn't seem to occur to priests or bishops that this kind of procedure will enjoy any credibility.

In the year between the publication of *Confessions* and its paperback edition I had learned for the first time about the sexual predators in the Archdiocese. In the paperback edition (1987) I had written a much longer chapter on celibacy to both defend it and to warn about the dangers the predators were to both young people and to the Church.[38] I had predicted that just as money was the scandal in the Cody Archdiocese so sex might become the scandal in the Bernardin Archdiocese—a prediction whose fulfillment was beyond anything I could have imagined.

A couple of years after I revised *Confessions*, a priest I had known for a long time proposed that we have lunch and he told me a horror story about how he had been "framed" by a false accusation of sexual abuse. He wanted my help, if only to be reassured that I believed him. I did. After all, he was a friend, wasn't he? Moreover, he was not one of the predators about whom I had learned. I wrote about a similar but utterly imaginary case of false accusation in my novel *The Cardinal Virtues* (1990).

This experience impresses on me today how reluctant I was to believe accusations against a fellow priest I knew, even though I was more aware of the problem than most others.[39] It turns out now that he was one of the priests removed by the cardinal's commission.

My column about *Judgment* led to an outpouring of letters from victims and parents. I realized for the first time that in addition to the ring of predators of whom I was aware, there were many more in the Archdiocese. The Church was still covering up. I wrote more columns and received more letters. A request was made from the floor of the "Council

[38]Gene Kennedy, always ready to play the coyote, twisted a passage out of context to make it sound like I thought that Cardinal Bernardin was one of them when I had in fact said just the opposite.

[39]Many priests, I believe, have hovered between ignorance and knowledge. They knew (and know) about the behavior of certain of their colleagues but they cannot bring themselves to know that they know. You talk to them about a given predator and they will tell you stories about him. Yet they won't admit that he is a grave danger to every young person with whom he comes in contact. This mix of knowledge and denial is at least in part culpable. Enough to require an apology.

of Priests" that the cardinal shut me up on the subject. He made no comment on the request (perhaps aware that he could not shut me up). Priests, including one who might be a predator himself, wrote to the *Sun-Times* attacking me. Not a priestly voice was raised in my defense. Nor has one ever been raised since.

The facts about sexual abuse in America are horrific. Seventeen percent of Americans (in the National Opinion Research Center's sex study) reported that they had been touched sexually before puberty, equally men and women. Two-fifths of the men and seven-tenths of the women reported that this abuse affected the rest of their lives. Eight percent of the men reported that their first sexual intercourse was forced, 14 percent of the women. Forty percent of the women and 20 percent of the men reported sexual harassment at work. In another national sample a third of the women reported some kind of sexual harassment from members of their family, 3 percent rape by fathers or stepfathers.

I doubt that these numbers represent anything unique in contemporary America. Rather they are a snap shot of the human condition. Defenseless men, women, and children have often been sexually abused. Only now has the horror come into the open.

I remember a weekend Boy Scout encampment when I was in late grammar school. I wandered into a cabin and observed a group of boys my age in the center of the large room whooping and hollering. I joined them to see what they were doing. A couple of them were holding a boy on the floor and another was masturbating him. Rape at thirteen. I didn't know what was going on then and I didn't know the word "rape." I left the cabin quickly because I was repelled by what I had seen, though I didn't understand it. It has never left my memory. I often wonder whether that assault affected the rest of the victim's life, and whether like most victims, he never told anyone about it. I was happy at our golden reunion to see that the rapist was not there.

There is obviously a psychological dimension to the problem. Those who prey on children and defenseless women (and defenseless men) are twisted emotionally. But there is also a more important sociological problem, that of what we in the trade call an "asymmetry of power," the strong prey on those who are weak, the powerful on less powerful. If one combines power with twisted emotions, one has a predator, perhaps a monster.

The pedophile problem is not new. A priest who said Mass on occasion in the parish in which I grew up (not one of the regular staff) made passes at altar boys (not at me).

The Church's usual procedure when accusations were made was to buy off the parents of the victim (usually by paying the costs of therapy though in some cases hundreds of thousands of dollars changed hands), send the priest into therapy, and then reassign him. It was felt that sexual abuse of children was a moral problem and that if the man "pulled himself together" the problem would not reoccur.

Catholic police and Catholic prosecuting attorneys in large cities where the population was Catholic had no taste for arresting and prosecuting a priest. He was the Church's problem. Then the Church would argue that he had been cleared by the police. Moreover, it would be said that he had also been cleared by psychiatrists. In fact, usually the psychiatrists (paid by the Church) would say that there was no absolute proof that the man was a chronic child abuser. Later they would insist that they never recommended that a priest be reassigned, but neither did they ever recommend, as far as I can learn, that a priest not be reassigned. Some Catholic lawyers quit working for the Church when they learned that despite promises, such men were routinely reassigned. One lawyer I know was propositioned by a diocesan official.

This symbiosis of neglect between the Church and the public authority was, from the point of view of both, a successful response for years, even decades. It was hard on victims, but neither institution worried much about them. Nor was there much concern that Church and State were conspiring, however implicitly, in the obstruction of justice. When finally they were forced to abandon this strategy, bishops said that they had only just realized that pedophilia was a psychological rather than a moral problem and probably an incurable one. Such a response is partially true but inadequate. It is interesting that bishops began to offer it only when the media broke the story of sexual abuse by priests and when victims' families all over the country filed damage suits. Moreover, the excuse that they didn't realize the nature of the problem is finally insufficient because they should have known about it. Maybe their psychiatrists, fearful perhaps of losing a client, didn't tell them, but the bishops are still responsible for seeming to solicit from their hired shrinks the opinions they wanted to hear.

Bishops did and often still do respond to the pain of victims and their families not as ministers of Jesus Christ should but with the adversarial style which their own lawyers propose. In effect, they become captives of their lawyers (who, be it noted, have earned huge fees off such cases). Thus in one case, an archdiocese sued the family of a victim, charging them with responsibility for the attack on their son because they had not warned the son about the possibility of such victimization. Even after the pedophile scandals became public the Church's approach, with many exceptions, continues to be legalistic, not pastoral. An iron law ought to be, as a senior American prelate remarked to me, you never, never let the lawyers take charge of your decision-making process. Their input is important, but it should never be final. Unfortunately in many cases, the lawyers took over completely, often with disastrous financial results and always with disastrous pastoral results.

At the root of the cover-up, however, is the traditional propensity of the Catholic Church in the United States to hide its scandals in every way it can, a propensity inherited from the early days of the immigrant Church when the Church felt it was a garrison under assault from nativist bigotry. Scandals also had to be covered up less the laity be shocked. Moreover, the intense loyalty of the priestly caste made priests most reluctant to admit that another priest had done wrong. It was (and still is) unthinkable to denounce another priest.[40] The clerical culture of the Catholic Church demanded that erring priests be treated gently, even when they had broken the law. Priests felt and still feel that they are entitled to a kind of quasi-immunity from the law, even if civil law patently does not accept the immunity which canon law grants the clergy.

More than anyone else, a New Orleans writer, Jason Berry, brought the situation to public attention with articles in the *National Catholic Reporter* and then in the *Chicago Reader*. Then Mary Anne Ahern, a young reporter for Channel 5 in Chicago, broke the conspiracy of silence with a story about a Chicago priest who had been charged with abusing a fourteen-year-old-girl, a priest who had been charged some years before by a mother with molesting her son and who had left a long trail of complaints around the Archdiocese.[41] The floodgates opened and Cardinal Bernardin began his reform which, while overdue, was nonetheless the best and the most comprehensive in the country.

Both Mr. Berry and Ms. Ahern were attacked, the latter from the altar of her parish church. Bishops and priests all over the country denounced the national media for programs on clerical sexual abuse. Cardinal Law of Boston literally cursed them by calling down the wrath of heaven on them. Yet the media was the last court of appeal for victims and their families who had been denied justice by both Church and State. They

[40]The loyalty vanishes when a priest is successful. Then he must be torn down.
[41]The mother had been beaten down by the Archdiocese's adversarial legal tactics and forced, because she had no money left, to settle her case for less than her legal costs. After the priest was convicted of abusing the teenage girl, the Archdiocese made no move to apologize to her, though she and the cardinal did meet personally several times.

still are because despite all the publicity and all the promises of reform, the predators are still on the prowl and the Church still has not put its house in order.

The priest whose case Ms. Ahern made public was convicted by an Irish Catholic judge in a bench trial and is now serving a prison term.[42] The argument Chicago priests offered in his favor is that the young woman has to be lying because the priest is gay and wouldn't abuse a girl. They closed their eyes to the fact that some abusers get their kicks from humiliating a victim and gender doesn't matter. Indeed, through the whole crisis, most priests have shown a dismaying inability to sympathize with victims and their families and to understand what it must be like to be sexually abused by a man you have trusted.

I am told that later the vicar for priests remarked that the problem would never have arisen if the priest in question had not been sent to the parish where he was caught. Did he mean that the cover-up could continue? What else could he have meant?

I do not know what the Church should do about pedophile priests. One of the reasons for reassigning them was that bishops saw nowhere else to put them, save in another parish. Now the Church tends to warehouse them until they get fed up and retire from the priesthood. Then the Church is no longer legally liable for their behavior. I'm not sure that prison sentences are appropriate either. Prison is not for those with (at times) irresistible compulsions. Pedophiles have been victims themselves and are caught up in a horror not of their own making (like the protagonist of *Interview with a Vampire*). They deserve compassion as much as their victims do, though I can hardly expect victims and their families to agree. I am not angry at the predators, not even at those who use their positions in the power structure to protect themselves. Rather I am angry at the bishops who have reassigned them and turn the victims and their families into "enemies." I am even more angry at their fellow priests who protect them.

I wrote in an op-ed page column in *The New York Times* that it was the most serious crisis in the priesthood since the French Revolution and perhaps the worse religious scandal in the history of our country. More priests denounced me. Blame the herald of bad news and not those who created the bad news.

Anti-Catholic bigots and angry Catholics had a field day. Celibacy

---

[42]It is the only case of sexual abuse by the clergy that States' Attorney Jack O'Malley has prosecuted. He staged a press conference to announce he would not prosecute a second priest who was later convicted of a pedophilia charge in Wisconsin.

was the problem. Abolish celibacy and there'd be no problem. Transform the institutional structure of the Church and the problem would be solved. Abolish the Catholic sexual ethic and the problem would go away. Give women more power and sexual abuse would disappear.

This was absolute and self-serving nonsense when offered by men who had left the priesthood to marry. Abusive personalities are trapped in a syndrome acquired early in life. In most cases they are married men, in a couple of cases married priests.

Journalists of every variety appealed to me to grant interviews on the subject. June Rosner, my media maven, selected carefully those to whom I would respond. Yet as the priest present, I was often under attack for the cover-up (especially by Phil Donahue) when I was one of those who helped (in a minor way) to blow the cover-up.

I spoke at a few meetings of victims' organizations, and even though I was the only priest in the country who was publicly on their side, many of them attacked me. I warned them if they beat up on their friends they wouldn't have any friends. However, so great was their pain that they could not see that truth.

I always tried to make several points, usually too nuanced for the simplistic world of the media—and especially for Phil Donahue:

1. Most priests were not pedophiles. In the careful study done by Cardinal Bernardin's commission, 3.27 percent were removed because of past charges. The national rate is certainly no lower than this.
2. Pedophilia is not merely a priestly problem. It affects the Protestant and Jewish clergy and professionals in all areas where there is access to children—education, sports, scouting, for example.
3. Pedophilia is not caused by celibacy. It is an obsession acquired very early in life and is apparently incurable. Most pedophiles are married men. If the pedophile priests were permitted to marry, they would continue to prey on children, often their own. One can perhaps make a case for the reform of the celibacy discipline, but pedophilia is not an appropriate argument for those who seek such reform. Quite the contrary, it is an intellectually dishonest if not bigoted response, equally so when advanced by Catholic "liberals."
4. The obsession is so powerful that the predators are often not responsible for what they do.[43] Often, perhaps always, they were victims themselves in childhood. The real villains are the bishops who reassign them and the priests who fail to denounce them.[44]

[43]I'm not sure that a jail sentence is appropriate for them.
[44]In response to my *NYT* column several priests wrote to say that they had denounced a child abuser. The accusing priest was punished by being trans-

5. Pedophiles are not necessarily gay. Girls as well as boys are targets of sexual abuse. Indeed, incestuous abuse of girls and women is one of the worst and most frequent crimes in the country (one out of five women have been the target of such abuse). Some predators don't care about the gender of the victim because humiliation is the goal of their obsession. However, it would appear that usually the sexual orientation of the pedophile priest is homosexual and a young male is his preferred target. Nevertheless, most gays and indeed most gay priests are not pedophiles.[45]

6. On the basis of the *Boston Globe* survey, the pedophile revelations had not caused Catholics to leave the Church or to lower their opinions of the priesthood. However, they demand honesty and quick solutions from their leaders. Many of them are thinking of lowering their financial contributions.

Such attempts at nuance were not reassuring to the victims groups which were forming to bring pressure on the Church and wanted more vigorous denunciations. But they did not diminish the animosity of priests either. When the two elected groups of Chicago priests—the Council of Priests and the Association of Chicago Priests—issued tepid and empty statements about the problems, I observed in print that they were weaklings who were not ready to face either the scope or the horror of the crises. The presidents of both groups demanded that I talk with them. I had been through such conversations before and know what they're like. All the emotions of loyalty to the priesthood would be invoked and I would in effect be put on trial.

I replied that I saw no point in meeting with them until their public statements indicated a willingness to denounce sexual abuse by priests and to apologize to the victims and their families. Like the equally ineffectual National Federation of Priests Councils, they were incapable,

---

ferred, suspended from the priesthood, and even compelled to take psychiatric treatment. As one of them said in his letter, when the truth of his accusations was finally sustained, no one apologized.

[45]A distinction is often made between pedophiles and ephybophiles. The former prey on children of either gender, while the latter prey only on young men—boys between twelve and sixteen. The former may have hundreds of victims, the latter, it is said, only a few. The value of the distinction escapes me. How many Catholic laity would want a priest in their parish who has abused only one or two adolescent boys? It may be that "treatment" works better in the case of ephybophiles. But in both types of cases, treatment only means "management"—constant supervision, participation in "twelve-step" groups, the use of medication such as depo-provera which diminishes libido (often called "chemical castration"). There are no guarantees that such "treatment" will work in the long run. Nor is there any "cure" at the present time.

then or now, of doing much more than expressing sympathy for priests and calling on the bishops to solve the problem.

Nothing has made me feel more contemptuous of my fellow priests—both as individuals and as collectivities—than their response to the pedophile crisis. Even though the image of the priesthood was and is in terrible jeopardy and devastating harm had been done to countless laity, they could do nothing more than sympathize with the accused priests, worry about their own rights, and blame the media. This reaction convinced me that our education (even in the seminaries of today) is sadly deficient, our levels of emotional maturity are tragically low, and our sensitivities to the laity virtually nonexistent.

The bishops in a way are worse. They responded as bishops usually do. After blaming the media for the problem, they set up a committee to study the problem, to make a report, and to issue vague and feeble guidelines. They were unwilling either to make a collective apology or to engage in a public penitential service.

Media pressure has lessened—for the time being—because the public has grown weary of a story that is no longer news and because the absurdity of the charges against Cardinal Bernardin cut the ground out from under further revelations. Dioceses continue to engage in tough legal tactics. Bridgeport, Connecticut, denies responsibility because, it argues, priests are not its employees but independent contractors. Dallas loses a judgment for more than a hundred million dollars. Prosecuting attorneys continue to duck indictments. Priests and bishops continue to refuse to apologize or do appropriate public penance. Priests continue to deny the obvious guilt of their colleagues and to blame the whole problem on the media. Nothing much has changed. Less than 10 precent of the priests in the country, according to the *Los Angeles Times* study of priests, see pedophilia as a serious problem.

The victims groups continue to apply pressure. Some priests have been removed. Suits are more likely to be settled now on terms favorable to the victims and their families. Only a few of the "review boards" around the country have or deserve much credibility. Prosecutors are a bit more wary of obstructing justice because they realize that the Catholic laity no longer wants priest pedophiles protected. Bishops are more hesitant about reassigning pedophiles, but mostly because they fear more suits. The national hierarchy protests that it doesn't know how many priests are abusers or how much money settlements have cost. And, one must add, doesn't want to know. Nor is it willing to take any vigorous collective action. Bishops and priests seem to think that if they continue to stonewall everything will return to the way it used to be.

There are some exceptions of course, including Chicago.[46] But even in Chicago, the ring of predators about whom I wrote in the paperback edition of *Confessions* remains untouched. There is no evidence against them because no one has complained about them and none of their fellow priests have denounced them.[47] Those who have been removed are for the most part lone offenders who lacked the skill to cover their tracks. The ring is much more clever. Perhaps they always will be. But should they slip, should they get caught, the previous scandals will seem trivial. Others like them still flourish all around the country.

There have been some improvements. The problem, however, is not solved, the crisis remains, the powder keg is still volatile, the bomb is still ticking. Keep your fingers crossed.

Do I regret my involvement in the crisis? Of course not. I spoke the truth when it needed to be spoken. I spoke it in as careful a style as possible. I earned a lot of animosity from my fellow priests because of what I said, but so what else is new. Did I have much impact?

I don't think so. If I had remained silent, I can't think of how anything would be different from the way it is. Moreover, you get no points in the institutional Catholic Church today for having been right. You may have been right when you made your first warnings ten years ago. You may even have been right when you wrote your first column. But you're not right now when you say the problem is almost as bad as it ever was.

My column in the *Sun-Times* was killed because, as the editor told my agent, there was too much about pedophilia in it—this two weeks after he had told the same agent that the columns were wonderful. Did the Archdiocese do me in? I am inclined to think it did. The cardinal did not complain, of that I'm sure. But lesser folk probably did complain, using his name without his permission.

I am convinced that the crisis will abate only when priests, individually and collectively, assume personal responsibility to end it, instead of un-

[46]The public relations staff of the Archiocese has not been able to explain effectively how the cardinal's reform program works either to the media or to the people of Chicago. In fact, they have made such a hash of it that I am tempted to believe that either they do not understand it or that they do not want to understand it.

[47]They are a dangerous group. There is reason to believe that they are responsible for at least one murder and may perhaps have been involved in the murder of the murderer. Am I afraid of them? Not particularly. They know that I have in safekeeping information which would implicate them. I am more of a threat to them dead than alive.

loading the responsibility on the bishops (as did the National Federation of Priests Councils). I see absolutely no signs that priests are prepared to do that. Ever.

In the next chapter I will describe how the pedophile crisis led to a reconciliation between Cardinal Bernardin and me, through a particularly ingenious (I've always thought) exercise of God drawing straight with crooked lines. Even after that reconciliation, however, the cardinal and I continued to agree to disagree about the case that brought me storming up to his house. He was absolutely convinced that the hardball tactics (including countersuits for libel) that the Archdiocese has funded in this case were necessary to protect an innocent man. I feel that the Archdiocese ought to have settled the suit out of court. While the priest won the suit brought against him, it would seem to me and to many of those who watched the case he did so only because the judge (whom the media people present at the trial thought was biased in favor of the Church) refused to let the parents of the victim present most of their evidence. Lawyers with no particular interest in either side in the case have told me that the judge committed reversible errors. However, winning a suit does not mean that the Church has seen justice done.

Moreover, the general opinion among Chicago lawyers is that you never want to get in a suit against the Catholic Church because it has deep—seemingly bottomless—pockets and that on occasion the playing field is tilted against the Archdiocese's "enemies."

The case occurred in the transition from the old "hardball" approach to families of victims or purported victims to the reform and the independent review board. If it had occurred later, I am convinced the outcome would have been very different. Whatever the final merits of the complaint in this case, the family was demonized and brutalized by the Church's legal team just as that team (or some of its members) had beaten into the ground previous complaints, including the woman who brought charges against the priest who was later convicted of molesting others.

The Archdiocese's lead lawyer earlier had said on the record (according to an article in the *Baltimore Sun*) that the families of alleged victims were the "enemy." From a lawyers' viewpoint they are, as is anyone who brings suit against the Church. I used to think that the lawyers gave the cardinal bad advice. Now I believe they gave him the advice that lawyers are supposed to give. The fault was not the lawyers' (though I have some problems with them) but the cardinal's for adopting a legal paradigm for dealing with victims' families. That paradigm has been put aside now, at least in Chicago. Better late than never.

There is a painful irony in all this. The cardinal's reform was the one outlined in my column, something he acknowledged to me before his death. But the idea for the reform was not mine. Rather it came from the father in this case. At one point he would have settled for the reform. No one has ever expressed gratitude to him for his suggestions, though at least some of the late cardinal's staff knew of its origins.

After the verdict in the trial, someone from the cardinal's staff (not necessarily at his direction) phoned me to say that perhaps I ought to apologize to the priest who had been "cleared." I had never once said he was guilty and had always argued rather that the Church ought not to have gone to court, especially because the "pit bull" style of the trial belied the compassion of the cardinal's reforms and provided the victims' groups with ammunition to denounce those reforms as fraudulent. However, I felt that I must consider the possibility that I had been mistaken. I asked a lawyer to read the transcript (which did not include the evidence that the judge had suppressed) and tell me how he evaluated the situation. His cautious and careful reaction was that the boy in question had certainly been sexually traumatized at the parochial school, though on the basis of the evidence presented he could not say with confidence by whom.

The disagreement between me and the cardinal illustrates one of the most difficult aspects of the pedophilia problem: how one determines the truth of charges. Many pedophiles are so disgusted with themselves that they admit their guilt as soon as they are charged (even though they may tell different stories to their fellow priests). But others are very clever and very persuasive liars. In the absence of a confession, it may be hard in many cases to know whether the victim or the priest is telling the truth. Usually the judgment about truth is based on the word of the "victim" against the word of the "perpetrator."

The Permanent Review Board in Chicago, charged as it is with protecting children, makes the decision for the Church (subject to the cardinal's final approval) of whether a priest is to be removed and whether he is ever to be reassigned. Civil trials lead to decisions based on the preponderance of evidence. Prosecuting attorneys and grand juries determine whether he ought to be brought to trial. A judge or jury must determine whether he is guilty beyond a reasonable doubt. In each of these three venues, a different kind of evidence is required, more probative at each level. Thus the PRB may refuse to reassign a priest after the civil authority decides that there will be no indictment because the PRB remains unconvinced that he is not a threat to children. Indeed the board may remove someone (and has) whose behavior is not such as to require a criminal investigation but whom it still thinks is probably a threat to children. The reason for something like the PRB[48] is that it provides the most impartial—and credible—method available to the Church to enable it to do what it should do. Like all human institutions it can make mistakes.

As a rough rule of thumb, the "victims" usually tell the truth. But there are enough cases when they do not or when they are manipulated by lawyers and psychologists to think they are telling the truth. Thus the legal area of sexual abuse charges has become a swamp and is likely to remain so. As long as the Church follows the advice of its own impartial panel it can usually avoid the swamp. For the Church the issue of whether a priest might be falsely accused ends with that panel's decision—though of course the priest has the right to defend himself in criminal or civil action.[49]

However, especially since the wide media coverage of sexual abuse by priests, the problem of false charges is now serious, one more result of the cover-ups of the past. The classic case of a false charge, blown out of proportion by a reckless TV correspondent, was the assault on Cardinal Bernardin in the autumn of 1993.

Before I left for Germany that autumn, I heard on the victims' grapevine that a suit would be filed against the cardinal in the next couple of days, a suit based on allegations of sexual abuse by a former seminarian who was dying of AIDS. The alleged "victim," I was told, had pictures of himself with the cardinal and presents the cardinal had given him. The victims' grapevine was delighted at the charges, as it always is. I was

---

[48]It is sometimes argued by those who don't understand the PRB (largely because of the hash the Archdiocese's public relations staff made of explaining it) that the Church should not be involved in such a determination and that it should report the problem to the criminal justice system and withdraw from the case. Of course the PRB does report charges to the criminal justice system, but the Church must also decide whether to remove the priest from a parish (which the state's attorney cannot do) and whether to ever reassign him (which is beyond the boundaries of the civil law's decision-making power). Even though a man may be "cleared" by the criminal justice system, the Church may still decide, through the PRB, that the protection of children requires that the priest never work with them again.

[49]Whether the Church should pay for such action is a much debated point. I gather that the current tentative policy is that the Archdiocese will lend him money for a criminal defense if he does not have money to pay for his own defense. Although the victims' groups criticize such "loans," I do not find them objectionable. I am not so sure about loans for civil cases. It would be better, I believe, if there were some kind of clerical "malpractice" insurance available to clergy in this litigious era. I reject out of hand the strategy of countersuits as unworthy of the Church and destructive of its pastoral goals.

profoundly skeptical despite the claims of rich documentation of the charges. I tried to reach the cardinal to warn him but he was out of town. I talked to a contact on his staff who said that they were aware that a suit was to be filed in Cincinnati which would charge the cardinal with neglect in his role as archbishop when he was there (as do most suits against dioceses charge the man who was bishop at the time of the alleged abuse) but that there was no reason to believe that the cardinal himself would be charged personally. I warned that my sources, usually very good indeed, were confident that the cardinal would be charged personally.

I then left for Germany to consult with colleagues in Mannheim[50] about research on religion in Western Europe and to lecture at Cologne about my work in the sociology of religion (more about this aspect of my life in a subsequent chapter). I was very uneasy about the prospect of the suit. I was sure it would be filed. I was convinced that it was the work of a lawyer whom many thought sleazy and of a sick man who was being manipulated. I was afraid that it would hurt and perhaps destroy the cardinal. I knew it would be a terrible setback for his efforts to deal with the pedophile crisis.

I did not imagine for a moment that there would be a link between the suit and an interview I had given the previous summer to Bonnie Anderson, a CNN reporter. Ms. Anderson had also interviewed the cardinal and he had told me that it was the best interview yet with a journalist on the pedophile crisis. It had seemed to me that the media had just about played out the subject and that for the moment there was no real need of or purpose for another TV special. But Ms. Anderson's approach seemed so intelligent and sophisticated that I thought the program might make an important contribution because of its balance and responsibility.

My first night in Mannheim I received a phone call from my contact in the cardinal's office—one of many late-night calls which would follow me to Cologne and Dublin and Kilarney in the next week. The suit had indeed been filed. The plaintiff had staged a news conference which CNN had covered in its entirety. Moreover, CNN was using segments from the news conference every half hour to promote its weekend special on pedophilia which would appear at the same time as the beginning of the meeting of the National Conference of Catholic Bishops in Washington.

If it looks like a plot and walks like a plot and smells like a plot, then there's a pretty good chance that it is a plot.

In the meantime the cardinal was being judged and convicted all over the world. In contemporary mass media culture, allegation is all that is required for conviction. The next night June Rosner called from Chi-

---

[50]At ZUMA, the German counterpart of NORC.

cago. She thought that the young AIDS victim had been persuasive in his tearful statement at his news conference, but that the cardinal in his own news conference the next day had been sensational. She thought the tide of local media reaction was turning toward him. However, CNN continued its drumbeat of promotion for the Sunday special.

Later I would learn from her that Ms. Anderson and her producers had interwoven some of my responses in the summer interview and the charges against the cardinal to make it look like I was supporting the charges and that Ms. Anderson had done the same with some of his comments to make him look like a hypocrite. Moreover, she had said quite explicitly that now the cardinal himself had fallen from grace—appropriating the title of the novel I had written about the pedophile crisis. I wrote a column in defense of the cardinal and suggested that it looked very much like a plot to promote a TV special. I also kept in touch with my contact in the cardinal's office and told him to pass on my faith and support, since I didn't want to bother him personally in such a difficult time.

When I arrived in Dublin several days later, the phone rang the instant I entered my hotel. The *Irish Times* wanted a statement about the Bernardin case. I repeated my line that the charges were surely untrue and that it all smelled like a plot. The Irish writer agreed with me.

How did they know I'd be in Dublin and what my hotel was?

Ah, that would be telling, now, wouldn't it?

Meanwhile, back in Chicago, the mayor had denounced the charge as a conspiracy against the cardinal and the city had rallied to him. Everywhere he went he was cheered, as he was at the bishops' meeting in Washington. Peter Steinfels of *The New York Times* remarked to someone that in Chicago 95 percent of the people believed the cardinal was innocent and the other 5 percent kept their mouths shut.

Through it all the cardinal never lost his cool with the media (as I would later discover when reading clips and watching tapes). He was at all times self-possessed, forthright, patient—the way an innocent ought to be. I learned subsequently that his public relations advisers (if one can use the name of such incompetents) wanted to keep him away from the media. I cannot escape the conclusion that they were more interested in protecting their jobs than in protecting him.

When I returned from Ireland I called him and began my conversation with the (typical, I fear) comment, "Joe, it's a hell of a way to raise money!"

He laughed. "You're right. Money for the cardinal's appeal and other contributions are pouring in. There have to be better ways."

Then I told him how moved I had been by everything he had said and done.

Chuck Goudy of Channel 7 took the lead in the positive response to the cardinal by the Chicago media (with TV doing a far better job than the two bumbling papers). In a remarkable series in Philadelphia, Goudy explored the credentials of the hypnotherapist who had "facilitated" the young man's "recovered" memories and the accreditation of the school where she had earned her master's degree in psychology. Both the credentials and the accreditation were nonexistent. I wrote more columns screaming plot.

One troubling event was an interview on a Chicago TV channel with a person who purported to know what was going on in the Church. He interpreted a previously scheduled visit of Cardinal Hickey of Washington to Chicago as evidence of an order from Rome telling Bernardin that he must resign and that his ecclesiastical career was over. I am forced to believe that his "source" was a disloyal person within the cardinal's staff. Actually the Vatican's support was unwavering.

It became increasingly clear in the new year that there was no evidence to support the charges: the picture was one of many taken with the cardinal by seminarians on their graduation day. There was no proof that the alleged gift was a gift. The psychologists involved made it clear that they had grave doubts. The lawyer may have filed the suit too late for the statute of limitations in Ohio. There was no case. Moreover the suit may have been filed without enough evidence even to justify a suit, the kind of action that could get the lawyer disbarred. Libel charges could easily have been filed against everyone. There was nothing there, nothing at all except highly dubious recovered memories, which probably would not have been admitted as evidence.

The plaintiff and his lawyer quickly backtracked and the suit was withdrawn with a semblance of an apology. It was an anticlimactic ending. Some lawyers in Chicago thought that the cardinal's lawyers had let the plaintiff and his lawyer off too easily. There should have been a trial to leave no doubt about the cardinal's innocence. An occasional objection was raised that it looked like the fix was in. In fact, people in Chicago and the rest of the country were delighted that the cardinal had been exonerated. The case was quickly forgotten and the cardinal emerged from it a more popular and powerful figure than he had ever been and, in my experience of him, a stronger man.

Not once in the whole ordeal had the cardinal missed a beat. Jack Rosenthal of the *New York Times Magazine* remarked to me that it was as brilliant a public relations feat as he had ever witnessed. Brilliant it might have been, I replied, but there was no public relations in it. It was simply the man himself.

It was a hellish experience for him and he survived brilliantly. Later he visited the plaintiff, reconciled with him, and said Mass for him. Again, that was not PR, that was the man. As I said earlier in this chapter, we have had our disagreements about the pedophile issue,[51] but I can only admire the brilliant and deeply religious way he responded to the charges. As Rosenthal observed, he's the only man to survive concentrated media assault after legal allegations. Anyone who is innocent *and* has as integrated a personality as the cardinal has can do it, I replied.

As I had feared would happen, the false charges against the cardinal were a severe blow to efforts to eliminate pedophilia from the Church. While the PRB continue to function vigorously in Chicago, priests now had a wonderful excuse to suggest that all accusations were false. Nonetheless, it will be a long run advantage to those of us who wish for a resolution of the problem to be able to say bluntly that some accusations are true and some are false and that's why something like the PRB is needed to make both short-term and long-term decisions about a case.[52]

Two questions remain: how valid are recovered memories? As my colleague and friend Erika From said to me, they are helpful tools for psychotherapy. In the absence of confirming evidence, they have no place in a court of law. It is surely true that many amateur therapists are using them as part of a campaign to convict as many men as possible of incest. While incest is a widely prevalent phenomenon and should be denounced repeatedly from the altars of every Church in the country, attempts to send men to jail on flimsy and unsupported charges based on recovered memories are as immoral as the incest itself. The controversy about whether such recovered memories (usually recovered through hypnotherapy) are of any value is a foolish one. They are of little legal value by themselves, but can be very helpful therapeutically when a skilled, patient, and nonideological therapist works with a client.

Finally there is the issue of CNN. I fail to see how it did not libel the cardinal and how its use of the charges to promote its own special, timed to coincide with the opening of the NCCB meeting in Washington, was not journalistically irresponsible. Moreover, since there was never any discovery deposition with CNN people, one cannot say for sure whether Ms. Anderson might have leaned on the plaintiff's lawyer to come up with recovered memories in time for her special. I don't think it would

---

[51]Though on some issues, like the closing of parishes, our differences narrowed.

[52]The cardinal was willing to submit his own case to the PRB (which then would report to the senior suffragan in Illinois) but neither the plaintiff nor his lawyer ever presented their complaints.

have been all that explicit. But the absence of the kind of explicit conversation which might be a violation of the law against conspiracy does not mean that there were not subtle and unspoken pressures. Anyone who understands how the media operates would be surprised if there were not such pressures. The timing of the suit, the CNN special, and the Washington meeting certainly created an atmosphere in which the smell of a plot seemed quite real. While I am glad the cardinal refused to sue anyone, I believe he had excellent grounds to go after CNN. It would appear that the upper brass at CNN still don't realize what they did.

Northwestern University's School of Journalism, in a blatant and to me offensive attempt to exploit the notoriety of the case, summoned a meeting to discuss the media ethics of the affair, a meeting which would include the plaintiff's lawyer and Bonnie Anderson. I replied to the invitation saying that I would not sit in the same room with either of them and that the School of Journalism was granting them a legitimacy they did not deserve.

As I expected the conference and the bland report it issued exonerated Ms. Anderson with mealymouthed "on the one hand . . . and on the other hard" rhetoric. It should have condemned her. There are, however, too many other journalists with guilty consciences to have condemned her for things they have done themselves, if not so blatantly.

The Church has brought the pedophilia crisis on itself by its previous policy of cover-up—often little more an obstruction of justice in conspiracy with civil authority. Other denominations have the problem too, but they have not used their power and prestige to hide sex abuse among their clergy—though of course they have not been eager to publicize it either. The Church penned up the problem behind a dam of dishonesty. When the dam broke the Church was inundated. It sowed the wind of pretense, and has now reaped the whirlwind not only of valid charges but of false ones. The damage to the image of the Church and of the priesthood has been enormous. Yet no one seems ready to convene either nationally or locally a service of public penance in which priests and bishops say that they're sorry. Such a service would go a long way to refurbish imagery. It is a measure of the continuing blindness of both individual bishops and the national hierarchy that they are either unwilling or unable to do so.[53]

No one even seems to grasp the relationship between pedophilia and declines in both vocations and contributions.

---

[53]Bill McManus, the late feisty retired bishop of Fort Wayne–South Bend (and a native Chicagoan), called repeatedly for such a service. No one seems willing to pay any attention to what looks like obvious wisdom to an outsider.

It's a hell of a way to run a Church.

Adversary: Did Himself promise that He'd always produce brilliant leadership for the Church? Gimme a break!

I don't regret the role I played and to some extent continue to play in the pedophilia mess, as disgusting as I think the abuse and the cover-up of the abuse is. I do regret that I did not stay in closer touch with the cardinal on this problem after our reconciliation (described in the next chapter). Yet he was busy and so was I. He was often out of Chicago and so was I. We both thought we had time and, as it turns out, he did not. I did not want to bother him. I sensed that those around him, the various vicars for the clergy and his legal team, had poisoned the wells. I had no desire to fight them, especially since I would have been doomed to defeat anyway. Still, perhaps I stayed too much on my high horse— if you want to believe them about me, Joe, that's your problem not mine. Maybe I could have tried harder before we ran out of time.

Only we didn't know we were going to run out of time.

During the high tide of the crisis, I visited Ireland. A certain bishop "rang me up" in my room at Jury's and asked me if I'd join him for supper in the restaurant. It turned out that, smart man that he was, he saw the same problem coming to Ireland. What should they do to avoid the American mistakes, he asked.

Enthusiast that I am, I thought perhaps I could help. We talked for hours. I repeated two themes—don't cover up and do apologize. He seemed to understand. But the Irish hierarchy learned nothing from the mistakes of their American brothers. They made their own mistakes and worse ones. So terrible was the impact of Irish pedophilia on the country (the flames being fanned by the justifiably anticlerical Irish media) that the image of the priesthood was shattered. Vocations have dried up— none at all to the Dublin Archdiocese last year. Younger priests who are scholars and writers and musicians do not even want to be identified as priests.

All of this was brought on by a policy that covered up the faults of a few priests to protect the image of the priesthood! And they had been warned beforehand, not merely by me but by many Americans.

Priests are not mere preachers of the word in the Catholic heritage. They are sacraments, revelations of the presence of God. When the priest presides over the Eucharist, he stands in the place of Jesus. He is touched, however lightly, by the transcendent. He is marked permanently, how-ever dimly, by his sacred role. Once a Catholic, always a Catholic. Once a priest, always a priest. The special horror of abuse by a priest is not that he is called "father" as the media idiots like to say. The worst of it is that it is abuse by one who is sacred.

Most priests don't get that. For the life of me, I do not understand why.

Adversary: They don't have enough imagination for empathy with those who denounced other members of their club. Your trouble is that you have too much imagination altogether.

Reconciliations

It was a bitter cold feast of All Saints' Day in 1992. I stormed up North State Street which becomes North State Parkway toward the cardinal's house. If he wanted a public fight over the seal of Confession, well, damn it all, he would have one. I had been subpoenaed to testify in a legal battle between the Church and a man who claimed that his son had been sexually abused by a priest, a man who had confided in me.

As proof of how rarely I entered that grotesque mansion, I rang the wrong doorbell and waited shivering in the cold. Sister finally opened the door a tiny crack and peeped out.

"Father Greeley to see the cardinal," I said, I hope now without too much hint of anger.

"Just a minute," she said as she closed the door in my face and left me still shivering in the bitter wind that was sweeping down the lake, across a brown and barren Lincoln Park, a wind that seemed aimed right at me.

Cooled down, perhaps by the icy wind, I permitted a rational thought to enter my mind. "I know this so-and-so. He's going to want to reconcile!"

I had become involved in the pedophile mess in the Church even before the crisis had broken into the public domain. I had entered a counseling relationship with the complaining parents in one of the cases. The archdiocesan lawyers had hinted sometime before that they would call me as a witness in the case. Someone had remarked to one of them that she couldn't call a priest to testify about what had been said in a confidential relationship. "He's not a real priest," she is alleged to have snapped back.

I wrote a letter to the then chancellor of the Archdiocese in which I warned against pursuing such a strategy. He had replied that there was no intent to do so. So I relaxed and stopped worrying about it. On Halloween I received a subpoena for a deposition. I called Tom Sullivan, my attorney, and told him that I would absolutely refuse to testify. He agreed that such was the stand to take.

So being a sensible and reasonable man I decided I would sleep on the matter before doing anything reckless. As usually happens after I sleep on something I was even more angry the next morning. Hence my stomp up to the cardinal's house.

Finally, the door opened again. Ken Velo, the priest who was the cardinal's administrative assistant (and had always been a friend)[54] opened the door. "Sister didn't recognize you, Andy. Come right in. The cardinal has just finished Mass. He will be down in a minute."

Ken had always tried to ease me toward reconciliation.

The whole problem, incidentally, was that Sister *did* know who I was. But that was all right. If I had been in her position, I wouldn't have let me in either. Subsequently Sister and I became friends.

In the years after Archbishop Bernardin had come to Chicago, we had avoided one another. I assumed he still blamed me for the leaking of my secret files which had proved an embarrassment to him. He was, after all, the cardinal, was he not? If there was to be a reconciliation, it was up to him to make the first move, was it not?

Moreover I knew that he had set up a secret commission at the request of Rome to "investigate" my novels. While the commission's report was what the cardinal wanted it to be—a "warning" about my fiction would be counter productive "at the present time"—he had not informed me of this Star Chamber procedure.[55]

Finally he had refused to accept a pledge of a million dollars I had offered to the Catholic School Endowment of the Archdiocese. He even refused to meet with the lawyers who were going to propose the offer. (So I set up my own foundation for inner-city Catholic schools.)

I did not sit in the front parlor into which Ken had shown me but remained standing coat on, pacing up and down, steaming with anger and doubtless looking like one of the eighteenth-century Irish "ribbon-men" (rural terrorists). Finally the cardinal walked down the stairs. He seemed nervous, even perhaps a little frightened, which under the circumstances was an appropriate response.

I threw the subpoena at him (I did, *really!*) and shouted something like, "If it's a public fight you want, Joe, it's a public fight you'll get!"[56]

I don't remember whether he caught the papers or picked them up.

---

[54]More than any priest I knew in such an important role, Ken has always seemed devoid of ecclesiastical ambition, an observation with which most priests in Chicago agreed.

[55]I would later learn that Cardinal John O'Connor had weighed in with a letter to the Vatican in which he argued that such a warning would be unwise. I owe him a favor.

[56]Rarely do I get that angry and never before have I shouted at a superior that way. All the craziness of the years since my files were raided had finally caught up with me.

"I didn't know about this till after it was sent," he said tentatively. "They are not our lawyers after all."

The Archdiocese maintained the fiction that the countersuits against the complaining family were being argued by lawyers hired by the defendants. I thought this was a disingenuous answer then and I still do. The Archdiocese was picking up the tab.[57]

"Don't try to tell me that," I shouted. "Your lawyer designed the strategy in this case and you're paying the bills!"

He looked at the offending paper. "I'll see what I can do," he said softly.

"You'd better," I said and turned to storm out, a blast of winter cold preparing to exit.

"Don't go," he pleaded. "Sit down and let's talk for a few moments."

So I sat down. He was my bishop after all. I knew what to expect and made up my mind how to react to it.

"I pray every day, Andy," he said, his voice uncertain, "that we be reconciled. Can we be friends again?"

---

[57]In the continuation of the countersuits at the time of this writing, the Archdiocese is no longer paying the legal fees. However, it still seems to me that this is a disingenuous claim. It did pay for all the discovery that preceded the suits.

The strategy of playing hardball against sexual abuse complaints was articulated at an informal meeting of diocesan lawyers sometime in the 1980s. They argued that they were being "nickeled and dimed to death" by settlements of the increasing number of sexual abuse claims and that the way to put a stop to it was to win several high-profile cases. Whether this was sound legal advice seems at this point problematic. Certainly it backfired. However, I fail to see that this was appropriate behavior for a Church.

Whether the counsel for the Archdiocese of Chicago was at this meeting I do not know. I do know that he was quoted by the *Baltimore Sun* as having said that the families of alleged victims were "the enemy." He certainly fought vigorously against complaints, including one case in which the mother of an alleged victim was forced because of lack of funds to settle for less than her legal costs. Subsequently the accused priest was convicted by an Irish Catholic judge (in a bench trial) on the charge of abusing a young woman. I could never understand why the Church stuck with that lawyer after such an egregious mistake. While the case which brought me to the cardinal's house was still being fought with the old-time strategy, the Archdiocese has abandoned that strategy since the cardinal's reform (described in a subsequent chapter) was initiated. Indeed I know of no other diocese in the country which has so completely dropped the hardball approach.

In any event, the hardball strategy was launched at precisely the wrong time—just before the epidemic of sexual abuse cases became public knowledge. I cannot see why any diocese continues to employ the lawyers who got them into this mess.

What do you say to that, O gallowglass warrior?

You say, "We'd better do it now, Joe, while we still have time. Neither of us are as young as we were when everything went wrong."

"What did go wrong?"

"There were false messages sent back and forth, for one thing."

"I know," he agreed.

"We should never have a problem again that we can't deal with by a phone conversation or a personal meeting," I said tentatively.

He agreed. We talked for some time and agreed to meet again to continue our exercise in clarification. In fact, we met twice and once more became friends.

As I hunted for a cab (too shaken to walk back in the wind), I said to myself, "Anytime in the last ten years I could have walked up here and ended this nonsense."

It is not up to me to suggest what the cardinal could have done or should have done. I can only judge my behavior in not ending the nonsense much earlier. I was angry and petulant, for which God forgive me. On the other hand, God works things out in Her own good time. Not as an excuse for my own mistakes, I believe that this might have been the right time. Perhaps we could not have done it appropriately much earlier.[58]

Well, that's water over the dam now. The cardinal and I became friends again. Until the time of his death we talked on the phone, we exchanged faxes, he visited my apartment, I ate supper at his house, he asked my opinion, we took each other to dinner, he visited Grand Beach. Our friendship was cordial, though not without difficulties sometimes. He was reluctant to call and say, "As a personal favor to me would you lay off that subject for a while." He did phone that request once and of course I agreed. We Chicagoans understand that when a friend asks for a personal favor we of course go along (and retain the right to pick up our marker on a later occasion). I was reluctant to intrude on his time of which he had so little and perhaps did not pick up the phone myself as often as I should have. Moreover there was necessarily a certain asymmetry in the friendship because he was my bishop and was subject to judgment by the priests of Chicago, by the other bishops of the country, and by the Vatican on whether he could "contain" me. On the other

---

[58]In our conversations he explained that he had turned down my offer of a pledge in support of Catholic schools because he did not want to stir up any more trouble from Rome. I don't doubt this explanation. However, I suspect that many of those around him warned him that I was seeking "respectability" by my offer.

hand, while I am a priest of the Diocese, I was about as independent as a priest can be and was accused often of writing "dirty" novels—usually by people who have taken a passage out of context—and sociological studies which are "obsessed" with sex. Moreover, most of the priests in the country could not and will not forgive me for my writing on the pedophile disaster. I do not want to suggest that our reconciliation was tenuous. It was not. But it certainly was intricate. I vigorously defended him on the public record when he was falsely accused of sexual abuse. He was, however, upset by my continuing attack on the Archdiocese's handling of a crucial sexual abuse case. I felt and still feel that the Church's lawyers had demonized and brutalized the family involved, even if there had been no abuse.

It was a private friendship, though not a secret one. Still, to be reconciled with the cardinal is in some sense to be reconciled with the Archdiocese, however informally and privately and unofficially. It is enough and more than enough.

The cardinal was clearly the most effective major leader in the American Church and also the most insightful. His response to the pedophile crisis once he understood pedophilia was light-years ahead of that of any other American bishop of whom I am aware (except the late Tom Murphy of Seattle, a West Side Irish Catholic). While some of the victims and their families may still be critical and while I myself disagreed with him on some matters, I have no doubt of either his sincerity or of the direction of his reforms. He did, after all, remove twenty-three priests, more than any other major leader has done.

His style of governance and administration was cautious, oriented toward compromise and coalition building. Many of the more liberal priests of the Archdiocese thought that he did not demonstrate enough "leadership." But when he did try to exercise leadership—as, for example, in his pedophile reforms—most priests refused to follow his leadership and some even tried to sabotage it. In fact, in the present chaos and alienation in the Church, I'm not sure that priests would follow the leadership of anyone.

Why didn't he speak up to the pope, some priests (and laity) demanded. On the public record he said that he has spoken to the pope both about married priests and the ordination of women. Obviously he did not change the pope's mind on either subject, but then who could? To fault him for not changing the pope's mind is absurd.

Consensus, coalition, compromise—I'm not sure that any bishop can govern well unless these are his goals. In Chicago, they are especially necessary. The late Cardinal Cody atomized the structure of the Archdiocese. Cardinal Bernardin inherited an archdiocese in which there were no structures and almost no administrative talent. Through no fault of his own he has been only partially successful in rebuilding the Archdiocese. The clergy have become so accustomed to hunkering down behind their own parochial bunker and viewing "downtown" with suspicion and distrust that many of them are incapable of behaving any other way.

Moreover, while there are still many talented priests in Chicago (and many, many more talented laity), the persistence of the atmosphere of the post-Cody chancery bureaucracy (about which in the beginning Cardinal Bernardin had little choice) inhibited men and women with talent from signing on. I am not saying that there were not able people around the cardinal. Quite the contrary, there are some such people, but not enough of them. Mediocrity, however, begets mediocrity. Moreover, the search committees who chose new appointees (in the finest traditions of consultative government) were not likely to recommend men and women who have more talent than they do.

Thus, when the cardinal was beset by the false pedophile charges against himself, his chief spokesperson was a woman whose previous experience was as the public relations director of a Catholic hospital. I have nothing against that background nor against the woman personally (as I did against her predecessor) but the Archdiocese of Chicago obviously needed someone in that position with much greater experience. Moreover, the spokesman who tried to explain the cardinal's pedophile reforms when they were announced made such a hash of it that the media people still don't understand how it works—to say nothing of the average Chicagoan.

His city planning advisers were innocent of both credentials and ability. Their style seems to have been to lay out a map and cross out parishes which they decided were unnecessary without much consultation (other than token) with the neighborhoods. Before the cardinal died he told me that he realized that he had closed many schools and parishes he ought not to have closed and that he would not make that mistake again—thus implicitly acknowledging the accuracy of my earlier criticisms of massive shutdowns.

Nonetheless, given the state of the Church and of the Archdiocese during his years in Chicago, the cardinal did a better job than most people could have done, indeed a better job than could have been reasonably expected, and he avoided some of the terrible mistakes that have been made elsewhere.[59]

During his illness, he called me often and Ken Velo kept me informed

[59]I was very critical of the massive school and parish closings a few years ago.

constantly. We were surely friends at the end. When the funeral cortege turned down Michigan Avenue after the Mass and began its sad but triumphal journey to the cemetery in Hillside, I almost broke down and would have if the TV camera was not focused on my face. (I was a commentator for Channel 5.) I will always miss him.

I have the feeling even today, however, that his sense that I had caused him enormous trouble at the time of the removal of my papers from the files at Rosary remained. He was willing to forgive that, but not to forget it completely.

Adversary: You scared him, boyo. If you didn't want that to happen, you should have kept your big mouth shut back in 1955 when someone asked you to write. If I were an archbishop you might scare me!

I hope I have learned something from our often tangled relationship— especially not to turn away from people with whose behavior I am disappointed and disgusted (and in some cases wrongly so). Rather than sulking I should confront them head-on and ask what the hell is going on. I should not wait till an explosion of anger forces me to do what I should have done long before.

I also learned that the later years in life are a time for reconciliations. I have pursued many such as a direct result of my renewed friendship with the cardinal. Some have been successful, others have been unsuccessful, and yet others are still in process.

In concluding my comments on this turning point in my life, I should add that the cardinal took the lead in the reconciliation and I did not (as I suppose is patent). If we became friends again, he was the one who deserves the credit.[60]

The other major reconciliation was at the University of Chicago.

Jim Coleman and I were sitting at lunch at the faculty club at the University (*The* University as it is usually called)[61] in the spring of 1993, chatting no doubt about the use of economic models in sociology (which

---

No more than anyone else did the cardinal like criticism (though he tolerated it better than most). Unfortunately his planning staff was totally incompetent.

[60]Will I ever be reconciled with Gene Kennedy or with the priests of Chicago? They are different problems. I have always agreed to do anything or give any talk that a priest of the Archdiocese has asked. I always will, as long as my health holds. What more than that can I do? Jim Roache, who was for a long-time Cardinal Bernardin's vicar general, told me that I would be accepted back in only when I did public penance for my novels. Now I would also have to apologize for my writings on pedophilia. Don't hold your breath, fellas. As for Gene, I certainly do not rule that out but only after I am persuaded that he has discarded his fixation on me.

[61]God forgive me for it, but I sometimes slip into that usage. To distinguish when I'm in Tucson, I refer to the University of Arizona as "the U" which is

I endorse, so long as they are not the only models permitted). Gerhard Casper, the courtly, charming, and witty German Lutheran lawyer who was then provost of the University (and now president of Stanford, mostly because the trustees of the University and especially their chairman messed up badly on not making him president of the University, where he belonged!), came over to our table, bowed, half seriously, half in jest, as he usually did and talked to us, I believe, about an exhibit of Celtic Revival art that the University's Smart Gallery was planning.

I had come to know Casper from dinners at Gary Becker's house and from meeting him often as I walked across the Midway to lunch and he emerged from the parking lot behind the Laura Spellman Rockefeller Memorial Chapel (as it is properly called). In our brief strolls from Fifty-ninth Street to Fifty-seventh Street he struck me as a brilliant and gracious man with just enough touch of the Old World to recall an ancient tradition of courteous scholarship and just enough of America to banter effectively with an American Celt. My friend Erika From, who, as a Holocaust survivor, dislikes Germans, always insisted that she excepted from this dislike Gerhard and his wife, Regina. You make one exception, I would tell her, and you have let the camel's nose into the tent.

After he had finished talking about the Smart Gallery, he leaned close to me and said, "I'm delighted that we have finally found a place for you in the University."

I responded with my best Irish smile and said thanks. After Gerhard had drifted away I turned to Coleman to see if he had heard Gerhard's last words. Clearly he had not. Had I imagined it? It was so quick and so soft I was not even sure that I had heard it. So I did not mention it to Jim or to anyone else. I knew there was a campaign under way, launched by Terry Clark, the director of the sociology program in the college, to win for me some kind of appointment in the University. I also had come to understand that most of my colleagues thought that what had been done in the early 1970s was a terrible injustice, though only one of the many that had been committed in those days. On the other hand, they did not want to repudiate one giant figure who had been the power behind the campaign against me and they did not comprehend why that battle was still so important to me.

I had come to the University in the time of the Confident Church in 1960, a priest studying to be a sociologist in and for that Church. Within the decade the Confident Church had been replaced by the Confusing

---

considered appropriate usage—also as "U of A." Sometimes the U is also referred to, though never by me, as "Wildcat Country." The University, however, as I hardly need remark, is never called by anyone "Maroon Country."

Church. I was a mostly unattached sociologist (save at the National Opinion Research Center) for whom the Church (as represented by Cardinal Cody) had no use and about whom the University had grave doubts.

Interestingly enough, the giant who opposed me on the grounds that the University had to protect its standards seems to have confused me with someone else since he reported that I had been a student of his and had an inferior mind. An inferior mind I may have but I was never one of his students. I congratulated him once in a restaurant on an article he had just published—long after he had done me in. "Thank you, Father, uh . . . what is your last name, Father?" After my appointment at Chicago he would nod to me and smile ever so slightly at the Quadrangle Club and on one occasion in public praised something I had said. It is a very strange world.

I had not been particularly optimistic about Terry Clark's initiative which was supported by Coleman, Gary Becker, and Charles Bidwell, among others. Such efforts had been tried before and failed. But I was pleased that they thought it was worth the effort.

I'm not sure any of my allies understood why I cared about it. Was I not a tenured[62] professor at the University of Arizona, certainly one of the top ten departments in the country? Hadn't the decision of the University of Chicago been repudiated long ago? My answer was to quote the late Mayor Daley when he was asked by a group of faculty wives from Roosevelt University why he always seemed to favor the University of Chicago. Da Mayor, with the usual puzzled expression when faced with a question to which he thought the answer was obvious, said, "Because it's the University of *Chicago*." It's my city, my alma mater, my department. For years I half believed that maybe I was not good enough to be there. The invitation from the U of A canceled that feeling (to say nothing of the absurd notion that I wasn't good enough for Notre Dame). Yet Chicago was where I belonged in the classroom—if not all the time, then at least some of the time, and I wanted, stubbornly perhaps, the record set right.

And so it was, much to my surprise. The offer that was made—visiting professor—did not have much dignity in it. But that didn't matter. As Senator Aiken of Vermont said about the Vietnam War, "Let's proclaim victory and go home." So we did and Jim Coleman had a grand party

---

[62]As I remarked in *Confessions* I gave up both tenure and salary at the U when my book royalties expanded. I saw no point in taking money from the people of Arizona or preventing the sociology department from bringing someone in to fill my line.

at his house to which virtually all the members of the new department came and we all celebrated. Only that night did I realize how much respect so many of my colleagues had for me. Again I had misread the signs because I had listened only to the adversaries, in part, I suppose, because the allies and friends were not so vociferous.

Jim is gone now too and I miss him. Norman Nie, a colleague from political science, had the brilliant notion that we should have a celebration of Jim before he died of cancer instead of afterward. I was deputed to do the after-dinner speech at the first night of the conference. It was the day that Jack Durkin, my wonderful brother-in-law, died. The computer had eaten my speech. I was in no mood for celebration, especially witty celebration. I guess I did all right when I argued that Jim was the product of a local culture (Seven Mile, Ohio) like everyone else. Everyone laughed and praised the talk. I got away from the dinner as quickly as I could.

But not before I met Robert K. Merton, Jim's mentor and the doyen of American sociology who has become a good friend and a great supporter of my work. He now tells people that sociology has not given me the respect that I deserve and that I ought to be elected president of the American Sociological Association. That will never happen, but it is nice to hear it from a man of Merton's stature.

I dedicated my major sociological work *Religion as Poetry* to Jim. Tears came to his eyes when he read the dedication. I also spoke about him at the ASA memorial service. When Jim died there was a remarkable burst of psychic phenomena among his colleagues and friends. (As always I was immune to such events. I study them, but I do not experience them.) A giant had fallen. I miss him. I always will.

A private friendship with the cardinal and a marginal appointment at the University? Could so little satisfy me? Were they not weak symbols of reaffiliation?

No symbol is ever weak, especially when full affiliation with either institution was the last thing I wanted at this stage of my life. Never fight Lady Wisdom (aka the Holy Spirit). I was much better off on the margins, even though I had not always realized that. At one time I would have liked to have been both a tenured full professor at the University and a sociologist for the Archdiocese. Either or both. What a mistake it would have been to go down those paths. Lady Wisdom didn't let me.

To renew my friendship with the cardinal and to be formally if only marginally part of the University were enough to end unhappy and depressing interludes. Proclaim victory and go home.

Where you belong.

Adversary: Now you have to learn to believe that!

The Rights of the Laity

In a certain diocese a newly ordained priest was sent to an active parish. His bishop told him that it was a busy place and that he shouldn't work himself into a state of exhaustion his first couple of months in the parish.[63] Upon arrival, however, he discovered that there was nothing for him to do. The youth minister forbade him to have anything to do with the parish teenagers. The liturgical minister insisted that he clear his Sunday homilies with her. The RCIA (Rite of Christian Initiation for Adults) director warned him to stay away from her people. The director of religious education would not let him into any of the classes. The minister of marriage preparation would not let him see couples before the wedding day. The deacon insisted that preparations for Baptism and the administration of the sacrament were his turf. The pastor begged the new priest not to upset the parish staff which, he said, was already volatile.

One can understand the concerns of the lay staff. Each had hammered out his or her own responsibility. Each was protecting his or her own turf. Each was concerned about his or her own employment future. Who needed a new priest?

A simple paradigm dominates the thinking of many elite "liberal" Catholics in the Confusing Church: the laity are good and the clergy and the hierarchy are bad. The more the laity gain active roles in the Church, the better it will be. This paradigm blinds them to the oppression of the faithful by parish staffs, often composed of laymen and laywomen who substitute ideological clichés for education. Not all of the neo-authoritarianism in the Church is lay. The clergy continue to oppress. The irony, however, is that the lay "liberals" are often equally oppressive—and sometimes proud of their authoritarian rules and regulations. Moreover, such Catholic journals as the *National Catholic Reporter*, which report clerical and hierarchial authoritarianism, ignore lay oppression of the faithful—understandably enough because the lay oppressors are often their clientele.

I began to hear horror stories. Just as I could not stay out of the

---

[63]This story like most of those in the chapter is a slightly fictionalized version of something that actually happened. It is fictionalized to protect the guilty.

pedophile fight, I found it impossible to keep my big Irish mouth shut. Freedom is indispensable for virtue. Those who take away freedom in the name of virtue make virtue impossible.

Among the changes in the ambience of the human condition in recent years, one of the most important, perhaps from the religious viewpoint the most important, is the expansion of choices which a person must make through the course of life. Choice means freedom. Freedom is a terrible burden, but there is no escaping it. Moreover, once humans have adjusted to a condition in which their lives are structured by a steady stream of choices, of personal decision making (especially when this structure is joined with much greater life expectancy), they are astonished and offended when they are told that in certain areas they must simply do what they are told without any input into the decision making or any persuasive reasons given for the decision.

Consider the situation of our ancestors, let us say, a hundred to a hundred fifty years ago. Most of their choices were already made for them. They would be what their fathers and mothers were, farmers and farmers' wives. They would, barring famine, live in the same villages in which they were born. They would marry someone from the same village or the next village. They would do what the priest told them because he was the absolute power in the village. There was dissent, of course, and some people did leave. But leaving or staying (or becoming a priest or a religious) were the basic decision alternatives. In the matter of a marriage partner, the range of choices was necessarily small. Life was relatively simple and uncomplicated. Most of us, despite nostalgic longings for the simple life, would go crazy in such a context.

Fifty years ago, when my generation was growing up during the war, between depression and prosperity (that we never dreamed possible), much had changed, but much had not changed. Few of us had cars. We dated people from the parish or the next parish or in some cases two or three parishes away. A romantic involvement with those mysterious and presumably uncivilized folk we called "South Side Irish" was as imaginable as a romance with a Tibetan. There was a theoretical choice to attend college, but, fearful of the return of the Great Depression, most of us opted for security—a nurse, a teacher, a secretary, a cop, a fireman, a clerk, an occasional (very occasional) lawyer or doctor. If we went to college, we went to a commuter college in Chicago. When we married we moved one or two parishes west. We intended to send our children to parochial schools. We were active in the Knights of Columbus, the American Legion, and the Altar and Rosary Society. We took the Legion of Decency pledge and some of us even kept it. Divorce was unthinkable. We tended to have large families and agonized over birth control, practicing it, but confessing it at Christmas and Easter. We voted Democratic (naturally). The parish priest was not automatically obeyed, but we listened very carefully to what he said and took his words very seriously, except when he suggested we should not vote for Franklin Roosevelt.

Our range of choices was considerably expanded over that of our grandparents, but our lives were not structured by the constant challenge of choice and the freedom which comes with that challenge.

Consider the present—at least for middle-class Catholics. Naturally we go to college (like 60 percent of all American high school graduates). We must choose among colleges as distant as San Diego and Miami. We must choose among programs that run from women's studies to oceanography, fields which were unknown to most of us not so long ago. Our possible marriage partners come from all over the country and indeed from all over the world. We have a smorgasbord of careers to choose from and sometimes we make several choices in the course of our lifetime. Depending on our employer or our own personal tastes, we will live anywhere in the country or anywhere in the world. We don't go back to the old neighborhood very often, in part because the old neighborhood isn't there anymore. We worry about where we will send our children to school, how to pay for their college education, and how to protect them from drugs and pregnancy. Orders from our pastor, our bishop, even the Vatican plus a dollar and a half will get us a ride on Rich Daley's subway. Divorce is a seriously considered option often in our marriages. Women have careers too. Choice, choice, choice.

Sometimes we make wise choices, sometimes unwise, but we cannot escape the obligation of choice. Our personalities, our characters, are shaped by a constant exercise of freedom—and the agony of decision making that freedom imposes.

The Catholic Church has yet to make its peace with the inevitability of the freedom of its laity. It does not like one bit the laity's assumption of the right to make its own decisions, and of its demand that it be persuaded instead of ordered. Indeed, the Church usually works on the implicit assumption that it is still dealing with peasants of a century ago who did what they were told (usually) without question, without argument, without the demand that it be heard, consulted, persuaded. Many pastors still assume that they have the same influence and power that their role models from a generation or two ago had. Catholics, they believe, still do what they're told.

It ought to be patent by now that this is not so. When Church leaders pretend to deny that the souls of the laity are now shaped by a constant exercise of freedom or lament the passing of the good old days when there was a lot less freedom, they have turned their faces against history.

Moreover, they miss the point of their own tradition which has believed that virtue is formed by the frequent repetition of *free* human acts. In any event the days of the docile peasant and the not quite so docile immigrant parish are gone and they will never return. The Church must adjust to the fact that in the European and North Atlantic world at any rate, the day of the free laity who make their own decisions after reflecting on the issues, who want to be heard, consulted, persuaded, is the world in which we live and work. In the present milieu, the laity reserve to themselves the right to say on what terms they will be Catholic. Nothing will change that fact, neither orders from Rome nor hysterical ranting from the tiny fundamentalist Catholic minority.

The failure of many, indeed most, Church leaders from top to bottom to perceive this new situation is a horrific failure of leadership. The Vatican Council warned us of the necessity of reading the signs of the times. Our leadership resolutely refuses to read these signs or sees them as a departure from the discipline and the order of the good old days. The leadership, in a monumental failure, urges rather a return to the old discipline of the 1950s—or the 1750s. In weal or woe—and patently I think it is weal—the leadership can no longer shape the Catholic laity by orders, rules, regulations, and commands.

To state the matter baldly: more personal pain is inflicted on the laity at the parish level than is inflicted by leadership at any of the higher levels. Before we blame the Vatican or the chancery, we ought to examine our own behavior.

No one gives up power willingly, especially power that one has exercised for a thousand years. So Church personnel, often thinking of themselves as "liberals," continue to search for ways in which they can exercise authoritarian control over the laity, to force them to "act right," to impose on them virtue as they define virtue. Believing as they do that the laity are secularists, materialists, consumerists, pagans, they feel that they must impose on the lay folk the practice of virtue in order to open them up to the work of the Holy Spirit. In this mindset, it is inconceivable that the Spirit might already be at work among the laity, blowing whither She will despite our assumptions. It is also inconceivable that the laity's experience of the Spirit is richer and deeper than our own. The authoritarian virus still permeates clerical culture and inevitably also affects the "quasi-clergy" who have emerged in the last couple of decades.

So we make rules and enforce them the best we can.

There are three differences between this new Catholic authoritarianism and the old: There are many more rules today than there used to be. There are a lot more rule makers, not all of them clergy by any means. Many of the laity are smart enough to know that there are parishes where such rules do not exist and that they can find one that for reasons of compassion or justice treats them like full-fledged, free human persons.

Since the power of the clergy and the quasi-clergy is severely limited by their lack of credibility as leaders, they tend to become neo-authoritarian in the one area where they do have power—access to the sacraments. They often violate the code of canon law in denying the laity the sacraments. The code asserts that the laity have the right to the sacraments, a right which only in rare and exceptional circumstances may be denied. Once, however, you are determined to "do good" by forcing the laity to be virtuous, canon law is hardly likely to stop you.

I herewith submit a litany of horror stories about the oppression of the laity by Church personnel. I lack empirical data to say just how typical these abuses of power are, but I have enough information to say that they represent abuses that are widespread. Many of my horror stories are clear violations of canon law.

1. A couple presents itself at the rectory and asks to be married in three weeks. The parents of the bride work overseas and have been granted an unexpected two weeks leave and the couple, graduates of Catholic colleges, want to get married when her parents are present. They know about the banns so they have come to the rectory in time for that requirement to be met. They also know about how many weddings there are on Saturdays, so they say that any weeknight or week afternoon will be fine. The unsmiling priest pulls out his parish file. It will be quite impossible he tells them. We have a rule here that you must be a registered member of the parish for six months before we permit you to be married in our church. Moreover, diocesan guidelines require six months of marriage preparation. We've been here at Mass every Sunday for the last year and a half, says the bride. I don't recognize you, the pastor replies, how do I know you're not lying to me. Guidelines are not rules, are they? the groom asks. Sure they are, the pastor replies, why else would we have them. You can forget about being married in my church. So the couple goes down the street to the local Lutheran church and are married there. However, after their honeymoon, they continue to attend the Eucharist at their parish. Their first child is baptized by the Lutheran pastor. (The clerical mind cannot conceive of anything but rules. "Guidelines," as worthy as they are, cannot be converted into rules that deny the laity legitimate access to the sacraments.)

2. A young married couple is delighted that only eighteen months after the birth of their son, they now have a little sister for him. The mother calls the rectory to arrange for a Baptism. She is turned over to the

director of religious education who informs her that she and her husband must come to class every Wednesday for six weeks so that they may be properly prepared to be parents of a newly baptized Christian. Another class will not begin for three months. The mother replies that both she and her husband have had sixteen years of Catholic education. The DRE dismisses that as irrelevant. But I work during the day and my husband works at night, we couldn't possibly come to a class and leave the two children home alone. Get a baby-sitter, the DRE says curtly. The mother admits that just now they can't afford a baby-sitter and that their daughter is too young to be left with a baby-sitter. That's your problem, she is told. We didn't have to do that when my son was baptized. That's because I wasn't in charge here then, the DRE says, hanging up. Once more the code of canon law is shattered.

3. A couple of academics, both with doctorates in policy studies, are told that their child cannot be confirmed unless they go to six classes on the Church and the Social Order. They both know the Church's social teaching and interpret it in a moderately right-wing fashion. The nun who teaches the class is a *National Catholic Reporter* leftist who has simple solutions for all social problems. They are horrified by the ideological rigidity and the ignorance of her pronouncements and the dullness of her presentation. But since she can decide whether their child will receive the sacrament, they remain silent.

4. An Episcopalian who is married to a Catholic, all of whose kids are in Catholic schools, and who receives Communion every week, decides to become Catholic. He is told that he must go through two years of RCIA before he is admitted and that he must leave Mass after the Gospel every Sunday for two years because he is a catechumen. He will thus not be able to receive the Eucharist. He wants to become a Catholic badly enough that he is willing to do it. His wife, however, a feisty woman, tells the RCIA director that it is only to be used for those who are not baptized. The woman responds that in this parish it is used for all adult converts. The wife tells her she is violating Church law. She also says that dismissing people after the homily is an anachronism dating to the time when the Church feared the Roman Empire, which she notes has not been around for fifteen hundred years. We will not receive your husband into the Church, the RCIA director responds. Whereupon husband and wife go to a neighboring parish where the husband, about whose Catholic faith and knowledge there is no doubt, is admitted to the Church.

5. Another RCIA horror story: I am a twenty-nine-year-old mother of four. Seven years ago I married a man who was born and raised Catholic. After some initial reluctance I began attending Mass and now

feel that I have found a home in the Church. I studied the teachings of the Church and compared those to my personal beliefs and life experiences. I have attended Mass and attempted to live my life as a Catholic in every regard yet the Sacrament of Baptism is being, in my opinion, needlessly denied me. In our parish there are quasi-catechumen classes. I say "quasi" because I attended all last year what turned out to be nothing more than round-table discussions with no real education given about the practices of the faith. After a whole year of classes I, in the view of the instructors, was not ready for Baptism. I believe that this was the result of me disagreeing with an instructor, a convert from an evangelical church, who in my opinion has not given up his previous denomination. The local priest often sides with me but the instructors have been given the power to determine who is baptized and who is not. They guard this power zealously. I believe that I am ready. I am charged with raising my baptized children in the faith but am prohibited from practicing it myself. The parish priest told my father-in-law that he felt I was ready for Baptism. Unfortunately, however, he is unable or unwilling to confront the instructors of the RCIA. I fear that if things continue as they are I will never be allowed to partake in the sacrament of Baptism or the other sacraments of the faith.

6. Because it gives enormous spiritual power to some people for the first time in their lives and because these people are often not competent, the RCIA is subject to frequent abuse of the rights of the laity. Consider the following case: "We sit in a circle. The woman has her big Bible. We sing a little song. We listen to a little homily of no content. We are asked for discussion. One or two of the devotees offer a supporting word or two. We eat cookies. I asked when we were going to discuss the nature of evil and how confusing it is to those who love God and was told that it was a matter of faith and no discussion was permitted." The woman who wrote this note to me has already been baptized. She knows much more about the Catholic faith than her instructors. Like the woman in the previous incident she desperately wants to be a Catholic. Yet she is excluded from the household of the faith.

7. In another parish, members of the "Baptism team" are sent to the homes of parents seeking Baptism for their children to determine whether they are worthy of the sacrament. They quote Father McBrien as denouncing "Baptism on demand."

8. A priest preparing the documents for a marriage discovers that the couple have the same address. Are you living together, he asks (which is none of his business). They admit they are. We don't marry people here who live together before marriage, he informs them. As a compromise

he insists that they must sleep in separate bedrooms if they wish to be married in this church. They promise him that they will and he's ignorant enough about the human condition to believe that they will.

Two other incidents which do not violate canon law but which do violate charity:

9. In a certain parish, the pastor noted at midnight Mass that while the church was filled, there were no throngs in the back. He wondered whether the predictions of erosion of Catholicism were at last coming true. He asked the head usher after Mass whether there had been any more people who tried to get into the Mass. Sure there were, the usher replied, hundreds of them. But I wouldn't let them in because of the fire rules. Some of them gave me a hard time so I had to call the police to take them away. As the pastor pointed out to me, the head usher had not bothered to consult with him before he enforced his new rule. Moreover, the people turned away from midnight Mass because there was no room for them (in the inn?) were likely to be the folks that were not on the parish rolls and hence there was no way to apologize to them.

10. A couple who have known each other since first grade have finally discovered that they are in love. They go to the parish in which both of them lived all their lives between Baptism and college graduation, a parish in which both families were almost compulsively active and contributed large sums of money—though only a year ago both sets of parents moved to condos downtown. There is a new pastor in the parish. He does not remember the young couple or either family. I don't know you, he informs them. You are not members of the parish. You may not be married here. But, say the young people, we have permission from the bride's pastor. I don't care, says the priest. I have a rule. I only marry people who live in my parish.

The proper approach to the sacraments is to make the ceremony of administration so charming, so moving, so celebratory that the nature of the sacrament is luminous to everyone who is present and to make the preparation sessions so intelligent, so excellent, so sensible that the people in the community will want to come. Guidelines, however, cannot and should not be enforced as though they are rules. Even the stern enforcement of the obligation to attend a "pre-cana" conference is wrong (and a violation of canon law). One persuades people to attend, one does not order, and one certainly accepts the decision of the laity.

What is wrong with this clerical neo-authoritarianism?

1. It often violates the rights of the laity as specified in the code of canon law.

2. It is almost always a violation of justice, charity, and compassion.

3. It doesn't work. The attitudes and behavior of the laity will not be changed by mini-courses. Only one ignorant of the nature of human nature would think that six sessions will change anything.

4. It ignores the truth that the liturgy of the sacrament, properly performed (which it usually isn't), can have a far more powerful impact on people than classroom instructions.

5. It makes the Church look terrible.

6. It drives people away from the Church.

Why then bother with such "rules"?

The most simple answer is that it's fun. One has power to deny the sacraments—or at least thinks one has the power; if one doesn't use the power often, then what is the point of having the power. To assume the seat of God and make such judgments about other human beings is an immensely rewarding experience. It's like being bishop or even pope in your own parish.

What can be done about these abuses of power by the neo-authoritarians?

The laity have the right to appeal to the bishop. Unfortunately most laypeople and clergy and some bishops are unaware of that right. In some dioceses you waste your time with such an appeal. (In my own the local vicar is sent to deal with the problem administratively, a procedure which usually is successful.)

You can also write to the pope. In a certain parish, the deacon absolutely refused to permit a couple to marry (even though they had known each other for five years) because he thought he recognized an attempt to get around immigration laws. They wrote to the pope. Two weeks later the local chancery ordered the parish to go ahead with the marriage.

Finally, the laity are the ministers of the Sacrament of Matrimony and are also valid ministers of the Sacrament of Baptism. When appeals fail to vindicate their rights, the situation becomes a "case of necessity." In such situations the laity can administer Baptism. Moreover, if it is impossible to find a priest who will witness the Sacrament of Matrimony within thirty days, then the couple is automatically excused from the form and may contract marriage without the priest and the two witnesses.

These are drastic measures. They deprive the laypeople of the splendor of liturgically elegant administration of the sacraments (which they often don't receive anyway). Yet they may in some cases be the only possible responses to irresponsible, power-drunk neo-authoritarians.

I confess that this is a windmill that I love to charge!

Adversary: Since you're never going to be pope, why should you think that you can make it change!

Catholic Schools

On a hot summer day in 1965 I paid my respects for the first time to the new archbishop, John Patrick Cody, in the Victorian mansion on North State Parkway with twenty-eight chimneys where Chicago's archbishops have lived for most of the century. I carried with me the galleys of *The Education of Catholic Americans*, the first systematic national sample study of the effects of Catholic parochial schools. I walked into a surrealistic world, an environment which I would later realize was madness. He began, as I had been warned he would, by attacking. Who authorized me to do this research? Who had paid for it? Who was paying my salary? How much did I make? Was I still hearing Confessions? What were my career plans? He didn't intend to leave me in that work indefinitely.

After I faced him down and he had backed off (as he always did), he invited me to stay for supper. Much of the discussion was about other priests. He tried his best to pump me for information about their faults. He also informed me that there was not enough money to sustain Catholic schools. There was no reason to keep them open for "Protestants" (meaning blacks). They would have to be fazed out. I left the house with the galleys under my arms. He couldn't have cared less about our findings.

In the blazing sunlight outside the house I realized my shirt was wet from perspiration acquired while I was inside in the air-conditioned rooms. The Vatican had sent us a crazy man.[64]

Not so crazy, but equally definitive has been the reaction of most Catholic leaders and clergy to the forty years of research on Catholic education which my colleagues and I have done. They couldn't care less about our data.

I am not a spokesman for Catholic schools, nor am I an advocate for them. Not since I taught eight grade at Christ the King grammar school in Chicago from 1954 to 1960 have I ever worked for or in Catholic

---

[64]Later I would learn that one of his techniques in Rome was to give an important curial bureaucrat a thousand-dollar bill and say, "Offer a mass for my mother."

schools. Catholic education has paid for none of my research. Many Catholic educators have attacked the work for reasons of their own. I am not a supporter of Catholic schools so much as I am a supporter of the research evidence. I came to my research with an open mind on what the Catholic schools were worth and a good deal of anger at the Catholic school officials who wanted to take over the project. My findings are not based on personal opinion as many priests are convinced, since all they know are personal opinions, but conclusions driven by data.

Catholic schools in the United States are called "parochial" schools. The word means "parish" schools and the close relationship between the schools and the neighborhood parish are an important, indeed crucial, aspect of the sociological reality of the schools. The neighborhood parish as it exists in America is, in my experience, a unique phenomenon, one that is hard to explain to those who have never lived there. After one of my colleagues described such a parish at, of all things, the Merryman Summer Institute in Ennis in County Clare many years ago, someone remarked in surprise—and I think dismay—"You're describing a West of Ireland village." She was right, at least up to a point. As I understand it, if you live in a West of Ireland village, you are part of the local community whether you want to be or not. In an American neighborhood parish, a product of the immigration experience but outlasting it, you have an option. Not all those who live within the geographical boundaries of the neighborhood parish are intensely involved in it. But many are, enough to make it different from almost any other form of urban community or quasi-community anywhere in the world. So strong is the parish identification that in many American cities, when Catholics are asked where they're from, they respond with the parish name—not Ninety-first and Hoyne, not Beverly, but Christ the King. (Bill Singer, a Jewish alderman in Chicago, used to respond that he was from "Our Lady of Peace." He understood how the game was played.) Despite the confident claim of some would-be Catholic intellectuals that this form of Catholic life is passing away, it persists vigorously in the professional class neighborhoods and suburbs of the big American cities and on many university campuses.

When one adds to the ties of immigrant and post-immigrant neighborhood and local parish, in which many people are intensely involved, the third factor of a school that is part of the parish buildings and to which many of the neighborhood children go, one has a remarkable triangulation of social energies—parish, neighborhood, and school—which seems to me to be absolutely unique. The neighborhood-parish-school becomes a center of what James Coleman called social

capital—overlapping social relationships—of enormous potential sociological influence. Indeed, Coleman used the parochial school as one of
the classic examples of social capital.

The Catholic elite, lay and clerical, in America ignore both the work
of sociologists who, like Coleman, are not Catholic and the unique nature of the Catholic neighborhood-parish-school. Immigrant self-hatred
and the collapse of the preconciliar "mortal sin" Catholicism have
persuaded them that there was nothing good in American Catholicism
before 1965. For virtue they must always look elsewhere. There is nothing to learn from their own experience. Curiously, now the strongest
supporters of parochial schools in America are scholars like Coleman and
Nobel Laureate Gary Becker who are not Catholic. Parochial schools
should be left behind like all the other "irrelevant" detritus of the Confident Church.

Catholic schools came into existence in this country as part of the
major effort of the Church almost from the beginning until the late 1950s
to protect the faith of urban immigrants from what was considered to be
a hostile public school system. Not only would the Catholic schools teach
religion—which the public schools eventually could not—they would
also be run by men and women who believed in the "traditional" educational techniques as opposed to the mushy theories of John Dewey
and the other "Progressive" educators.

It remains to be seen how necessary the parochial school was as a
defensive measure against a hostile Protestant culture. The culture was
indeed hostile and to a considerable extent still is. However, the immigrants never found the Protestant option particularly alternative—who
wanted to give up their statues and vigil lights? That the Catholic schools
did preside over the acculturation of the immigrants and their children
and grandchildren into American society now seems to be unquestioned,
though there is a lurking suspicion that the young people who attended
them would have been even more successful if they had attended public
schools "like everyone else."

Let us move back to the late 1950s and consider the conventional
wisdom about Catholic schools. The first four were the conventional
wisdom of the professional education fraternity. The latter three were
the conventional wisdom of many, if not most, Catholic "liberals"—lay
and clerical.

1. Catholic schools were academically inferior because of overcrowded
   classrooms and the lack of sufficient teacher training for their staffs.
2. Catholic schools were anti-intellectual, in part because they valued
   obedience and faith more than critical thinking and the quest for truth.
   Monsignor John Tracy Ellis's work had shown, had it not, that those

who went to Catholic schools were not part of the intellectual life of America.

3. The rigid, doctrinaire atmosphere of Catholic schools inhibited the social and economic success of those Catholics who attended the schools.

4. Catholic schools were divisive because they isolated Catholics from other Americans and thus, perhaps unintentionally, encouraged racial and religious prejudice. Moreover, by rejecting the "common school" of Horace Mann, they resisted the assimilating energies which were necessary to unite American society and culture.

5. The students who attended Catholic schools showed little evidence of being better Catholics. Articles appeared in Catholic magazines (with pictures) that contended the young people who attended these schools participated in race riots.

6. To the extent that those who had attended Catholic schools were better Catholics, the reason was that they came from better Catholic families.

7. In a "changing Church" (in a few years that cliché would be change to "postconciliar Church"), Catholics could no longer afford to put so much of their resources into a separate Catholic school system. Something new, different, and better was needed. The only candidate seemed (then and now) to be the so-called Confraternity of Christian Doctrine (C.C.D.) programs, renamed "religious education" programs.[65] Available resources, it was said, should be divided equally between the schools and religious education—as though the schools somehow did not engage in religious education.

Among those who still supported Catholic schools, debate raged about which level—primary, secondary, or tertiary—was most important for the impact of the schools, such as it might have been. Not surprisingly those who worked for each level contended that their was the most important.

I think it safe to say that these two sets of conventional wisdom are still intact. Although the academic test scores for Catholic schools are consistently higher than those of the public schools and this fact is accepted by everyone save for former UFT president the late Al Shanker in his vanity column in *The New York Times,* the results are usually dismissed on the grounds that they represent merely the extra motivation and the higher economic status of those parents who send their children to Catholic schools.

---

[65]"Adult education" is also mentioned on occasion, though it is usually not clear what the term means.

The three great enemies of Catholic schools in the United States—professional public educators, the leadership of the American Federation of Teachers, and many Catholic "liberals"—have not modified their positions. They are not likely to because research evidence never changes the minds of ideologues. Nonetheless, it is safe to say after four decades of research, not a single item in the seven objections listed above has been sustained by the empirical data.

The beginning of systematic research on Catholic schools was the 1958 Fitchburg, Massachusetts, project of Peter and Alice Rossi. Although, to my knowledge, only one article appeared about that project it was important in two respects: the Rossis were impressed by how poorly the conventional wisdom about Catholic schools fit the schools they were actually studying. Moreover, they were also convinced that the proper subjects for research were not schoolchildren but adults later in life. The decisive question, according to Rossi's laws,[66] was what residual impact the schools had on the lives of Catholic adults. This law ought to be self-evident but somehow it is not, perhaps because it implied probability sample research on Catholic adults, a process which is far more costly than sampling from a list of students or a list of people who have been identified as parishioners. It has the distinct advantage of being the only valid way to do it.

At the same time, James Coleman's classic study, *The Adolescent Society*, appeared. One of the schools studied in that project was a Polish Catholic high school in Chicago. Clearly it was an excellent place. Jim's curiosity was aroused and later would manifest itself in his work on a national sample of high school students.

The first national data collection research was done in 1961 in a study of the career plans of a sample of June 1961 college graduates. My job was to analyze the impact of religion on these choices. The most important finding was that Catholics were one-quarter of the graduate population, the same rate as for the whole country (the rate is more than one out of three now, Catholics are one and a half times as likely to graduate from college as is the average American). Moreover they were even more likely than other Americans to plan arts and science graduate school enrollment. Finally, the graduates of Catholic colleges were even more likely than other Catholic graduates to plan academic careers. The theories of Monsignor Ellis and Professor Gerhard Lenski about Catholic anti-intellectualism simply collapsed in the face of the data. I assert then and I assert now that the only thing wrong with their conclusions was

[66]There are many such laws and I'm not altogether sure what number should be assigned to this one.

that they were dealing with data from the past—in the monsignor's case from the 1920s.

Reaction to my findings was underwhelming. Even if I was right (and I was accused of being an "optimist" or of wanting to be a bishop), these graduates would not make it through graduate school, would not receive quality academic appointments, would not attain tenure, and would not end up at distinguished national universities. Follow-up studies or similar studies would prove that all of these predictions were wrong, save perhaps at the elite private universities which for many years discriminated against Catholics, though even among those schools resistance has diminished. At the major state universities it went away a long time ago.

This enormous change in Catholic culture is no longer denied (2 percent of American Catholics can be said to be members of an "intelligentsia," about the same as the national proportion). It has made the journey, commonplace for many research findings, from what no one believed to what everyone knows.

Pete Rossi decided that it was time to do a full-scale national sample study of the effects of Catholic education and obtained a grant from the Carnegie Foundation for the project, after, he insists, a stop at St. Paddy's to light a vigil. The decisive comparison would be between those who went to Catholic schools and those whose parents had the same level of religious practice and would have sent them but no Catholic schools were available.

Many of the issues in the debate were settled intellectually with the publication of *The Education of Catholic Americans* in 1965.

- There were statistically significant correlations between years of attendance at Catholic schools and religious knowledge, religious practice, doctrinal belief, and social attitudes (rejection of racism and anti-Semitism).

- The strongest impact of the schools was on those adults whose parents had been devout Catholics. Far from causing the school effect, parental background specified it. This is a distinction which some clergy seem unable to comprehend. But I try: if family background explained the Catholic school effect, there should be no difference on the scales between those from devout families who went to Catholic schools and those from devout families who did not go to Catholic schools.

- There were no signs of any discernible effects in later life of having participated in what then was called C.C.D. None. Nor have I ever seen serious evidence and any impact now that the program has been relabeled "religious education." This was again not a matter of personal opinion or an ideological bias. It was and is simply a research finding.

- Students who had gone to Catholic schools were more successful economically and educationally and occupationally in later life than those who had not attended them, even when parental social and economic backgrounds were held constant.
- No level was any more important than any other level. What counted was the cumulative number of years in Catholic schools.
- Catholics who had attended Catholic schools contributed more generously to the Church as did parents who had children in Catholic schools.

The book was treated very unevenly. *Commonweal, National Catholic Reporter,* and *The New York Times* attacked it. (John Cogley, then of the *Times,* apologized later. The other journals characteristically did not.) With this sort of launch the book became a kind of inkblot which was quoted to support many different ideological positions, usually out of context. Mostly, however, it was ignored. During the years after the publication of the book, some sort of national policy was formulated, perhaps implicitly, by the hierarchy and school superintendents that no more Catholic schools would be built. Since that time only one new Catholic school has been opened in my diocese, and that one is enormously successful.

One thing can be said about the book, however. No one has ever been able to refute its findings. Few have even tried.

In the seventies we did two major projects on Catholic schools at NORC—in 1974 a replication of the 1963 study and at the end of the decade a study of Catholic young people. Data were collected for the 1963 project before the implementation of the reforms of the Second Vatican Council. That made possible an intriguing natural experiment: with data from before the council we could study ten years later the changes which had occurred in Catholicism and in the Catholic schools as a result of the council, one of the most dramatic, and arguably traumatic, events in the whole history of the Church.

In the intense controversy which raged around *Catholic Schools in a Declining Church* (which I wrote with William McCready and Kathleen McCourt), the specific findings about Catholic schools were often overlooked. The findings are simple enough to summarize: the relationships between having attended Catholic schools as children and adult Catholic behavior had grown stronger than they were in the 1963 study. Those clergy and religious and "liberal" laity who were antagonistic to the schools and who argued that in a "postconciliar" Church that Catholic schools were no longer necessary could not have been more wrong. They had become substantially more necessary in a turbulent and restless

Church. Moreover, it was precisely those who had attended Catholic schools who are more sympathetic to the conciliar reforms. There were two other important findings in the book:

• The mechanism which seems to explain the impact of Catholic schools was how "close" a given person felt that she or he was to the Church (holding everything else constant, of course). I speculated then that their presence on the physical grounds of the parish and the contact with clergy, religious, and dedicated laity—that is from the Catholic community—were more important than anything taught in the classroom. This finding would appear even more important in the light of the work of Coleman and Bryk I will report on shortly.

• The bottom was dropping out on Catholic financial contributions, in great part because of increasing rejection of Church authority and sexual teaching. Bill McManus and I would turn to that question again in the middle eighties.

In the late 1980s with Bill McCready again and also Joan Fee and Terry Sullivan we turned to a large sample of Catholic young people between fifteen and thirty in both the United States and Canada and, if they were married, their spouses. This provided a treasure trove of useful and interesting information about young Catholics and about their religious imagery, most of which was dutifully ignored, because everyone seemed to think (wrongly) that they knew what we would find without reading the two books (*Young Catholics* and *The Religious Imagination*).

On the subject of Catholic schools we would be able to see the impact of the new, post-conciliar Catholic schools on those who grew up for the most part in the years during and after the council. There were four findings which are worth noting here:

• The correlations between Catholic school attendance and Catholic adult behavior were stronger than ever. Catholic schools seemed even less optional for the Church than they had been in the years before the council.

• Despite complaints from many parents about what was being taught in the Catholic schools, the young men and women who had attended these schools were if anything more sophisticated Catholics in most respects than their predecessors. In particular they were more tolerant toward minorities, more committed to the rights of women, and more intensely Catholic in their religious imagery.

• Moreover, granted the life-cycle pattern of alienation from religion (and everything else) which emerged clearly for those between fifteen and twenty-five, those who had attended Catholic schools were less likely to leave, left later, or came back earlier. For those over twenty-five there was a *negative* correlation between attendance at "religious education" programs and a return to the Church.

In 1988 NORC included in its annual General Social Survey an extended battery of religious questions. I purchased time for a question about Catholic school attendance. The basic findings (which I reported in the Jesuit magazine *America* with the title "Catholic Schools: A Golden Twilight") the following year had a certain monotony to them. Correlations were becoming higher yet for Catholic school attendance and no influence of "religious education" could be found.

Yet within that context the findings were truly astonishing.

- Those who had attended Catholic schools scored systematically higher on measures of support for the equality of women.
- They were more likely to describe themselves as "liberals" or "moderates."
- They were more likely to have high levels of psychological well-being and were more likely to have benign views of their fellow humans. They were also more likely to have benign views of God.
- They were half again as generous to the Church.
- They had greater awareness of the complexity of moral decision making and were half as likely to have drifted away from the Church.
- They were also more likely to say that intense sexual pleasure had increased their religious faith.
- These correlations were even stronger for those under thirty.
- Moreover, controls for education, income, and parental church attendance did not diminish the power of the correlations.

I noted in the article (and forgive me for acting like the pope or a bishop and quoting myself):

> *Virtually all the criticism aimed at the Catholics schools are refuted by these data: they are not rigid, repressive, dull or restrictive. On the contrary, they seem to facilitate greater happiness, more support for the equality of women, more confidence in other people, more willingness to see sex as a sacrament, greater generosity to the Church, more benign images of God, greater awareness of the complexity of moral decision making, and higher intellectual achievement. Not bad.*

Subsequently Bill McManus and I returned to the question of whether the Church could afford to build more Catholic schools. Using a large number of surveys between the middle 1960s and the middle 1980s there would have been no problem sustaining the Catholic schools if there was the will to do so. Catholic contributions had declined (as percentage of income) from 2.2 percent in the sixties to 1.1 percent in the eighties while Protestant contributions remained at 2.2 percent. The Church had lost six billion dollars annually because of this decline. The hostile response was vehement: the problem, we were told, was that Catholics went to church less frequently than in the past. But if they had bothered to read the book, the clergy and hierarchy would have noticed that most of the decline in giving was precisely among those who continued to go every week. We could account for most of the decline by taking into account changing Catholic attitudes on authority and sexuality. The laity, I insisted, were angry and the only thing which would diminish their anger was a real share in decision making and/or an effective parish priest. At first Bill was dubious about the anger. Later he agreed with me.

Again the results were attacked and ridiculed, but they never have been refuted. In fact, no one to my knowledge has ever assembled a longitudinal data file (one with different measures at different time points) which would be necessary to attempt a replication. A recent excellent study of Catholic finances by Joseph Claude Harris generally sustains the arguments that Bill and I advanced: the money is there, the Church for various reasons is unable to collect it.

At the beginning of the decade, NORC began a monumental study of high school students in the famous *High School and Beyond* project. The late James Coleman was the director of the project and the guiding genius behind it. Noting that there had been a large influx of minority students, especially African American and Hispanic American, I asked whether this was a wise investment of resources by minority group families. Many of those who had observed this phenomenon argued that the apparent results were in fact a function of the family background of the students whose parents opted for Catholic schools and of the ease with which Catholic schools could dump the large numbers of discipline problems. A nun at a very difficult inner-city school lamented to me, for example, that they were not really responding to the worst of the problems of her neighborhood.

In fact, this expulsion of problem students is a myth. For my book I surveyed twenty dioceses and found only a tiny number of expulsions. Subsequently, Bryk reported that on the average Catholic high schools expelled only two students a year and suspended three more. However, myths are not refuted by data. Al Shanker of the United Federation of Teachers, whose dislike for Catholic schools bordered on the pathological, continued to insist that vast numbers were expelled.

But the question remains as to whether the academic outcome of minority students at the Catholic schools can be accounted for by the positive family background from which these students come. It was the same issue, you will perceive, as was raised earlier about the religious effects of Catholic schools.

I was astonished by the finding, which was exactly the opposite of what one might expect: even holding family background constant, the payoff at Catholic schools was not for the upper-middle-class young people who came from stable and well-educated families and who had not experienced emotional, academic, or disciplinary problems. As I said in the book, parents of that kind of young person might just as well send their child to the public schools as far as academic outcome was concerned (though patently there were other reasons for choosing Catholic schools—like physical safety for example). The payoff came for those young people who are disadvantaged in one way or another—broken family, poverty, low education of parents, emotional, academic, or disciplinary problems. And the more these disadvantages were piled on top of one another, the more effective Catholic schools were. Such a finding, I said, ought not to have been so astonishing. After all, the Catholic schools had been founded to educate the children of impoverished immigrants. They knew how to do it.

The same year as the publication of *Catholic High Schools and Minority Students*, Coleman and his colleagues Tom Hoffer and Sally Kilgore published their first report on the *High School and Beyond* study—*High School Achievement: Public and Private Schools*. Their findings were the same as mine, but in the context of a much broader assessment of American secondary education. The public education fraternity had a field day denouncing both books. I let Jim, perhaps the best sociologist of his generation, fight the battle. He was a born fighter and I was as fed up with the rigid supercilious public educators as I was with the ignorant and stupid Catholic educational administrators.

Jim began to speak of the Catholic schools as the real "common schools" in the sense of Horace Mann, schools which tended to equalize opportunity for everyone.

If Catholic educators were aware of this battle about their schools or even interested in it, there were no sounds heard from their side of the playing field.

The critics' most serious complaint against our books was that we had no longitudinal data—that is, we needed measures of sophomores and then the same students as seniors two years later to measure school outcomes. The sophomore scores would definitively hold constant family background. Anything added by Catholic schools in the following two years (over and above what public schools added) would be a pure school effect.

I howled gleefully at that last-ditch argument, because we were about to repeat the study when the sophomores were seniors and there was no doubt in my mind what the results would be.

Coleman, Hoffer, and I joined forces in publishing the results of that second wave in *Sociology of Education*. Far from diminishing the Catholic school effects, the second wave presented them as even stronger than they were in the sophomore years—even though the public schools had lost many of their poorest students through dropouts. If this was not a school effect, then there were no school effects anywhere in American education. I am convinced that such effects in any other institution would have been hailed as a great educational achievement.

The battle continued. I continued to let Jim fight it out. I was sick of the whole subject and convinced that we would never change the minds of anyone. Christopher Jencks offered a not unreasonable conclusion to the argument: the average achievement in Catholic high schools is somewhat higher than in the public high schools and there is evidence that Catholic high schools were particularly helpful for minority students.

Coleman subsequently developed his theory of "social capital," one of his major contributions to American sociology. Simply put, social capital is the pattern of overlapping relationships that develop in and around an institution and make it even more effective in its work—such as the lab school at the University of Chicago at which the parents were not merely members of the parent community but also university colleagues; a school in a small town where parents knew one another as friends and neighbors as well as parents of schoolchildren; and Catholic schools where parents share denominational membership, religious heritage, and even (in the case of the grammar schools) parish membership. It was this social capital, he suggested, that would account in part for the success of Catholic schools.

Finally in 1993, Anthony Bryk, Valerie Lee, and John Holland published their book *Catholic Schools and the Common Good*, the best report on Catholic education ever written. I do not know whether Professor Bryk is or ever was a Catholic, but the book is written with a balanced objectivity that makes that question irrelevant.

Graciously he and his colleagues acknowledged their debt to those who went before them, but observed that neither Coleman and his colleagues nor I were able to identify and explain (save at a very general level) the nature of the institutional mechanisms and dynamics which account for the apparent success of the Catholic schools studied in *High School and Beyond*. Using sophisticated mathematical models which were not generally available earlier they offered powerful evidence of why Catholic schools work.

Basically, Bryk and his colleagues described three mechanisms which seem to be explanations for the success of Catholic schools:

- Institutional arrangements which require more advanced work in subjects like math and English for those on the college track, assign relatively few students to the general track, and insist that even they take advanced academic courses.
- A personalist institutional philosophy which emphasizes concern for each individual student.
- A community spirit which seems to animate the Catholic schools.

Not only were these explanations offered, but they were also tested against the data and generally sustained. They were all part of Jim Coleman's social capital and, oddly enough, what Catholic schools had claimed to be doing all along—often, I fear, with little confidence that they were living up to the claims.

But they were. In fact, they were doing a much better job than they suspected they were doing.

There is still room for research on Catholic schools, but I think the basic questions of the late 1950s that I raised at the beginning of this chapter have been answered beyond any reasonable doubt: Catholic schools have been enormously successful in both religious and academic terms and are doing today a better job than they have ever done before.

There is some satisfaction in pursuing a problem like this for forty years and achieving accurate answers to its basic questions. However, I'm inclined to think it was a waste of time. One received no points in the academic world for doing it because by definition research on Catholic schools was not proper work for a scholar. (This position has changed, at least to some extent.) And no one in power in the Church listened to the results. Indeed, just as the Catholic schools were emerging as astonishing institutions and as extremely important resources for the Church, we have been closing them down and not building new ones.

At first I thought the reason that no one listened was me. Why take a sociologist who is a priest seriously, especially when he is also a successful novelist? But they did not listen to Jim Coleman or Tony Bryk either, so it wasn't just me.

The visceral dislike for Catholic schools of some Catholic "intellectuals" was revealed once again recently in an article in *Kappan*, the magazine of Phi Delta Kappa, the educational honor society. The authors dismissed the Catholic schools of the 1950s and '60s as "sleepy," arguing from a memoir of columnist Garry Wills and a play by John R. Powers—ignoring the research from that time of Rossi, Coleman, and myself. Then they said that the schools were no longer Catholic because a quarter of their students were not Catholics and indeed not white (a curious implicit racism). Finally they suggested that the costs of Catholic schools were pushing them out of the reach of working-class Catholics; it never occurred to them to ascertain whether scholarship programs were not already dealing with that problem.

At the same time, a committee established by the late Cardinal Bernardin recommended the closing of more Catholic schools in Chicago because they could not afford modern technology, especially sophisticated computers. None of us, Catholic and non Catholic, who had performed the research on Catholic schools for the last forty years were asked to testify before the committee. Who needed research? That there were almost five thousand children on waiting lists for admission into Catholic schools in Chicago was apparently not proof that parents were looking for something more than computers.

Yet for the first time in a long time I'm beginning to think there is some reasonable hope that the social capital in parochial schools will not be wasted. Our new cardinal has read the research, astonishingly enough. Moreover, he believes that Catholicism is a teaching church and must therefore teach. He is about to launch a hundred-fifty-million-dollar fund-raising campaign for Catholic education. His most pressing pastoral concern is the nine hundred thousand Latino population of Chicago, for whom the parochial schools can be a critical pastoral resource, just as they were for earlier immigrants.

Can Chicago afford that kind of money? The answer is that an archdiocese like Chicago can afford anything it wants. Astonishingly, there is considerable enthusiasm for his campaign, though not among the clergy. However, a memory of a similar fund-raising drive by Cardinal Cody from thirty years ago continues to simmer. Archdioceses like Detroit and Minneapolis may have carried out similar campaigns. But the history—and the bitterness—in Chicago is much different.

We will see.

Adversary: I'm not going to argue with you about this chapter. You've too much data!

III

Interlude

Prayers

When I was writing *The Cardinal Virtues*, a story about contemporary suburban parish life (which had originally been designed as a setting for a TV series), I decided that the reflections of Father Laurence O'Toole McAuliffe, the pastor of the People of God in Forest Springs (an imaginary west suburban parish which many people wrongly thought sounded like CK, which as every Chicagoan knows is on the *South* Side), ought to appear in two forms—his interior monologue, which suggested an exhausted and disillusioned man, and his dialogue with God, which suggested a man of deep faith. As I began to compose his nightly prayers I realized that I was praying through him, that while we were different men with different experiences, we had similar relationships with God. Might this be a good way for me to pray? Not using "Lar" (pronounced to rhyme with "care" and not "bar," if you please) as an intermediary, but talking directly to God on the computer screen?

It seemed a strange idea, a mix of spirituality and technology that would not appeal to most masters of spiritual life. One shouldn't need the keyboard and the monitor (at this moment a Compaq Qvision 200) to focus one's attentions on the deity. Perhaps not, but it might be a help. So for seven years now I have done my daily spiritual reflection in the form of a conversation with God on disk. One of the advantages of such prayer, incidentally, is that if your machine eats up passages (or whole months' worth), you don't have to redo it because God remembers even if your hard disk does not.

So every day for the last seven years (well, most days anyway) I begin the day with a swim and a conversation with Lady Wisdom (well, usually in the morning). I do not mean to suggest that such a "prayer journal" is the way everyone should pray. But it is a form of prayer which forces me to concentrate my energies and my attention on God and has been an enormous help to me, in part because I have to ponder during the day what I'm going to talk to God about on the morrow. I don't read them myself after I've written them, but I suspect that often the human side of the dialogue is pretty pathetic, an exhausted and discouraged human complaining to Lady Wisdom. On the other hand, if God really is a lover (and She really is), then like all lovers She wants to know what's on your mind. Or rather more precisely (and with a greater care for orthodoxy), God wants to hear *from you* what's on your mind.

I use the womanly pronoun here because the God I talk to is an opposite gender God (Lady Wisdom is not just a tip of the hat to being politically correct). This was not part of the plan, it just worked out that way. I did not try to convert God into a mother and lover, though I was not worried when those metaphors began to emerge because our research on young people had shown that an image of a cross-gender God had a powerful impact on the religious and social and sexual lives of young men while a womanly image of God had no effect at all on young women. Moreover, a third of Americans, regardless of gender or age, imagined God as more Mother than Father or as equally Mother and Father. As Marilyn James, a grammar school classmate, said to me, if you have ever held in your arms a baby you've just brought into the world and been filled with love for that little mite, you know that's the way God feels about us. The image has been out there for a long time, it would seem. Only now are the religious elite becoming aware of it.

In the TNK (the Jewish Scriptures) such images abound. The Lord sometime compares himself to a mother struggling to bring forth a child and a mother bending down to nurse a child, especially in Isaiah and Deuteronomy.[67] Jesus compares Himself to a mother hen gathering her chicks around her and to a mother nursing her child. Medieval spiritual writers and theologians often compare grace to mother's milk we suckle from the breasts of God. Pope John Paul I, the September Pope, in one of his audience talks said we must imagine God as our Father, *but even more*, as our Mother. Methodius of Olympus in 310 wrote of the womanliness of God as represented by the Holy Spirit related to Jesus as Eve did to Adam. Sophisticated philosophers like Nicholas of Cusa contended that in God opposites were combined, including man and woman, because God in their perfection has the attributes we commonly imagine as paternal and maternal. So the image has always been a part of the tradition if only in a minor key. In contemporary theological parlance God is both male and female and neither male nor female (and these terms are used symbolically of course and not for purposes of sexual stereotyping). It is therefore legitimate to imagine God as either gender. All God talk is necessarily metaphorical, even the most abstract of Thomistic theological terms such as *Ipsum Esse*, Being Itself. The most we can say is that our relationship with God is like a human relationship

[67]Check out Isaiah 42:13–14, 45:10, 49:15, and 66:13.

which we know—Mother, Father, Master, Judge, Spouse, Lover, Friend, King (to use the images we use in our research at the National Opinion Research Center). Implicit in all metaphorical talk is the assumption that God is also unlike the person described in the relationship. But the "unlike" comes from defect and not excess. To say that God is a spouse—a powerful image in both Jewish and Christian tradition—is metaphor which fails not because God is less passionate, less dedicated, less implacable than a human spouse, but more so.

One hears objections on occasion from theologians (especially Protestant theologians or Catholics who have absorbed much of the Protestant tradition) that such terms are anthropomorphic and hence idolatrous. Yet since we are imaginative creatures and cannot pray without imagining and hence must imagine God to pray, we have no choice but to use metaphors. My friend Hans Küng is fond of saying, "Ya, but God after all must be God."

Right on, Hans! But even that sentence has an implied metaphor in it. Paul Tillich's "God beyond the Gods" is a useful theological concept, but *you* don't pray to that image (which is still metaphorical in any case) and it is a long way from Jesus' "Abba," which might be translated "Daddy." The fear of tainting God with human imagery is legitimate enough—though I don't imagine many people have ever prayed to the Great Architect of the Universe either. One certainly must be wary of making God too human and equating Her/Him with the Olympians of Greek mythology, though I don't think all that many people do that today. On the other hand a God of whom we claim to have no tentative picture is likely to be a very distant God and one whose absence leaves a very bleak universe.

Moreover, most religions do have a woman deity of one sort or another. Only Protestantism and Islam lack such a metaphor for the life-giving, life-nurturing dimension of God. In Catholicism the function of Mary the Mother of Jesus (obviously I would say) is to reflect the mother-love of God and prayer to her is to the maternal dimension of God. In the folk Judaism of the years before the prophets, the Holy One was thought to have a spouse who was called the *shekena* of the Holy One, His Glory. She apparently appeared in statues in some temples outside of Palestine and in the Scriptures remains as His presence going before the armies of the Children of Israel. Both the Hebrew name for her and the Greek translation "Spirit" are feminine in gender. Thus in Catholic and Jewish traditions the metaphor of woman for God has existed for a long time and need not deteriorate (though on some occasions it may have) into fertility worship.

I do not want to impose this imagery on anyone. But I insist that it is a legitimate and orthodox imagery for those who wish to use it. However, those who oppose it (about a quarter of the letters I get which are critical of my stories[68] complain, usually hysterically, about Blackie Ryan's propensity to refer to God as "Herself") want to deny the right of such imagery to others. It is permissible for God to be imagined as a spouse but only a male spouse. No one, however, has the right to deny metaphors that are in the tradition to anyone else.[69]

Moreover, the God to whom I am speaking in my prayer journals is not only womanly but vulnerable. God a lovely and vulnerable woman? I can hear Küng saying again that "God after all must be God" and warning of the dangers to which the *Patripassiani*[70] succumbed. In the Greek philosophical perspective which has shaped so much of Christian theology, God has to be invulnerable, immutable, and utterly independent of his human creatures. So, for all practical purposes, He cannot give a damn about our suffering. (Contemporary Process Theology approaches the matter differently and argues that vulnerability is a perfection and that to deny it to God is to deny God a perfection to which he is entitled.) I am not a theologian but I cannot see how this component of traditional theology can be harmonized with the overwhelming data of revelation. Repeatedly in the Jewish Scriptures God complains that He is hurt because Israel has rejected His love. In some passages He claims to have suffered not only for Israel but because of Israel.[71] I fail to see how the theologians can ignore or dismiss such data. Certainly they are poetic images, but poetry is the only way we can talk about God. Dismissing the images as merely poetic simply won't do. The task for theologians is to try to explain how the imagery is consistent with the traditional theology of God. Very few have bothered to try. However, I will not permit them to deprive me of the imagery of the Scriptures in my prayer life.

Paul Murray, an Irish Dominican priest and poet (and patently a mystic), describes what God is like:

[68]About one out of thirty letters are hostile.

[69]As far as I can determine there are no depictions of God as a womanly spouse in the high art of the tradition. Bob Fosse in his remarkable film *All that Jazz* seems to be the first one to image God as a woman—not for reasons of political correctness but because of the nature of his own religious experience.

[70]A Christological heresy in the early Church described the nature of the relationship between the Father and the Son as being such that God the Father also suffered on the Cross. But that's not what I'm talking about. Can one really insist that the Father did not in some fashion share in his Son's sufferings? And if He didn't, what kind of a Father would He have been?

[71]See Terence E. Fretheim's book *The Suffering of God*, Fortress Press (no date given).

He who brings the gifts we give
He who needs nothing
His need of us and . . .
If you or I should cease to be
He would die of sadness.

That, I believe, is what God is really like. As Robert Barron of St. Mary of the Lake Seminary puts it, once God creates us, He becomes like a mother to us and is as involved with us as every mother is with her children.

I write the first draft of these pages on the anniversary of the liberation of Auschwitz by the Red Army. I cannot believe that God was immune to the sufferings of the people who died there. Nor do I think God wants us to believe that. Moreover, the refusal of theologians to address the issue of the suffering God has caused enormous pastoral problems. How can one say to the family in which a young father has died that his death is God's will? What kind of God could superciliously dismiss their suffering? I think it much better—and more consistent with the scriptural data—to tell them that God suffers with them. As the Russian mystic Berdyaev once said, when the little baby weeps, God cries.

Obviously such words are metaphors. God's suffering is not the same as our suffering. The words are used analogously of God and us. But they still reveal something important about God. Indeed, as always (or almost always), the metaphor errs by defect rather than excess. God's suffering with and for us is more intense than our suffering. I don't know how this can be, but it is up to the theologians to figure out how it can be and they're much too busy with other things (mostly what they think to be politics)[72] these days to be interested in that question.

If God is vulnerable and suffers with us, then does it not follow that She needs our love? But the theologians (and the clowns that write catechisms) insist that God does not need us and that whether we exist or not is therefore a matter of indifference to God. I am baffled that they can really propound such nonsense in the face of the obvious message of the Scriptures. God clearly depicts Himself as wanting human love in return for His love. What kind of a lover is it that would not want a response? If we exclude God from wanting a response to Her love, then how can we claim the term "lover" is not used with two utterly different meanings of God and us and that therefore the metaphor means nothing at all?

[72]I do not know of a single theologian who could deliver a pack of starving vampires to a blood bank.

I can see how some kinds of Protestant theologians might accept the notion that the metaphor "God is Love" tells us nothing about God. But I cannot see how Catholic theologians can do that, not if they accept St. Thomas's notion of analogy or David Tracy's notion of the analogical imagination.

The way God wants us (and how can you have a "want" without a need of some kind) is clearly different from the way we want our human beloved, but not completely different, and to the extent that it is different, God's want surely must be more intense than ours rather than less so.

I don't deny that there are problems with this image of God, but there are a lot more problems with the one which denies any similarity between human love and God's love. It seems to me that, for all practical and pastoral purposes, to deny the passion of God (in both senses of the word "passion") is to reduce to meaninglessness the core of the most important metaphor for God that is available to us: God IS Love. Moreover, the pastoral problem is that the theology by which we have tried to explain that metaphor has reduced it to meaninglessness. Most Christians simply are unable to make anything out of the metaphor. If God's love is so unlike our love that it is utterly different from our love, then what does the metaphor tell us about God? What happens to the story inherent in the metaphor of God's romance with Her creatures?

The result of taking this metaphor seriously (though not literally) suggests that God is a strange kind of God. How could the Person who started the Big Bang, the God of supernovas and black holes, of billions of galaxies and perhaps billions of universes, the God of hurricanes and tornadoes and typhoons and floods and earthquakes, also be a vulnerable God, a God who wants and needs our love?

Beats me.

But this is the God with whom I dialogue every morning and whom I must tell on many occasions that She is a strange kind of God.

I had no intention of publishing these prayer journals. However, the late Dan Herr begged me to come up with a book on spirituality at a time when, he insisted, Thomas More Press needed such a book. I argued that I didn't have anything and I didn't have time to do anything. He continued to push (inappropriately, I told him, for a man whose column was called "Stop Pushing"). So finally I printed out the 1991 diary and said, "Here it is; you can have it. I refuse to look at it again. You go through this stuff and cut what you think might be a problem and publish it. And leave me alone."

After I had turned the manuscript over to him, I wondered if it was not a terrible mistake. Yet, if my prayer journal could help other people pray, then I didn't care what people would say about its author.

After Dan died (and God be good to him), Mike Leach at Crossroads Books took over the editorial task and so far four volumes of the prayer journals have appeared. They were not widely reviewed (which was fine with me), but all the reviews that I saw were, to my astonishment, quite favorable. So too were the letters I received. Several priests—such as Jack Egan and my late classmate Frank Gill—told me that they read one dialogue (or implied monologue since I have to guess at what Herself is saying) every day. Some secular colleagues tell me they see themselves in my reflections.

I truly cannot imagine why people find the journals useful. I know why people read my novels: they like the stories and often "get" the religious illumination in them. But I don't know what they see in the journals. Nor will I ever know because I am incapable of reading them.

I do know, however, that writing the journal reflections every day is a tremendous help to my own spiritual life—which is why I began to write them. Along with the reunions and the reconciliations (and perhaps age and maybe a tad of wisdom) they have played a major role in the slow transformation of my life during the last fifteen years.

They are not diaries, by the way; I note only in passing or not at all what has happened to either me or the world. If anyone wants to know what I think about the events of the world, they can read that in my columns. They are, rather, attempts at intimate conversation with the Absolute who also can legitimately be imaged as a loving and vulnerable woman.

Another form of prayer is writing poetry. The function of a poem is to capture the images of a transient moment of grace. Consider my lunacy, that is my romance with the moon.

Autumn Moon

I looked out the window late last night
And saw there the moon, lurking in the trees,
How rich and full she was and silver bright
She wanted only to pose for me and please,
A sacrament of woman, love, and God
Beguiling me with her radiant, magic light.
Yet I turned away—how terribly odd—
And, O, pushed my naked moon out of sight.

No time . . . away with her seductive tease!
She tried to ravish me, poor thing, but lost the fight.
For my precious work I must each minute seize;

Thus I rejected her and, Ah! destroyed delight.
Moon and God, I love you both, but on my knees
I plead: not now, come back some other night!

Moon, however, does not give up. She has after all played the game a long, long time. So she returns. Only to be rebuffed again:

Sly Moon

Sly and crafty moon came snooping round again
Bright orange and lush she was and oh so sleek
And shapely out there on the desert rim
An irresistible and seductive treat
O Moon, my love, you're gorgeous tonight, I said
If I had time I'd compose for you a hymn
But I must work tonight and then to bed
Sorry, drapes will keep your luminescence dim
Like Lady Wisdom, Lady Moon plays to win
She turned away so I saw but half her face
And, as she faded, her knowing crooked grin
I'll be back, she laughed, same time same place
And with me you know well what I will bring:
The first Sunday after the first full moon in spring

If Moon is benign, thunderstorms are not. They remain in their worst manifestations a reminder of my childhood fears, especially when they sweep across Lake Michigan and assault my dune with ferocious fury.

The Storm

I was afraid when I was a little boy
A storm like this might herald the world's demise,
The day of wrath to end all hope and joy
As sun and moon vanish from the skies.
The clouds are dark and mean and low,
The air is heavy, thick with portent and dread,
The angel might any second blow
His trumpet to wake the living and the dead.

The apocalypse is now long delayed
And only in wild metaphor described.
Yet of this autumn storm I'm still afraid

And tremble at the thought of God defied;
For someday soon my fragile life will end
Pie Jesu, domine, dona mihi requiem

A churlish Catholic reviewer, tearing up my *Confessions of a Parish Priest*, was particularly harsh on the poems I included. I was certainly not a great poet. I am no Hopkins or Thompson. If he were more literate, he might have said that I am no Seamus Heaney either. I cheerfully admit that I am none of these three gentlemen. I fail to see why I have to be one of them. Or why I have to be a great poet to attempt to record passing moments of grace or to share these moments with others. We are all poets, we all experience moments of grace, and we all have the capacity to incarnate them in metaphors. The demand that we be a great poet before we try to do so is an absurd constraint of the literary elite. Thus when I stood on the north coast of County Mayo, shivering in a wind coming straight from the North Pole, and thought of the men and women who had lived on this coast five thousand years ago when the average temperature was several degrees warmer than it is today and crops could be raised year-round, I could not help but try to incarnate, to capture, that moment of grace in words:

Mayo 5000—the Céide Fields

The seabirds screech as they did long ago,
Hinting at tragedy, pain, and death,
Over a bog, brown, lifeless, and cold.
Yet my imagination squeezes time
And I quickly slide back to my stone age past:
A wide screen panorama—green tillage
Blooming all year round under a warmer sun,
Rocky tombs and thatched stone huts
Busy workers, measured fields, stone fences—
A stone age people living peacefully
Not unlike the Mayo of only yesterday,
The first Irish, ten thousand of them along this coast,
Singing and dancing and storytelling no doubt
And probably drinking too much if truth be told.

Then came global cooling; rain and bog
Slowly ate away their farms; they vanished
In a proto-famine perhaps, the first of many.
Or maybe they survived, moved down the road,

And lived and loved and begot more children;
Perchance their genes endure in me.
With scientific knowledge of ecology and climate,
Am I not wiser than my stone age cousins?
Can I not smile at their frantic work
And naive, perhaps destructive, farming art?
Or, in evolution's time, were they born but yesterday?
Am I only a stone's throw ahead of them?
Irish, I grieve for your loss, Neolithic cousins,
And praise your diligence and faith!

Perhaps the poem I wrote immediately after our 1992 class reunion captures the wonder of those moments better than the half chapter I have just written about the event:

Golden Reunion

Marked by the ravages of life and age
Dubiously we came to the white stone church,
Mourners perhaps at a requiem Mass—
Fifty years is, after all, too long a time.
Yet baptismal smiles crept across our faces
And then, as if at a wedding, we laughed!
Exuberantly we clung to each moment
And wished the reunion would never end.

What did we celebrate that golden day
Memories recalled from when we were young?
Nastalgia on an autumn afternoon?
Or in a sacrament of friends rediscovered
The faith that we would all be young again?

I like angels. I refuse to believe that creatures like the protagonists of my three angel novels (*Angel Fire, Angel Light*, and *Contract with an Angel*) do not exist somewhere in the universe. It seems to me that Lady Wisdom, exuberant in everything else She does, would have constrained to produce only one rational species in the whole expanding cosmos (to say nothing of all the other cosmoses which may exist). So I think rational beings like ourselves are all around. We are not alone, oh no, not at all alone. Our dignity and worth do not depend on us being absolutely alone and unique. I don't like the inanity of the current angel cults. As Raphaela, the seraph in *Angel Light*, observes, angels have a lot more important things to do with their time than pull humans out of the paths of buses or trucks that they should be watching for themselves. Yet, when her jet-lagged, motion-sick Tobias (Toby) steps in front of a number 12 Dublin bus, she pushes him out of the way.[73]

Anyway I believe in celebrating angels, narrative symbols of God's love for each of us as an individual person:

Michigan Avenue Angels
(On observing crowds of shoppers on the Magnificent Mile and
wondering who protects them from constant collisions)

If there be truly spirits of Love—
And surely there are such wondrous beings—
Guardian angels hovering above
Shadowing us under God's bright wings,
Then there is an angelic traffic jam tonight
As in spirit dance both subtle and wild
In the waning pre-solstice misty light
They whirl to guard each their beloved child.
Or is their dancing (on the head of a pin?)
Led deftly by an agile seraphim?
Floating serenely on the evening breeze,
A gentle umbrella above star-studded trees,
Does Bethlehem's choir on the Magic Mile
Now hum us softly as mother and child?

For the Angels
(to mark their appearances on the covers of Time *and* Newsweek*)*

Once they were white fire exploding in the night
An awesome choir dispatched from heaven's height
Swift messengers of dense impassioned light
Too beautiful for lowly human sight
Now celebs like wretched British royals
Cuddly pets in the newest Gnostic thrall
Domesticated, obedient to our call
Yes, Angels of the Lord, it's been quite a fall!

[73]I am amazed at how many contemporary people, even those who are religious, have not read the book of Tobias and are even prepared to deny that such a book exists. I had thought that when I told them that *Angel Light* (perhaps eventually to be renamed as *Angel Lite*) was based on the book of Tobias they would know what I was talking about. No such luck.

What say you, Michael, Gabriel, and Rafael?
About this newest dizzy human craze
In your fury do you want to end us all?
Or do you smile gently at our foolish ways
And chuckle at our unmitigated gall
As older sisters laugh at childish play.

Robert McGovern, editor at the Ashland Poetry Press at Ashland College, who had read some of my poems, asked me to submit a bundle of them for publication and chose enough to publish an eighty-eight-page booklet called *The Sense of Love.* He says in his introduction that I have the "modern lyrical ability to examine the self for what it is." Well, maybe. I would not have thought of it that way surely. But I like what he said, even if I am a bit skeptical about it.

All I was trying to do was capture moments of grace, moments of love, for myself and family and friends. If other people liked these depictions of grace, well, wonderful. If they didn't, they didn't. Hey, they didn't have to read them. Surely they are under no obligation to like my "Passover" song.

Passover

Water, fire, and pale desert moon,
Cross venerated, feet washed clean,
March Easter come and gone so soon
Quick moving festival of spring
Chocolate eggs and hot cross buns
Time and my life on speedy wing
The steed of night so quickly runs
Yesterday's child in Easter hat
Now proud mother of many sons
Three precious days escape too fast
I hum "Exultet" once again
Will this paschal hymn be my last?
Bunny and lilies, and that's the end
But did not Lent begin last week,
A fresh chance to renew and mend?
Christ is Risen, Alleluia
Russian greeting at Easter time
Risen indeed, Alleluia

All poems are stories, all metaphors imply narrative, no matter how obscure or how difficult. I'm afraid that I could not write narratives or poems that were obscure. Certainly not this one into which narratives are densely packed.

Pictures at an EXHIBITION:

Grand Beach 1991
"Grand Beach is grand again!"
—BISHOP JOHN BLACKWOOD RYAN

An art gallery in summertime
Of deftly painted impressions
Pigment on canvas of sand and water—
The beach delights my devouring eyes

Sweating bodies crowd around the net
Contorted in desperate agony
Against the plunging ball
And the sedentary week before

A little boy in his kind's endless war
Against the patient lake
Skips stones across the waves
Undistracted by the world's ought else

Authoritative matriarch,
His "big" sister bustles to his side
Mummy says it's time to leave
Stalks off offended that he does not hear

Graceful haunches and naked backs
Of two young matrons strolling
In pretense that they are unaware
Of envious and longing eyes

In their fruitful confidence
A contrast to bikinied teens
Uncertain of brand-new bodies
And fresh, fabric-jamming breasts

A symphony of dazzling colors
Sailboard, Hobecat, beach boat

Bob and twist in counterpoint
To the blue rhythms of the lake

While, stately acolytes in procession,
Cruisers and racing yachts,
March by solemnly off shore
In sedate worship of wind and wave

A puppy, by law forbidden,
Chases a stick into the foam
Pumps mightily to swim ashore
And proudly, refuses to give it back

Ski boats and wave runners
Slice dollops of white frosting
And in manic abstract motifs
Spread it on the purple lake

An old couple toddles carefully
Avoiding rocks and torrid sand
Hand in hand, their enduring love
As passionate as mighty Michigan

Seabirds watch with indulgent smiles
It is their gallery after all
When September comes, they know,
The exhibition at last will end

I do not hide my pain at the death of marriages over which I had presided and whose partners I had known for a long time in this lament.

The Death of Love

Can anyone tell me why love should die,
Infected by the fatal disease of fear
Sickened by anger's deadly virus
Or consumed by cancerous hate?

At its obsequies blame and recrimination,
A wake with no forgiveness
And every treasured pain
Thrown in each other's face?

A corpse for which there is no grave
No decent burial of corruption
In consecrated ground which hides
Till Judgment Day what used to be?

So many Nuptial Masses
So many celebrations
So many wedding toasts
So much loving dance

All this love turned sour
All this hope now bitter
All this passion gone cold
All these dreams destroyed

A tunnel which does not end in light
No rebirth of springtime love—
No happy ending that romance demands
No promise of trying once again

If married love is of God's a sacrament
A hint of cosmos animating fire
The promise of these unions was lost
Proto-sacraments gone wrong

A flower withering
A plant shriveled up
A bright morning ruined by rain
Now desert without life, once a fertile plain

The priest who presided at the Eucharist
Feels sad and helpless, responsible
Somehow, but paralyzed and powerless,
Admits easily the tragedy of life

It is sad but so and so and that is that
But did it have to be?
Was there a turning point,
A time the path might have changed?

God knows and Her help was not enough
Like the priest She mourns this ending

Not the timeless love affair She wanted
Not what He planned at the story's start

So God's delicate mother work
To wipe away the tears, bind the wounds,
Ease the pain, end the blight,
Bathe with grace the injured soul

And promise somehow a happy ending
When bitterness has had its final say
And all first loves do not die
At the dawn of the everlasting day

I wonder as I read that story again whether my response is too easy. God, *You* take care of it all because I couldn't.

Yet one must still praise God for all Her goodness. She does lurk everywhere in creation if only we are open enough to find Her and listen.

Psalm

I praise You in the cold half-moon
Stark above the mountain
In the wildflower
Peeking round the rock
In the yellow cactus fruit
And the darting chipmunk
In windless calm at sunrise
And glorious crimson at the end of day
In the royal blue sky above the desert
And in the soothing peace of blessed night
In the child's happy smile,
And the old woman's glowing eyes
I praise everywhere You lurk,
Teasing me with Your love
I praise you in Mozart's melodies
In the matin songs of the bustling birds
In the evensong of hungry coyote
In the rush of river waters against stone and rock
On the telephone, a familiar voice
In the raindrops against my roof
In the surprise of a doorbell chime
In the implacable ticking clock

I praise You in the expressway curve
In the new terminal's sweeping arch
In the monorail's graceful bridges
In the skyline's shimmer
And the L station's walls of glass
In the dome of the old Polish church
In the white lights of the avenue
In the quiet neighborhoods dusted with snow
In the peace of coming home.
I praise You in the ingenuities of my life
The jet's hovering wings
The cheerful electric light
The VGA's rainbow screen
The auto's solid push
The phone's link with distant home
And the medicines which guard my health
I praise you in the smell of creosote after rain
In the aroma of a Sonoran enchilada
The scent of the lake on a hot summer day
Cinnamon buns baking on the stove
Evergreen needles at Christmastime
The rosemary bush at the dawn of spring
Chanel number 5 on an opera night
Hot chocolate frothing in a mug
I praise You in all my loves
Amen

The Sense of Love was not, as far as I know, reviewed in any Catholic journals. However, it did receive some attention from the people who review poetry in the secular press and they seemed to like my poem prayers, which pleased and flattered me.[74]

I confess that my attempts to capture moments of grace are intermittent. I have to be in a certain mood—unhurried, playful, reflective—to attempt poetry. In the last couple of years I have not been in such a mood. Mostly because I was winding up four sociological books, including one called (ironically in the present context) *Religion as Poetry*. I must try to get back in the mood again now that the ordeal is behind me. I already have a third Moon sonnet in my head and must return to her.

[74]All the poems in this chapter were written after publication of *The Sense of Love*.

Prayer journals and poetry prayers—these two perhaps unorthdox prayer forms have made a major contribution to my spiritual life and my maturing (I hope) wisdom during the years since *Confessions*. There is, however, a third kind of prayer I should mention, though I do so cautiously because I have a very hard time thinking of myself as a contemplative. Nonetheless contemplation is the only name I can think of for it.

One afternoon in Tucson, after working all morning on sociology, I curled up in the shade outside, warmed by the desert sun, to begin to read a book. It was a quiet afternoon and the desert can be very quiet when it is of a mind. No sound of cars on nearby Ina Road, no chirping birds, no breeze rustling the palm trees (which have no right to be in Tucson), no phone (O blessed gift!). Peace, temporary but wonderful!

Then my consciousness changed slightly. It was as if the peace has temporarily bemused me. I had eased into a reflective mood of the sort I had known before, though not regularly in my hectic life. Then, suddenly, someone else was there. Or Someone. I don't mean I saw anyone. But I was aware of a reality that was intensely personal and right next to me, all around me, inside me, outside me, everywhere.

The reality was utterly benign. She made me smile, as She always does when She comes. No, that's not the proper word. She's always there. I smile when I permit myself to be aware of Her presence. I use the womanly gender here because the reality is profoundly maternal, amused by me perhaps, but loving me no matter how distracted my attempts to stay in touch with Her might be. Moreover, I realize that She has always been there, that I've encountered Her before, albeit briefly, and that I could have always been in deeper and richer contact with Her. She doesn't seem to mind the many lost opportunities or my failed and distracted attempts to reach Her since that first afternoon, though if I were in Her position I would mind. Even now as I write these words, I am aware of Her presence and find myself smiling, perhaps because She is amused at my clumsy attempts to describe Her.

(Like everyone else I know, She becomes part of a character in one of my novels, this time playing Herself in *Contract with an Angel*. The God I describe in dialogue with Ray Neenan at the end of that story about whether he should return to life from his near-death experience is the Person who visits me when I give Her a chance to.)

There are brief moments in these interludes of prayer in which I experience an almost intolerable sweetness. Sometimes the color white in flowers or clouds or walls seems suddenly unbearable. I do not know what to make of either of these phenomena.

Is this lurking presence the Infinite, the Absolute, the Ground of Being, *Ens a se*, the Totally Other, the initiator of the Big Bang, the Reality of which the whole exploding cosmos is but a pale reflection? If She is, why is She so gentle and why is She bothering with me?

I have tormented myself with the experience as a good, skeptical scientist must. Is it merely an exercise in self-deception, a game played by my brain chemicals? Maybe. I think not, but maybe. After all such analysis I no longer really care. It is goodness and beauty that I encounter, probably Goodness and Beauty and that is enough.

Any God who is not like the Person who comes to me in theses interludes is not God. God, as St. Therese of the Infant Jesus (and the Holy Face!) said, is nothing but mercy and love.

This contemplation of mine is low-level stuff. I will never be a mystic, never reach such terrifying experiences as the Dark Night of the Senses or the Dark Night of the Soul. That doesn't matter. Neither will I ever play basketball like Michael Jordan. There was still a thrill in my free-throw contest with Phil Doran.

Somehow or other, God comes into my life in vivid experiential mode and that is enough, much more than enough. I write about this third kind of prayer only because perhaps I will be able to persuade some of my readers that if we give God an opportunity we can become strongly aware of His presence, the presence of the one who provides the illumination in all the stories I write, indeed in all stories.

Clearly in this chapter I define prayer in a very broad sense of the word. But I think that's how prayer should be understood. If prayer journals written on the computer screen every morning and attempts to incarnate grace experiences in words are for someone a useful form of prayer, well, fine. If there are some who might be encouraged to do their own prayer experiments, well, that's fine too. If there are some or many who dislike or disapprove of such prayer forms, then, that's also fine. They don't have to engage in them. But they should not assume the right to denounce anyone that does. The Spirit, after all, blows whither She will.

But not so much to placate the liturgical fanatics[75] as because it is true, I must report that I also enjoy, benefit from, and love liturgical prayer, especially if the circumstances of the parish liturgy (choirs, readers etc.) make the service tasteful and beautiful. A good liturgy is another example of a Durkheimian "collective experience." A certain effervescence pervades the congregation; priests and people leave the church exhilarated, renewed, refreshed—often despite the efforts of the local liturgist belief

---

[75]One has heard perhaps of the difference between a liturgist and a terrorist? You can negotiate with a terrorist.

that the only good liturgy is a slow, long, and preachy liturgy. A good liturgy is one from which people depart feeling happier than when they entered. The Eucharist is a celebration and both priest and people should feel when it's over that they have indeed left a celebration. Indeed, the celebration must be joyous, which is why I ask the kids to come up to the altar to help me during the Eucharistic prayer. They love it, their parents love it, everyone loves it. So does, I think, God.

Once a man swept out of church and barked at me as he went, "It's supposed to be the holy sacrifice of the Mass, Father. You have turned it into a circus."

Dummy that I am, I asked whether that was a complaint or a compliment. One *celebrates* Mass. Without joy, without smiling faces, there is no celebration. The Eucharist is indeed a sacrifice, but a joyous, celebratory one.

All prayer ought to be a celebration. What other way is there to respond to a love affair than to celebrate?

As I reread some of my story poems, I become conscious that I have failed miserably in many of the crises in my life. By definition a crisis is a stressful situation that you don't expect and are unprepared for. In many of those situations I have behaved badly, particularly by walking away from unpleasant confrontations which I should have faced, by permitting the critics to dominate my perceptions, and by losing my cool at the wrong times.

My worst mistake was not to see the love that existed all around me, especially the love which I cling to for my being itself, the love I celebrate in my story poems. I don't think that I will repeat those mistakes, but I have little confidence that I will not make others, though hopefully not as bad.

IV

Stories

Sometimes I suspect that my obituary in *The New York Times* will read, "Andrew Greeley, Priest, wrote steamy novels." Most readers don't think they're steamy. Quite the contrary, from *The Cardinal Sins* on, mail from readers indicates that they understand that my stories are theological novels, tales of God's unremittingly forgiving love. Each year I bind up these letters, now many on E-mail, and file them, just in case anyone in ecclesiastical power wants to make the case that they cause "confusion." The stories are the major accomplishment of my life as a priest and I'm proud of them and delighted by the fact that so many people read them and understand them.

Stories as Pictures

Stories begin with pictures. You look out your window at night. The full moon illumines the vista. You see something strange. It scares you. The next morning you're still scared. The picture and the experience it represents is something that has been common in humankind since before we were human. All right, as a storyteller I want to recall from your memory an image of fear in the moonlight to captivate you for my story *Irish Eyes*. At this point all I have is a picture and a brief hint of a story.

Consider the situation: Dermot Michael Coyne and his wife Nuala Anne McGrail are at Grand Beach in late October with their family, which includes their six-month-old daughter Nelliecoyne (always called that, with her names combined) and their Good Dog Fiona—an Irish wolfhound. Nelliecoyne, as might be expected of a daughter of Nuala, is a good baby and sleeps all night long. However, one night she wakes up screaming furiously. Her parents can't believe it. However, the wolfhound nudges them out of bed. Nuala sighs that the little brat is probably hungry and goes into the nursery to feed her. The fretful, anxious child is not hungry. Rather she wants to be held in her mother's arms. Thus protected she slowly calms down and to the tune of an Irish language lullaby goes back to sleep.

The next morning her mother tells her father that maybe it was the dark schooner that lay offshore in the moonlight that upset the little girl. What dark schooner? Oh, the big one with five masts, that's a football field long.

There are no schooners that long on the lake anymore, Dermot realizes. They're all on the bottom of the lake. Then he realizes that not only is his wife fey, so too is his infant daughter.

Another Nuala Anne mystery begins (the fifth in a series which includes *Irish Gold, Irish Lace, Irish Whiskey,* and *Irish Mist*).

What will happen in the story? What is the schooner that upsets Nelliecoyne and Nuala Anne sees, even though it was sunk long ago?

Ah that would be telling now, wouldn't it?

The Nuala Anne series labors under certain constraints. In each chronicle the young couple must solve a mystery from the past as well as the present, the former mystery stirred up by herself's psychic propensities.

Moreover, their personal relationship must grow and develop through various crises, this time the unease created by the arrival of their daughter (whose Irish eyes give the book its title). Finally, forgiveness and grace must flow through the story. I am at least as interested as are my readers in what happens to the people involved in the stories.

But they all begin with pictures. They have to. I do not begin my stories without a clearly thought-out theme, much less a moral to drive home. Thus my image of Nelliecoyne wailing fiercely at the great black ghost ship in the moonlight came while I was reading a book about the Great Lakes. I will tell that story without worrying about the illumination in it. That will come.

If I am to judge by the thick volumes containing reader reactions (also available in the archives), my stories have been an enormous success in revealing God's forgiving love to the readers. The letters leave no doubt about that in my mind, whatever some critics might say, that the books in fact are not steamy, not racy, not raunchy. They are not pulp fiction or potboilers. They are stories of grace, patently to my readers if not to others who may not believe in grace and certainly not in grace in popular storytelling.

Having made those statements, I dismiss the critics who have missed the point. As far back as *The Cardinal Sins*, many reviewers, especially if they were priests, missed the point, but I was inundated by letters from readers who got the point. It is from that perspective that I write about how a storyteller works. In its essence a story is an attempt by the storyteller to intrude into your memory with a picture—like the dark schooner in the moonlight off Grand Beach.

Storytelling establishes an intimate relationship between the storyteller and his audience, an intimacy that is a necessary precondition for the storyteller to preach his good news. This intimacy is essential to the storytelling exchange because the storyteller is trying to short-circuit ordinary propositional discourse and make a leap from his imagination to the imagination of the listener/reader, from his memory to their memory, from his life to their lives (or to push the metaphor a bit, to her life), from his story to their stories. The storyteller shares himself with the audience as a necessary attempt to create a bridge between two imaginations and thus to provide illuminating good news.

All storytelling is autobiographical. However, the autobiography is almost always fictionalized to provide the illumination, the epiphany, the author intends. One must change one's own biography somewhat for the sake of the story. Stephen is not Joyce and Joyce is not Stephen, though they have much in common. Joyce is supposed to have remarked that he "gave that young man a hard time." Nor is Marcel Proust or

Proust Marcel, though they shared many experiences. They both lost a lover, but a different kind of lover.

Despite the fact that these quintessential autobiographical novels are fictionalized (Nora Barnacle herself does not appear in *Portrait*, though there is a strong hint of her in the seabird girl, a barnacle goose being a seabird), we learn more about the authors than we could learn from any autobiography and indeed from any biography, no matter how sophisticated. We do not need an academic critic, for example, to tell us that Joyce was never able to leave his religion or his country behind and that Proust had an almost obscene obsession with being accepted in elite Parisian society. Nor do we need a psychoanalyst to provide us with insights into the souls of both authors. They provide richer and deeper insights on every page of their work.

They must, you see, if they are going to tell their story.

But even stories that are not so patently "portraits of the artist" are still essentially autobiographical. Even when I tell you a joke I am telling you something about myself, more perhaps than if I showed you my curriculum vitae.

The storyteller, the seanachie (the professional storyteller), wants to share his life with you, whatever the risk might be, because only by doing so can he intrude into your life and stir up reactions within your memory that will enable you and him to share experiences. One tells stories not to edify or educate, much less indoctrinate, but rather to illuminate (as Jack Shea has observed), to send forth from the story interlude the listener with a heightened sensitivity to the possibilities of life, to give you greater insight into things you dimly thought might be true or hoped to be true. One is able to do this only if one is willing to trust one's own experience of life with the other, to indeed share one's life and one's self with the other. In *Portrait*, Joyce shares his own Genesis experience on the strand with us, allowing us into the very depths of his soul, and thus illumines for us the possibility of such re-creation experiences which renew life and hope. I put it to you that we learn more about the soul of James Joyce from this interlude than we would from Elman's monumental biography or from all the dissertations that have ever been written about him. One could read all the analyses of this interlude and not know Joyce. One reads the passages in *Portrait* or Molly Bloom's "Yes" and one knows Joyce and goes forth from that communion with an illuminating challenge to one's life that neither scholarship nor careful biography could possibly occasion (and which of course they don't try to occasion).

Why does the storyteller want to intrude into your memory to activate images that parallel his own? He does so to engage in ancient human (and arguably prehuman) activity which Mark Turner calls "parable," the "projection" of a story we already know to explain a new story that is emerging or has just emerged. What is the kingdom of heaven like? Well, it is like a farmer who went out to hire laborers for his field. We know what the latter story is because images of it fill our harvesttime memories (if we live in Palestine at the beginning of the Common Era). Jesus "projects" that old story on his new story of God's implacably forgiving love. The storyteller is in a certain sense an evangelist. He invades our memory to tell his story and thus offers the possibility of an illumination which perhaps will add a new dimension of meaning to our lives. Why does your man tell us of his vision of the seabird girl? He wants us to recall our own experiences of seeing a lovely young woman on a beach and the touch of hope which such experiences can bring (where there is fresh beauty there is perhaps life) and send us forth from the land of story with a new or renewed sense of the possibility of meaning in life. The seabird girl story is in that sense a parable.

Was it the intent of your man to share his very being so intimately with us? Of course it was, why else tell us about it? Did he want to provide us with the possibility and the opportunity to transform our lives in a similar fashion? Perhaps not explicitly, but surely all storytelling is evangelical in that the storyteller wants to entertain us, but also to transform us with good news of what might happen in our lives, even if the storyteller is an existentialist for whom the good news is that there is no good news so therefore we are free to be brave.

Is that illumination of good news, that transient epiphany a brief, momentary contact with the "companionable void," the Other? Does God lurk in every story that deals with the "inscrutable person" that a human is? Is every "serious" story at least implicitly theological, even if, unlike mine, it is not explicitly so? Does "illumination" necessarily evoke the Other? Is every "serious" story, a story of God?

How could it be otherwise?

In passing, I must observe that the Irish Church, having obliterated both the pre-Christian wake and the pre-Christian holy wells, now is beginning to understand that there might have been grace in them after all. Thus formal Irish Catholicism catches up with the Celtic maidens who danced around the fairy tree.

If one tells stories one puts the self at risk. When *The Cardinal Sins* appeared, a priest said to me that it was a shame I had to reveal so much of myself in the story. I could have said that there was no danger of his doing the same thing because he was and is an exceptionally private and even hidden person. Or I could have said that if you are not willing to do that, then you shouldn't be writing stories. Finally I could have remarked that if you want to create the possibility of transformation (*metanoia*) for others, you must first of all illuminate them and you cannot do that unless you share yourself with them (in a nonobtrusive way), even in a Sunday homily.

Must the storyteller be satisfied with herself to run the risk of storytelling? Quite the contrary, if one waits till one has made oneself so perfect that everyone will like the person revealed in one's story, then one will never write (or speak) at all. I suspect that those who write but never show their stories to anyone else or those who are paralyzed by the need to present a perfect story are (quite properly one might say) terrified of self-disclosure.

Rather the practicing storyteller is one who is sufficiently confident in her own worth, that she is not afraid of what people will say about her even if she should hear the classic Irish put-downs, "What will people say?" or "Who do you think you are?" This does not mean that the storyteller is immune to what others might say. You like my story, you like me; good for you! You don't like my story, you don't like me; your name goes down in my black book with a line through it! If you don't like me (or don't like what you think I am) and hence don't like my story, then your name goes in a separate black book with a red line through it!

Immunity to critical nastiness[76] is not granted to our species (and possibly not to any species with mind and will). The storyteller cares about what people might think of her as she reveals herself in her story, but not badly enough to shut up and stop telling stories. In the absence of that relatively modest level of maturity and self-possession, one would not become a storyteller.

In my work as a storyteller, none of my novels are autobiographical and all of them are. They are not autobiographical in the sense that Stephen is somewhat like Joyce. I am not Kevin Brennan or Laurence O'Toole McAuliffe or Blackie Ryan in the way Joyce might be said to be Stephen. I admire these admirable men. Sometimes they are my spokesmen. I would not be ashamed to claim them as look-alikes. However, for reasons of my own (the exact nature of which need not detain us)[77] I maintain a respectful distance from them. However, they certainly do reveal me and more adequately than any memoir possibly could. So do all my characters, including (perhaps especially) my women charac-

---

[76]An experiment: code the reviews in, let us say, *The New York Times Book Review* each week as to whether they tell you more about the reviewer than about the book.

[77]Especially since I'm not sure what they are.

ters.[78] How could it be otherwise? They all emerge directly out of my memory and my consciousness and my experience. Of course they reveal me! The storyteller in this respect is something like God—more precisely a metaphor for God: just as God discloses Herself through Her creation, so too the storyteller discloses himself through his creation.[79] If you write stories, you write autobiography, just as God writes autobiography in His creation. As Elie Wiesel once said, God creates because He loves stories. Our lives are the stories God tells. (The last sentence is Jack Shea's comment on Wiesel).

Storytelling, I have implied, is an act of intimacy similar to the relationship between human lovers (as well as a metaphor for our relationship with the divine lover). It is the transient sharing of the self with the hope of capturing transiently the self of the other so that the other might be transformed (and hence be touched momentarily by the Other) or at least more open to transformation. Storytelling is patently not as physically powerful as sex or as emotionally demanding and it need not and cannot be sustained (save perhaps if it wins over the reader sufficiently that she will read more of your books!). Yet finally the storyteller is in the seduction business. He shares his life with others to win them over to share their lives with him, if only for a few moments and perhaps to have a more sustained influence on their lives.

So too, I may add, does the divine storyteller.

Memory is the matrix of storyteller, the wedding bed where storyteller and audience meet for the purpose of possible epiphany. The storyteller reaches into his own memory to find pictures, scenarios, experiences which might somehow parallel pictures that lurk, perhaps unremembered, in the memory of the reader or the listener. The most important and powerful tool of storytelling is the picture. Perhaps indeed it is the only tool.

Stories are fragments because memories are fragmentary. No memory can possibly encompass a whole belief system, but a memory retold can be an occasion for an epiphany, both for the storyteller and his audience. We storytellers paste together fragments into larger fragments to entice you, to seduce you, to intrude in your memory, maybe even to share an epiphany with you.

[78]Perhaps because they disclose the womanly aspect of my personality. Do I, incidentally, fall in love with my women characters as novelist John Fowles admits he does in his story *Mantissa*? Who could not fall in love with someone like Nuala Anne McGrail?

[79]This utterly unexceptional statement once led two writers in the *Commonweal* to claim that I think I am God, a twisted lie that only the *Commonweal* would print. All humans are metaphors for God in their work and in their lives.

Our memory fragments are retained lest we lose our necessarily transient grace experiences. Proust goes back to the memory of lying in bed as a child because that fragmentary image recalls so many other fragmentary memories of his childhood. In my most recent novel about the late 1940s, appropriately called *Younger than Springtime*, the key fragment is my memory of an exuberant softball game (sixteen-inch ball, the only kind) played by the St. Angela Chapter of Catholic War Veterans of America on a summer evening in 1948. That whole dazzling era is recaptured for me in my memory of that game—and hopefully preserved forever.

In the story it is not any particular softball game, but a fragment pasted together from many different fragments and peopled with characters, none of whom may have been in the picture that originally jumped into my mind when I wanted to convey what the world of the returning vets was like when they were still young—as all the world was or seemed to be. When I finish with this composite fragment, I want to activate your memories of softball games in school yards and your memories of returning war veterans. I also want you to understand how this particular time, when most of you were not yet alive, was different from similar times in your memory, though that is a subtle aspect of my picture. Most of all I want to invite you into the "post-war" world and illumine you with both the fragility and durability of youthful hope as my generation experienced it in those astonishing years.[80]

Storytelling is a delicate and ambiguous business precisely because the pictures that lurk in our memories are dense, multilayered, polysemous. My picture is not the same as your picture and can never be. When my memory touches your memory, you may see more (or less) than I see, but you will certainly see differently. Therefore you might find in my stories meanings of which I am not not aware or which I do not intend (at least explicitly).[81] Thus "interpretation" is a tricky business. Pictures, metaphors, symbols, have many implications. Yet there are interpretations which not only go beyond the structure of the symbol but violate it. Does the storyteller have a privileged interpretation? When someone interprets Blackie's Eucharist on the aircraft carrier USS *Langley* in *The Bishop at Sea* as evidence that Blackie does not believe in the Real Presence and neither do I, it is my privilege to reject that interpretation as a violation of the structure of the metaphor and therefore corrupt—and

[80]This is the first time I've made explicit even to myself the goal of *Younger than Springtime*. I surprise myself when I say this is what I'm about in the novel.

[81]How many different and valid meanings can be found in the parables of Jesus, for example?

quite possibly evil. Metaphors can mean many things, but they do not and cannot mean anything the reader wants them to mean.[82]

Similarly, if Flann O'Brien, the Irish novelist, chooses to interpret Joyce's episode on the Strand as pro-Jesuit propaganda, Joyce if he were still alive would have been within his rights as a storyteller to engage in pungent Irish obscenity. (Though he might have laughed too.)

Can your man on the beach communicate effectively with anyone who has never experienced the revitalizing power of watching a young woman walking down a beach? Memory speaks to memory and in the process brings alive again pictures and hopes that lurk at the far edge of consciousness. You let Jimmy Joyce into your memory with that picture and he's got you, he's seduced you for at least a couple of pages. Or you let Proust into your memory with a picture of Gilberté or James T. Farrell with a picture of Lucy Scanlan and your own memories of young love come rushing back with the hint, ever so slight, that perhaps such love, shallow yet intense, need never die, not at least so long as it is remembered. Not as long as it is caught in the safety net of memory.

Here your man (I mean this time your man Proust) had it absolutely right. We tell stories about times lost so that they might not be lost. We say in effect if you can remember your Nora, your Gilberté, your Lucy because I have seduced you with a picture of mine (a certain Rosemarie Helen Clancy in *Younger than Springtime*),[83] maybe that interlude in our lives has not died and—here comes the big leap—*need never die*. And if that be true, if memory conquers time, if memory defeats time, might it also be possible that memory can also defeat death.

That is the ultimate bet of the storyteller: nothing ever remembered in story will die. My life which I share with you in story is, in the words of the *Song of Songs*, as strong as death. Even those storytellers who do not in their heads believe that such survival of memory and memories is possible still wager (along with Blaise Pascal though for somewhat different reasons) that stories, once told, can never die.

The crucial scene in *The Cardinal Sins* is the scene in which Ellen Foley tells Kevin Brennan that she wants to be back inside the Church with all the wondrous images and experiences of Catholics, and that she wants these for herself and her children.

---

[82]Priests will tell you that research assistants do the research for my novels and write large segments of them. They don't cite any proof; it's merely something that they *know* to be true. In fact, while I have no objection to writers using research assistants, I do all the research as well as all the writing in my novels—and in my sociology too.

[83]A composite young woman. She has dark black hair while the woman closest to being my Lucy is blond.

She goes through the usual sins. Kevin is not satisfied. She has not yet told the real sin. She resists and then breaks down.

> *"Only one sin does matter," she said. "All right, Kevin. I'll say it, and you'll have to mop up the tears on this hard floor of yours. I blamed the Church and God for things that were inside me and my family. I focused on all the ugly things and forgot about Father Conroy and Sister Caroline and first Communion and May crownings and high club dances and midnight Mass and all these wonderful things that I loved so much. I gave them all up because I was angry. I blamed the Church for Tim's death. I loved him but I couldn't save him, and I thought the Church should have saved him. Even when I was doing it, I knew I was wrong and that someday I'd be kneeling on a tile floor before you and pleading to be let back in."*
>
> *"And now you have done it," I said, feeling a huge burden lift away and go spiraling off to space.*
>
> *"The damn fool Church," says Ellen Foley Curran Strauss, "we really didn't notice you were gone, because we never let you go."*

I did not plan to write that scene when I began the novel—though I did know where the story was beginning to go. I did not even know that I would write it when I started at my typewriter (before the days of personal computers) that morning. I knew that there would be a reconciliation between Ellen and Kevin and Ellen and the Church. It was only when I actually saw and heard the characters talking to one another that the scene exploded in my head. I knew in the writing of it that it would be very important for the book, indeed an encapsulation of the illumination of the whole book.

In the scene I was not telling people that the Church will take them back (presumably they know that anyway), much less trying to persuade them that they should return. All I was doing—and I think this is everything—was telling a story about a woman who does return, and thus illumining perhaps for others the path home.

John Shea says that my stories exist on three levels—the level of plot, the level of history, and the level of illumination. For those who grasp the illuminating scene, he says, it lights up the rest of the story like a Christmas tree.

This exchange between Kevin and Ellen, without my realizing it when I began to write it, was the star on the top of the Christmas tree. Or the Angel. Or Santa Claus. Or the Madonna and Child. Moreover, the reaction from readers—hundreds writing or phoning that the scene had attracted them back into the Church—persuaded me that I was correct in judging the illumination of the scene as crucial to the book.

Yet in the controversy that the book stirred up, the scene was never mentioned. In all the cries of protest against depicting sinful priests, corruption in the Church, the sexual desires of priests, a priest writing about sex, the similarity with Cardinal Cody (there wasn't any), a priest making money by telling "steamy" stories etc., etc., this scene was never discussed—by either friendly advocates or hostile critics. I don't think that it has ever appeared in any of the venomous articles in Catholic journals in the last decade and a half. Only some of the scholarly critics have discovered it.

I ask myself how could they have missed it? How could anyone read *The Cardinal Sins* and miss that scene? I conclude that one could miss the scene only if one was rushing to judgment and was not ready to explore the story for illumination. Every reader has the right to do that of course. But to do so is to violate the storytelling process.

The issue of the effectiveness of a story cannot be judged either by a book reviewer or by the author. The worth of a story depends on how much wonder and surprise it creates in the audience and how much illumination it offers them while they are inside the story (whether actually reading it or reflecting on it afterward). If I am to judge by my mail, many people do go forth from my stories with some such illumination. This illumination comes hardly at all from what I plan to write. Rather, it comes from the elements of the story as they emerge in the process of writing it and thus from my preconscious, my agent intellect, my poetic imagination (call it what you will).

Another illumination scene, which readers loved but which critics never notice, is the dialogue between Daniel Farrell and his presumed cousin teenaged Noele Farrell. Daniel has returned from twenty years in a Chinese concentration camp. The difficulties of reentry are proving too much for this modern Ulysses. Noele has had enough of his self-pity. "Daniel Xavier," she says, stamping her foot. "Resurrection isn't supposed to be easy!"

My stories are about second chances, about rising from the dead, about at last finding your Holy Grail, about reunion and reconciliation, about coming home. Noele's impatient cry is a warning to one and all that the rebirth of love, the second chance, does not provide any free lunches.

What will be the illuminating scene in *Irish Eyes*? I don't know yet. You can't plan things like that. It will come in due course and it will surprise me. It almost certainly will involve the little girl child Nellie-coyne.

John O'Donohue, an Irish theologian and poet and spiritual writer, expresses this insight when he suggests that since memory is part of soul and since soul (in which, he says in a nice Celtic twist, the body lives) is eternal, the stories we tell ourselves (and everyone finally tells stories) and tell others are eternal.

> *Human memory is . . . refined, sacred, and personal. Memory has its own inner selectivity and depth. Human memory is an inner temple of feeling and sensibility. Within that temple different experiences are grouped according to their particular feeling and shape. . . . Your soul is the place where your memory lives. Since linear time vanishes, everything depends on memory. Our time comes in yesterdays, todays, and tomorrows. Yet there is another place within us that lives in eternal time. That place is called the soul. The soul, therefore, lives mainly in the mode of eternity. This means that as things happen in your yesterdays, todays, and tomorrows and fall away with transience, they fall and are caught and held by the net of the eternal in your soul. There they are gathered, preserved, and minded for you.*

The net of the eternal!

Ah, that's where the stories are to be found, more stories than if we wrote them for a thousand years! Memory, O'Donohue tells us, is a festival. He quotes Czeslaw Milosz about the marvelous festivals of our lives.

> *I would prefer to say I am satiated,*
> *What is given to taste in this life, I have tasted.*
> *But I am like someone in a window who draws aside a curtain*
> *To look at a feast he does not comprehend.*

The storyteller in effect says to his audience, here are the pictures that lurk in my memory, here are my yesterdays, todays, and tomorrows. I have spun them together to amuse you, to entertain you, to seduce you into liking my stories and liking me. If I am fortunate, my stories may touch some of the pictures in your memories. If I am very fortunate, that touch may make a change, however small, in your life. If I am fortunate beyond all reasonable expectation, then the "companionable Other" may intrude along with me into your life. Maybe after the story is over you will remember a little bit of it and a little bit of me and a little bit of the burst of light, however tiny, that exploded inside of you when my memory and your memory touched and you discovered that some of the things you hoped were true—in fact, might be true. Maybe in the story there was the possibility of a very minor epiphany.

Does that sound like a modest ambition? Ah no, it is a monumental, almost a megalomaniac ambition to want to influence the lives of others by sharing fragmentary memories with them. We try to rediscover and re-create the "way" "(*à la côte de chez moi?*) of our past, our epiphanies on the strand, not only to make them real again for ourselves, but by making them real also for others, to bestow on the stories an eternity for those who hear them or read them. The storyteller wants to catch himself and his audience in the net of eternity.

Sociology and Fiction—Two Muses or One?

There are two myths that seem to have affected my writing, not exactly consciously but not exactly unconsciously either—the myth of Ulysses and the myth of the Holy Grail, the latter clearly Celtic and the former transmuted into something at least partially Celtic in this century (oddly enough by a man who didn't come home physically, though he never left home spiritually).

I am surprised when I consider my novels at how many resurrections there are. Lisa Malone revives from a deathlike coma in *Happy Are the Clean of Heart*. Catherine Collins's grave has become a shrine in *Virgin and Martyr* but she returns. Paul Cronin in *Thy Brother's Wife* is reported dead in Korea but comes home when the prisoners of war are finally released, as does Leo Kelly in *Summer at the Lake*. Daniel Xavier Farrell is presumed dead in a Chinese prison camp and disrupts his whole family when he returns in *Lord of the Dance*. Ciara Kelly disappears from the face of the earth in *Rite of Spring*. Mary Anne Haggerty in *Happy Are Those Who Work for Justice* vanishes on prom night in 1946 and is presumed dead. She reappears forty-six years later. Jerry Kennan says a prayer at the grave of Maggie Ward in San Diego and yet that worthy reappears in other books to give almost as much advice as Blackie Ryan.

Moreover other protagonists have gone away return home to wrestle with the demons and the loves they have left behind—Neil Connor in *St. Valentine's Night*, Kieran O'Kerrigan in *Fall from Grace*, Maura Meehan in *Wages of Sin*, Lisa Malone as a young woman, Jim O'Neill in *Death in April*.

Clearly there is a kind of Ulysses theme (whether in the Greek or Hibernian versions) in my stories. Men and women go away, sometimes, it seems, even into the valley of death, and then come back to deal with the problems of winning their Penelope again and routing out those who have taken possession of her. In *Fall from Grace*, the smooth, handsome, ingenious clerical chorus, Father Brendan McNulty (who is half in love, as anyone would be, with the wondrous Kathleen Leary), even announces that he has become Telemachus to Kieran O'Kerrigan's Ulysses.

I did not consciously set out to use the Ulysses myth (though in *Fall from Grace* I was clearly aware that it was operating) any more than I tried to write stories about resurrections and the struggles involved therein. Intellectually I believe that death and rebirth are the paradigm of human life, experiences that happen often to us before the (apparently) final resurrection. But it was not my intent to teach that lesson. All that I wanted to do was to write stories which were hopeful, though not quite happy. Resurrection symbolism arose on its own. Indeed, in the one story in which I explicitly involved your man from Dublin, *Happy Are Peacemakers*, the resurrection/return themes are at most latent.

I am happy that upon reviewing these stories I have discovered that I have kept some kind of gender balance. Women as well as men must rise from the dead. Women as well as men must woo their old loves. Penelope returns to recapture Ulysses from the women who have made his life miserable since she went away, most notably Moire Meehan of *Wages of Sin*.

Unlike the rebirth theme, the other major theme which runs through my stories—the quest motif—was self-conscious at the beginning, though later it sank into my preconscious where it continues to have a lasting effect on my stories. I wrote my first novel, *The Magic Cup*, as a deliberate retelling of the Irish version of the Holy Grail quest in which the hero finds the magic princess and the magic cup (with considerable help from the princess). The Celtic version of the Grail quests, unlike the version served up to us by the French and the British, is life-affirming, flesh-affirming. It would appear that in its original form it was a narrative to accompany a spring fertility ritual. The girl and the grail and the god were all in some intricate fashion identified with one another. Cormac MacArt finds the magic cup and wins the girl (though she might be the one who does the winning) and through the girl (who is not a Christian) discovers what the Christian God is really like.

In most of my novels there is, as a number of the academic critics have observed, a Holy Grail theme. The pilgrim, who is often someone who has returned from the dead or from distant places, is seeking a second chance at an old love which she/he has foolishly lost in the past and through whom perhaps she/he can fill aching emptiness and find a new direction for life. Clearly the symbols of resurrection and second chance, of return and search, of old love lost and found anew, are closely related to one another. In thinking about my novels, I find that Ulysses and the Holy Grail create the matrix out of which most of my stories come (not all of them—some of the Blackie mysteries, *God Game, Angel Fire, Irish Gold,* and *Love Song* have different symbolic orientations). I'm quite sure, however, that my imaginative repertory is less shaped by the two myths than drawn to them. I would probably have written stories about questers who often return if I had *per impossible* never heard of

Homer or your man from Dublin and never read about the Irish version of the Holy Grail story (in a book by the Breton scholar Jean Markale).

Why is the combined myth of quest and return, of return and quest, so much a part of my own preconscious? That is another story and one that I am yet unable (not unwilling) to tell.

Not all my seekers are successful, though most are. Thus Sean Cronin in *Thy Brother's Wife* does not get Nora (and as a compensation for his loss Blackie Ryan is sent by God who is a comedienne). Nor is Mary Elisabeth Quinlan, heroine of *An Occasion of Sin*, able to hold on to Jumping Johnny McGlynn. There are women searchers too. Usually my Woman who is the Holy Grail who is God is also looking for her own Holy Grail, her own lost love, and her own God. It is debatable whether she is the pursued or the pursuer. Or to put the matter more positively, the rhythm of death and rebirth, of lost and found, of pursuit and counterpursuit, moves back and forth between the two genders as it often does in life. Danny Farrell, Lorcan, Neil Connor, and Kieran O'Kerrigan are as much captured by Irene Farrell, Moire Meehan, Megan Keefe, and Irene Farrell (respectively) as they capture these lost loves. The difference between the two genders as they close in on their Holy Grail is that the women know that they are pursuing as much as pursued and the men don't know it. Moreover, while the women seem hesitant to the men for whom they have become a Holy Grail, in fact it is the men who stumble and bumble and vacillate while the women, when they have made up their mind that this guy is truly their Holy Grail and can trust themselves to him (more or less), are direct and decisive in their actions. Thus Kathleen Leary, clad only in her underwear and a robe uncertainly clutched at her waist, rushes from her house and shouts "Kieran!" when, thinking there is no one home, he is about to drive away. In the subsequent love scene poor Kieran thinks he is the aggressor.

And both genders learn that Noele is right: resurrection isn't easy. Once you have found your lost love and taken that love as well as given yourself over to the love you must learn to live with the love on a day-to-day basis—a task which, as Eileen Ryan Kane, perhaps more than the others, comes to understand, is neither easy, nor dull. A saint in the house can try the patience of a saint, no matter how good he might be in bed— or in the other places he corners her.

Some further observations about these loves when they come together in sexual union:

Such unions are the culmination of quest efforts of the people involved, the moment of high passion in which the Holy Grail is claimed. They are special sexual interludes which renew old loves (which is one of the traits for which the evolutionary process selected when it developed human sexuality), but do not eliminate other problems, decisive turning points, but not complete solutions. Noele again:"Resurrection isn't supposed to be easy."

True to the Irish version of the legend, both the man and the woman are seeking the Holy Grail. Both come close to the recovering of the lost love. Then they hesitate because they dread more pain and because they are not sure of their own adequacy as either a man or a woman. Finally sexual desire, designed as it was by the evolutionary process, to bond and to bind, drives them out of the trenches in which they have been hiding and into each other's arms, often against what they might construe both before and after as their better judgment.

The men are patient and tender, healing (though they probably do not realize it) the woman's fear that she will not be good enough. The women, once they are assured of their sexual worth, are as passionate as the men and more confident and direct than the men. They reason more clearly about their relationships and are more realistic about the possibilities in them. Perhaps like Annie Reilly they also have more creative and more erotic fantasies.

These interludes of passion are not ordinary sexual interludes between a man and a woman. Rather they are ecstatic turning points in two lives. The argument that they are not typical of human sexual encounters is not relevant. These are very special lovemaking episodes though not uncommon experiences either. They are neither graphic nor pornographic, save to those who for reasons of their own wish them to be.

The most ecstatic of the sexual rebirths is that between husband and wife—Red and Eileen Kane. For most humans the chance to rise from the dead and to take the second chance, to be both Ulysses and a Searcher, is between married lovers after their marriage has endured for a couple of decades.

Kathleen Leary Donahue, Megan Keefe Lane, Irene Farrell, Maria McLain, Anne O'Brien Reilly, Eileen Ryan Kane, and Moire Meehan Hanlon are all women in their forties and fifties, yet irresistibly appealing to the men who love them, in part because they have kept themselves in good physical condition, but mostly because they are the beloved. As Leo Kelly, half fun and full earnest, tells Jane Devlin Clare in *Summer at the Lake*, a woman does not become really interesting sexually, if she ever does, until she is forty. Whatever may be said about Provost Kelly's reverse ageism, my own research suggests that sexual love can and often does become more passionate as lovers age. One goes forth on a search and returns home to finish the search. The theme of G. K. Chesterton's *Colored Lands* and of Eliot's the end of all our searching is to return home and know it for the first time.

There are other themes I find in reconsidering my novels which are either a surprise or would have been a surprise if some of the scholarly critics had not called them to my attention: sacred time in the Church's liturgical year and sacred place in the parishes and neighborhoods and in the city and the lake (and even in the river). Sacred persons in angels and saints and of course priests.

If you believe the writers in Catholic journals, both on the left and the right, I write about priests who violate their vows. In fact, only one of my priests leaves the priesthood (Hugh Donlon) and three others (Patrick Donahue, Sean Cronin, and John McGlynn) break their celibacy vows, for which they do appropriate penance. Such critics pay no attention to all the good, virtuous, hardworking, and wise priests who inhabit my stories—Kevin Brennan, Dick McNamara, Laurence O'Toole Mc-Auliffe, John Raven, Mugsy Branigan, Brendan McNulty, Packy Kennan and his nephew Jamie Keenan, Sean Cronin in his later days, and especially John Blackwood Ryan.

The issue of the effectiveness of a story cannot be judged either by a book reviewer or by the author. The worth of a story depends on how much wonder and surprise it creates in the audience and how much illumination it offers them while they are inside the story (whether actually reading it or reflecting on it afterward).

All right then, you've described how creativity works, how come your creativity produces so much? How do you do it all?

These questions often become an accusation, as if writing a lot is to some an offense which must be explained. Are you a workaholic, as Gene Kennedy told *Time*? Don't you have a large staff which does much of your work? Do research assistants do the legwork for your stories and even write some of the text? Do they do preliminary data analysis for you? Do you stay awake all night? Don't you have a rigid time budget from which you do not ever depart, no matter what else may happen? Isn't it true that you refuse to revise or rewrite your work?

Many priests will swear that the answers to all those questions have to be yes. In fact, the answer to all the questions is no. I'm not a workaholic. I can easily stop to swim or water ski or go out for supper or read a book or talk to a friend. My "staff" consists of one administrative assistant (Roberta Wilk, who presides over the chaos of my life with grace, elegance, and charms)[84] and one half-time sociological research

[84]In my mail as I write this chapter are nine books which authors or publishers have sent me to read and provide comment on that can be used for publication. Nine. How can anyone do all of that? I'll try to help some of them if I can. Yet I can't help feel that this is exploitation.

assistant. I do all my own research for my stories and write every word myself. My research assistants work with data sets for analysis (transfer files from the main frame, create system files, merge data sets, assign variable and value labels), but if they do any of the analysis, they are always given full credit. I sleep eight hours a night. My life contains too many juggling balls for me to have any kind of a schedule. I revise all my work repeatedly. Almost always I accept editorial recommendations—sometimes, it turns out, mistakenly.

How do you do it all then? Are you some kind of freak or something?

Arguably, as Blackie Ryan would say.

When I work, I work hard. I hoard time, making the most of every opportunity to sit down with my laptop (on which I am writing these lines at the new Denver airport). I'm facile, glib, quick—call it what you want.

And, no, I never have writer's block.

In truth, I have no confident explanation of why I can write so quickly, why I hear the words in my head even before my fingers type them on the screen. In *Confessions* I suggested that the various boundaries of my personality are permeable, which would mean I have more direct and easy access to the creative dimension of the self than many other people. Not only do I know how a story is going to end before I start to write, I also know the words of a sentence even before I type the first word.

This is a great curse, some say, because you never have to take time to think.

I don't believe that.

It is a great blessing because words flow so quickly.

Maybe.

It is a great curse because it makes so many people envious and angry.

Too bad for them.

It's a great gift and you should show your gratitude by using it.

Yeah.

Is it hard to switch from a novel to a newspaper column to a sociological article to a *New York Times* article to a book like this to one of your poems about your friend Moon?

Not at all, for reasons I've explained in the first part of this chapter. In effect they all require the same skill if not the same rhetoric.

Do you ever get tired of writing?

I get tired often. I am especially likely to get tired when I have spent a whole day working in front of a screen. Who doesn't and who wouldn't? But I never get tired of writing. It is too much fun.

Are you ever going to stop writing?

Not as long as God gives me life and health.

So my love affair with the muse, whichever one is stuck with people like me, goes on.

Where do people like Dermot and Nuala, Cindasue McCloud and Peter Murphy, Blackie Ryan and Sean Cronin, come from?

In the film *8½* Federico Fellini shares with us the confusion of a filmmaker who has lost his muse. It's a film about making a film when you have no idea what the film is about.[85] The white-clad muse, portrayed by the wondrous Claudia Cardinale, slips by him occasionally with a magic smile and then vanishes. Once she appears in his bedroom at night, straightens it out, makes modest romantic advances to him, and promises to remain and bring order and love to his life.

Then the phone rings and the muse disappears once again. She comes back at the last moment to lead Anselmi (the filmmaker) and his cast of characters in search of a plot in a madcap parade down the beach, a parade which, astonishingly, crystallizes the disorder in the filmmaker's imagination into a work of art.

During the film the muse occasionally seems to blend with an actress (also played by Ms. Cardinale and called appropriately Claudia) and Anselmi's wife (Anouk Aimee). The muse is somehow related to real-life women, reflects and is reflected by them, and eludes the filmmaker just as they do.

Inspiration, Fellini seems to be saying, is rather like a lover, a notion which he shares with the Greeks; but she is also rather like a wife—a partner who maintains cleanliness and order and serenity in the imagination as well as whispering in moments of ingenious passion the creative themes with which the artist will work.

Such is the nature of the relationship between discursive mind and creative mind, between rationality and imagination, between, if you will, left brain and right brain, between full consciousness and the preconscious daydream world which lurks on the threshold of the unconscious. There are times when the voice we hear in this daydream world are the adoring whispers of a tender lover. There are other times when she is imperious and demanding like a full partner in a complex relationship. And yet other times when she's not there at all.

[85]I began to develop the ideas in this chapter for a centennial convocation at the U. Later I updated them for a talk on the fiftieth anniversary of the National Opinion Research Center and still later presented them as an article in *Society* magazine. This is a fourth and expanded version of how I think the creative imagination works and why sociology and novel writing are not all that different.

Should we, Fellini asks, treat her as a partner or a handmaid, a spouse or a slave?

His answer seems to be both, depending on her mood, a thoroughly Mediterranean answer it might be noted. A Celt, wiser perhaps in the matter than his southern cousins, already knows that the only possible response to a woman, simultaneously lovely and demanding, is to straighten up, get one's act together, act right, and do what one is told.

It is enough to say that anyone who has chased creativity around the park and has been chased by her knows that she is both an erratic if tender lover and a loyal if often absent friend. And can be exorcised, as in *8½* by the ring of the telephone.[86]

The creative dimension of the personality must be treated with respect, a partner in the human enterprise and not a slave to be summoned when we are in need of the slave's services.

Creative artists of every sort report similar experiences: suddenly, almost without warning, they hear and see what must be done, as though a lover is speaking softly to them and telling them what they must do. The Greeks may have been the first one to call this opposite gender inspiration a "muse," but they were by no means the last to have such an experience.[87]

What do I mean by creative imagination? Either you have it, like rhythm, and no definition is necessary, or you don't have it and no definition is possible. Leonard Kubie called it the preconscious; the scholastics called it the agent intellect. Mihaly Csikszentmihalyi called it "flow," Michael Polyani called it "personal knowledge," Bernard Lonergan called it insight, others call it the creative intuition, nondiscursive knowledge, an altered state of consciousness, the process by which you know the answer to a problem even before you have defined the terms of the investigation, the dimension of the self which knows the end of a journey before it even begins, the skill by which researchers pursue the truth long before they get around to describing their theories for the first few paragraphs of a scholarly article.

[86]I jump—it seems like half a foot out of my chair when the phone rings while I'm working on a story. "I know you're writing," the caller often says, "so I won't bother you for more than a minute." There's no way to explain to such a person that the damage has already been done. I have been wrenched away from the story and must wrench my way back in.

[87]I leave it to a woman artist to describe for us who is the other they experience whispering softly to them. Would it be someone of the opposite gender or, as a woman has suggested to me, a woman friend? Who, she noted tartly, would expect inspiration from a male?

It is that experience when something inside the self takes over and tells you, often quite imperiously, what comes next. Did I say something? But those who know the experience realize that I understate what happens. Someone tells us what comes next. If we are forced to imagine what that someone is like, there is no reason to deny the power of Fellini's picture of the white-clad Ms. Cardinale—a gentle and demanding lover, a handmaid and a spouse.

We hear the answers, often with the grateful humility of an amanuensis who knows that he does not deserve credit for what he is writing down.

A software programmer on a roll, a poet racing through a sonnet, a storyteller watching the actions and listening to the words of his characters as they take over the story and write it themselves, a data analyst constructing ingenious models out of the blue (or so it seems), a quarterback observing a pass pattern open up and the other team responding to it, a surgeon reacting with quick and sure instinct in a crisis during a long and complex operation—all of us knows that someone else takes over. Demon, god, muse, call it what we will, we are in the grip of a force which seems outside of our self, at least outside of the normal rational self of everyday life.

Afterward we ask: how could I have possibly written that line, devised that plot, conceived that model, thrown that pass? Let others praise me for it if they will. I know that I don't deserve the credit.

Adversary: You're right! You don't deserve the credit, because I do the work.

In other words, thank you, Ms. Cardinale.

Adversary: I'm flattered that you compare me to her.

There is a dimension of the self, resident perhaps to some extent though not exclusively in the right hemisphere, which seems to continuously scan—like a radar scanner or a computer compiler—the image traces of our memory in a mostly silent lunatic game of bricolage. It playfully juxtaposes and separates, combines and readjusts, changes and undoes, assembles and tears down, and then reconstructs again complex, intricate, brilliant, and absurd imaginative structures—and patiently waits till we fall asleep so that it can really have some fun.

Creativity seems to be nothing more than the accessibility of this scanning, compiling dimension of the self, an ability to slip through the boundaries of discursive reasoning and join the fun and games going on in the preconscious. Crossing such barriers requires patience, respect, craftspersonship, determination—like all love affairs. There are no shortcuts, no wonder drugs, no weekend seminars, which will make us creative. But there are skills and disciplines that facilitate the access to our creative intuition and our ability to express what we find there when we return from the journey.

I often think that the difference between God and us is that in the former rationality and imagination are combined. Creating a whole poem in a marvelous burst of energy in which rationality and creativity combine to produce the total work is rather like creating a cosmos of your own, a godlike experience. Characters in stories are not the result of carefully engineered construction work in which bits and pieces of people we already know are carefully assembled in conformity with a detailed plan. Rather, Venus-like the character bursts forth, a creature of passion with which to contend as well as love. Is that not what God experienced when She made us?

Recognizing the double helix or the weak force or the right model or the fitting equation, do these experiences not make us want to laugh and celebrate because now we understand too how the machine works and in some sense are the creators of it? The way She felt when She jumped over Planck's wall in the first fraction of a second of the Big Bang?

The creative imagination lurks in the preconscious self where we hear its promptings as if from an "other," and indeed a loving other. The dance with the muse is essentially an act of play, a bricolage with materials dredged up from the trash cans of memories. The playful dance in creative social research is not dissimilar from that in which artists of various sorts engage with their respective muses. The dance among the trash cans is driven by the storytelling impulse, an impulse which, I suggest, involves an affective relationship with our data. Social research is indeed driven, not quite by the data, as our colleague Norman Nie has persuasively argued, but rather by narrative. Thus fiction and social research are both off offspring of the narrative impulse by which we humans strive to make sense of the world around us.

The distinction between theory and data with which social scientists are obsessed is a post-hoc reflection and a very inaccurate one on what actually happens in the analytic enterprise. To the extent that the distinction means anything at all, theory and data are merely part of the playful dance which goes on in the creative imagination as we dance with whomever we wish to define as the Claudia Cardinale of social research.[88]

[88]As everyone knows the nine Muses are Calliope (epic poetry), Clio (history), Erato (lyric poetry), Euterpe (music), Melpomene (tragedy), Polyhymnia (religious music), Terpsichore (dance), Thalia (comedy), and Urania (astron-

The creative imagination (the preconscious, the agent intellect if you wish) is a scanner which is constantly reviewing the bits and pieces of image and story which are stored in our memory, arranging, rearranging, accepting, rejecting, juxtaposing, separating, integrating, taking apart these pieces in a bricolage[89] game that ends only when the self ends. Note that to describe the creative imagination I have used a metaphor from electronics (scanner) and told a story, a story which is built into the metaphor that is in fact a narrative symbol.

Where do my stories come from?

Do I sit down and search in my mind for a theme around which to build a story? Hardly. Rather one opens up the conscious self to the ceaseless flow and drift of images and partial stories that are constantly bubbling up in the preconscious. The story which the writer happens to tell is only one of perhaps thousands that are served up to him in the course of a day (and a night). The conscious self becomes passive, listening and watching and perhaps choosing among the rush of constructions in which the scanner is engaging. The work is being done, it seems, by someone else, by a friendly, helpful, and loving other who is offering a seemingly endless supply of possible tales. The conscious self may know that it is only another dimension of the self, an altered state of consciousness perhaps, that is at work, but the experience is of someone else distinct from the conscious self.

Hence the Greek Muse and Fellini's Ms. Cardinale. A writer's block or a filmmaker's block is in fact a breakdown in communication, for whatever reason, between the conscious self and the preconscious self or, if one wishes, an inability to move into the altered state of consciousness in which one has access to the work of the scanner/muse/preconscious self.[90]

How does the muse work (and now I embrace the metaphor and the story embodied in the metaphor)? She is, I submit, an unpredictable, endlessly darting, fast-moving poltergeist, a Tinker Bell–like sprite (think of her as Julia Roberts instead of Claudia Cardinale if you wish) who rambles and roams about and among the luxuriant garden of our memory

---

omy). All the Muses are what the Irish would call seanachies, tellers of tales. In fact, the Muses are not Greek at all, at all, but Irish.

[89]Bricolage is a game that French agricultural workers play, if Levi-Strauss is to be believed, in which they see how many clever constructions they can make out of the bits and pieces of string and rope and wood chips and other odds and ends left around the yard.

[90]Some people, for reasons of nature or nurture or a combination of both, have more ready access to the preconscious self, thin boundaries perhaps (to put the matter differently) between various states of consciousness.

and pokes in the various trash cans in which we have discarded memories, experiences, images, pictures, all the partial and fractured stories of our life story, assembling them, holding them for us to see and hear and then, perhaps, with a clap of her hands or a wave of her magic wand, tossing them aside to find another construction and then another and then yet another.

One uses the metaphor of a love affair to describe a relationship with a muse (with the creative imagination) because it is a process not unlike a love affair in which one is attracted, captured, made prisoner, led on, satisfied, and then challenged again and because while it is an often frustrating and demanding process, it is also a delightful experience.

Does one write stories out of experience or tell stories about people one has known? The answer is both yes and no, yes one writes out of experience, but only as the bits and pieces of experience and experienced people are pasted together on the fly by the dancing Tinker Bell. The story one finally settles down to write is a story that one has frozen in time and space before the creative imagination can toss it aside and frolic on to another construction, another madcap game of bricolage.

Where then does the story come from? The author is forced to say that he doesn't know. It just happened to be there and he is as surprised by it as anyone else. Did he do it? Yes, of course, but his conscious activity was simply grabbing on the run the construction pieced together out of the trash cans of his memory, pieced together, the author supposes, by some dimension of his self, but not one over which he has much if any conscious control.

It is precisely because the muse is a cavorting spirit that her work and the work of dancing with her must be playful. Storytelling, song singing, poetry writing, are necessary playful acts. It does not follow that they are not hard work or that storytellers are dispensed from skill, practice, discipline, concentration, attention. Play is not random behavior, it is not "doing your own thing," it is not "letting it all hang out." It only follows that storytelling must be as light as a Mozart gigue—and as controlled, as sensitive, as responsive, as graceful as the gigue. Or to change the Ometaphor it is as precise and as practiced as a pass pattern executed by, if you wish, Eric Kramer and Curtis Conwayu. Or if you don't wish, by Steve Young and Jerry Rice. Tinker Bell is not a random spirit but an experienced and demanding one.

What she is not is heavy-footed, stodgy, methodical, or dull. Unless an author is willing to play with the materials she tosses from the trash cans, she will quickly outrun him and leave him in the lurch.

When storytelling stops being effective, when it loses the agony and the delight of a love affair, it stops being fun. When storytelling stops being fun, it stops altogether. The word "dance" implies affection, an intimate relationship with the other, a relationship of friendship or even of love, perhaps a form of foreplay which prepares for a total union with the preconscious self that if it is never quite completely consummated, still is overwhelmingly enjoyable in the anticipation. The storyteller is deeply involved with his materials; but, no, that doesn't put it strongly enough. He is possessed by the story and possesses it. He is caught up in a love affair with the story and with the one who seems to be telling the story to him.

Some authors tell me that their work is driven by language and not by story. I don't know quite what to make of this assertion or whether I even believe it. But it does sound like drudgery. They will say that it is what distinguishes literature from popular fiction. Perhaps, but it doesn't sound very playful or affectionate; and as far as literature goes, I very much doubt that, for example, it was the way your man from Dublin worked.

Was there ever a man who played more with his story, who danced more maniacally with his muse—who in whatever form she revealed herself (Gerda Conroy, Gertie MacDowell, the seabird girl, Anna Livia Plurabelle, Mollie Bloom) was always Nora. What else would one expect from the most playful product of a culture which is drenched in playfulness?

The sociological act, the analysis of data, proceeds in roughly the same process. I don't want to say that the playful spirit of the sociologist is exactly the same as Tinker Bell or Claudia Cardinale. And I don't insist that all artistic or scientific effort proceeds in exactly the same romp through the trash cans. There is no point in succumbing to unnecessary reductionism. I'll be content with the more modest assertion that when Leonardo was imagining a statue or a painting the activity was not dissimilar from that in which he engaged when he was designing a submarine or a helicopter. Such narrative symbols as "black hole," "great attractor," and "big bang" have been enormously successful and fruitful in astronomy. Stephen Hawking attributes some of the progress made in analysis of the superdense matter which is called a black hole to the name itself (a metaphor with a story lurking inside it). If Urania can be tolerated by astronomers, I see no reason why whatever sister of hers is assigned to sociology cannot also be recognized and praised.

Do mathematicians have a muse with whom they engage in loving dance? Never having been one I can't say for sure, though I note that when my friend Leo Goodman describes a new model he has spun out of the air, his eyes light up very like a man who is caught in an intricate and pleasurable dance.[91]

At first blush this suggestion will seem offensive to some sociologists. Are we not, after all, serious and responsible men and women? Are we not committed to rolling back the frontiers of science and perhaps saving the human race at that? How dare anyone suggest that we are, in our best moments, engaging in affectionate, playful dance with a muse, an intimate other with whom we are in a relationship not unlike love?

Do we not carefully define a problem, review the research literature which discusses that problem, formulate (null) hypotheses based on that literature, seek data sets which enable us to test the hypotheses, operationalize our hypotheses, run the models, and conclude, with the proper levels of confidence, that the null hypotheses must be rejected or cannot be rejected? What could be more methodical, careful, cautious, and pedestrian?

I respond that we don't do that at all. Or if we do, it is a ritual we go through to propitiate the gods much like the South Sea islanders do before they venture forth on the open sea. The gods in our case are the referees who determine whether our articles are published. Or perhaps devils.

Rather what actually happens is that a question pops up in our head, our creative imagination begins a game of bricolage in our sociological trash cans with bits and pieces of dimly remembered data, hunches, "theories," previous findings, expectations, half-told stories, other people's work, our own back alleys, and blocked paths. A story erupts, we turn to the data as fast as we can, run the required tables, look at the numbers, and begin to find and put together the building blocks of a new story which almost tells itself as we dance with our data and with the muse who tells us what questions to ask of the data so that we may refine and develop the story that is rapidly emerging. We rush as rapidly as time and circumstance permits to keep up with the story so that it does not lose us.

Only when the story has been told do we, perhaps shamefaced, outline the half-remembered literature, the pertinent research traditions, the required obeisance to the fathers (Weber, Durkheim, Marx, etc.) and formalize the hypotheses which we had pursued as implicit and hardly recognized hunches.

The quicker we can play with our data (in some form of interactive model building) the more ingenious becomes our story—that is, the

---

[91]Leo confirmed this in a recent conversation in rain-drenched Berkeley: "It's still fun," he said.

better we are able to keep up with our madcap sociological muse as she runs amok in the various trash cans of data and theory and insight.

In his presidential address to the American Sociological Association, Stan Lieberson, now of Harvard and sometime beloved head of sociology at Arizona, argued (persuasively in my judgment) that theory and data interact. I quite agree, but they interact at the preconscious, creative, muse dancing level—if we let them. Norman Nie in an address to the Interuniversity Consortium for political and sociological research argued that data drives much of our research. Indeed it does, but it is data that strives to form itself into the patterns of the half-formed story which is struggling to be born in our creative imagination.

Sociological analysis is poetry not prose. It only turns prosaic when we write it up.

The half-remembered, imperfectly formed stories in our trash can are, for example, about immigrants choosing to vote Democratic, about affluent people choosing to vote Republican, about democratic conflicts in printer's unions, about overlapping communities of neighborhood and school, about parents passing on the advantages (or disadvantages) of their social status to their children, about immigrants taking on the culture of the host society, about actions shaping beliefs, about beliefs shaping actions, about hardworking Protestants and otherworldly bemused Catholics, about exuberance in collective rituals, about small groups of true believers becoming institutionalized bureaucracies, about rich people exploiting poor people, about poor people rebelling against rich people, about the state oppressing its citizens, about the state imposing social justice on its citizens, about military industrial complexes wanting war and intellectuals wanting peace, about waiting in line for jobs, about concentric circles around the city, about gold coasts juxtaposed with slums. All these stories, I submit, exist in our trash cans of memory, first of all as vivid narrative images before they emerge as prose propositions in our verified or falsified hypotheses.

I have no objection to propositional prose. Quite the contrary, since we are reflective creatures we need such formal statements. I object merely to the notion that propositional assertions, deracinated from their roots in poetry and play, are the only or the best form of knowledge. Our work begins with old, twice-told stories, passes through a process of formalization, and then becomes the raw material for new stories to be stored in the trash cans for the muse on her next romp.

Ken Woodward of *Newsweek* tells me that he is writing a cover article on prayer and asks if I have any data. Do I have data? I work at the National Opinion Research Center, of course I have data! And theories, and expectations, and vaguely remembered findings from previous romps, and hunches, all juxtaposed in the mess of a trash can in the form of half-finished or partially told stories.

Later I formalize what I was doing by saying that the relationship with the Other as expressed in prayer might be expected to be a paradigm for relationships with others, the intimate other who is the spouse, the distant other who is the criminal, and the absent other who is the lost loved one. These are the stories which are struggling to be born as the muse in the creative imagination rummages through the trash cans and plays with data, hunch, instinct, and expectations. In actual experience I come to know the story in the telling, just as I do when I am writing a Blackie Ryan mystery. But the hypotheses, the theories, and the data are scarcely attended-to components of the exercise in bricolage at which I am frantically playing as I dance with the muse. What compels me and impels me, what possesses me and obsesses me, is not the interaction of theory and data but the story I am discovering in the telling, the tale that I am passionately uncovering as my dancing partner maniacally arranges and rearranges the bits and pieces of memory with which she is playing.

This is not, of course, the way I will write up my report. I will follow the conventions lest referees accuse me of being "flip" or even, heaven save us, "Irish." There is nothing wrong with the convention, I suppose, so long as we don't deceive ourselves—or, more importantly, our students—into thinking that the way we write about what we do is the way we actually do it.

Graduate education often seems to be designed to destroy what little creative playfulness our students have when they emerge from undergraduate education—not much if they have attended an elite undergraduate institution. Often we seen to turn out young men and women with a repertory of mathematical models who then search for realities that might fit their models. In our legitimate concerns that they learn all the skills of the trade, we seem to forget that the skills of the craft are not much good unless the sociological imagination (what Peter Ors used to call "the green thumb") is freed up by the skills instead of being entombed in them. The skills, as Mike Hout once observed to me, are only tools in the toolbox of storytelling.

In a certain sense none of this is new. Michael Polyani long ago suggested that our "personal knowledge" knows "tacitly" the outcome of our investigation before it begins. If this romp of mine adds anything new it is the suggestion that "personal knowledge" is emergent, it is a narrative image striving to emerge out of the preconscious (the creative imagination), as a story to be told in the actual telling of it.

Here I think is where the distinction between theory and data falls apart—and where the beloved Lieberson is correct that they must interact with one another. The muse does not know from theory or data. She knows only images, pictures, partial stories bouncing back and forth against one another as she rattles the trash can. If you tell her that some images are mathematical models, some are theoretical paradigms, and some are statistical tabulations, she is likely to stamp her foot impatiently and insist that *all* of them are stories.

Both the Blackie Ryan mystery and the paper about prayer are exercises in the narrative art, perhaps not of quite the same aspect of the narrative art (and thus avoiding reductionism) but not all that dissimilar either. I make that assertion because all knowledge is story and all intelligence is storytelling intelligence.

The muse may occasionally deign to use general world memory as a source of minor parts of the bricolage construction in which she is engaged. But she sniffs impatiently at that kind of memory. Her game depends on rummaging in the trash can to find story-based memories from which she weaves her tapestries. The dimension of the self which plays games with stories is, for the most part anyway, the dancing muse, Claudia Cardinale leading the parade down the beach, Julia Roberts calling us back to Never-Never land.

Somehow or other this romp, dense with story and metaphor, through the subterranean realms of creativity will seem offensive to many somber and serious social scientists. It will never appear, you may be sure, in the *ASR* or the *AJS* or *Footnotes*, the newsletter of the ASA. Storytelling is stone age stuff, a manifestation of the primitive mind, an activity of archaic culture, a folkway, behavior appropriate for *gemeinschaft* society, for a given instead of a socially constructed world, not the kind of thing in which rational choice operates. Have we not left storytelling behind? Is it not prescientific or pseudoscientific? Are not stories imprecise, obscure, even perhaps superstitious? Am I not calling on sociologists to be poets?

In answer to the last question, yes.

It follows then that the distinction between art and science, however useful it may be, is ultimately invalid. Science is certainly artistic in its procedures. Now we admit we seek elegance, beauty, symmetry. Perhaps only the social scientists, still pathetically eager for acceptance in the world of "hard" science, are reluctant to admit the artistic aspects of their craft. But even we, as we become addicted to model fitting, are charmed by the elegance of the real and are willing to readmit creativity into our lexicon.

Whether art is also science might be another matter, one perhaps to be hotly disputed by the humanists among us—many of whom are simultaneously envious and contemptuous of the respectability of the world of "hard" science as they see it—the kind of humanists who see the typewriter as the last bastion of defense against the mechanization of the word processor (though they are not willing, as logic demands, to retreat to the quill—or the chisel).

Perhaps it is enough to say that both are committed to the pursuit of truth with no holds barred and the expression of that truth, once discovered, in the most charming and attractive models. We seek the charms of the real in order to charm others with what we have discovered. The tools may be different, but the core of the method of both discovery and method are the same.

(I should add here by way of assertion to be debated on another occasion that I think the personal computer may be the greatest blessing for human creativity since the alphabet.)

Peace will no more be declared in this battlefield than it will be in the conflict between science and religion or in the lanes and fields of Ulster. Perhaps in the next century, however, some of us will come to realize that we have a common interest in and dependency on the creative imagination which necessitates at least an armed truce. In the absence of the muse, you see, science becomes pedestrian and art becomes dull. Both artist and scientist need her—and, one adds, both had better accept her as a full partner to discursive reason. For it is in the combination of the rationality and imagination, in the fertile and passionate union of the two, that the work—whatever the work might be, Rasch model in sociology, unified field theory in physics, sonnet, story, painting of a beach in summertime—is born.

Hopefully, I have made it clear that I am not advocating the abandonment of reason, of rational and discursive knowledge. I am not supporting the surrender of intellect to the wilder and more demonic dimensions of the self. The image of the muse as lover should make it clear that the appropriate goal is union, not disjunction, comprehension not isolation, both and not either/or. Because "creativity" has often been a password for those wishing to depart on a far-out trip to the Never-Never Lands of substance-induced dreaming or mystical voyages to what the Celts called the multicolored lands, it does not follow that we should consign the muse to the bleary-eyed concern of the psychedelic pilgrim. She is too wonderful, too lovely, and too important to be left in their dubious care.

The creativity in each of us—radar scanner, compiler, manic bricolage game—is in the final analysis Herself (to use a Celtic expression), a beauty ever ancient, ever new, charming, attracting, drawing us on, seducing us along the beach of life with a promise of yet more beauty to be found farther down the beach.

And whether you spell her name with a capital "H" or a small "h" doesn't matter, not so long as you know that once she's captivated you, she'll never let you go.

Adversary: Would you ever believe that I'm the one that does the work!

Characters—Blackie and Nuala Anne

Who's Blackie and where did he come from?

As he would say: Arguably you should consider *Who's Who*:

Ryan, John Blackwood. Bishop; philosopher; born Evergreen Park Il., September 17, 1945; s.R.Ad. Edward Patrick Ryan, USNR(ret.) and Kate Collins; A.B., St. Mary of the Lake Seminary, 1966; S.T.L., St. Mary of the Lake Seminary, 1970; Ph.D., Seabury Western Theological Seminary, 1980. Ordained Priest, Roman Catholic Church, 1970; Ass't Pastor, St. Fintan's Church, Chicago, 1970–1978; Instructor, classics Quigley Seminary 1970–1978; Rector, Holy Name Cathedral 1978–   ; created Domestic Prelate (Monsignor) 1983; ordained Bishop 1990; Author: Salvation in Process: Catholicism and the Philosophy of Alfred North Whitehead, 1980; Truth in William James: An Irishman's Best Guess, 1985; Transcendental Empiricist: The Achievement of David Tracy, 1989. Mem. Am. Philos. Asc., Soc. Sci. Stud. Rel., Chicago Yacht Club, Nat. Conf. Cath. Bshps. Address: Holy Name Cathedral Rectory, 732 North Wabash, Chicago Il. 60611.

And now a self-description:

"Call me Blackie . . .

"In fact that sentence is misleading. It conjures up Melville and the Black Prince and Chester Morris playing Boston Blackie on late night (very late) cable films and the Black Knight and the Black Horde. Or perhaps Black Bart or maybe even the Black Death. Or perhaps Chicago's historic Black Horse Troop.

"Actually I am the most innocuous and least romantic of men. You could enter an elevator I was riding and not even notice I was there. Indeed, often I am the little man who wasn't there. Occasionally even I manage to be not there again today. My siblings' offspring claim that I deliberately cultivate the appearance of G. K. Chesterton's Father Brown. One of their parents, my sister Mary Kate, the

*distinguished psychoanalyst of whom you've doubtless heard, comes
closer to the truth when she says, 'The Punk [a normally affectionate
diminutive to which she is addicted] was born with the personal and
cultivated the personality to fit.' "*

How did Bishop John Blackwood Ryan (aka Father Blackie) come
to be? My explanation will illustrate my theory that characters are not
made but discovered. The books which tell us how to write fiction (and
they are not all useless by any means) have chapters on character construction which provide detailed instructions on how to create our characters. I do not want to fault these books because at a minimum they
provide a checklist of things we should keep in mind when we look
over our manuscripts to see if our characters will appear to the reader as
they appear to us.

Moreover I do not claim that my way of "character creation" is the
only way or the best way. It is merely the way "character creation"
happens to me.

I did not so much make Blackie as discover him. I learn more about
him (that he has a brother, Packie, and three sisters, Mary Kathleen,
Mary Eileen, and Mary Anne, known as Mary Kate, Eileen, and Nancy)
not by making up things about him and his family, behavior they would
all find offensive, but by getting to know him better.

I have only recently discovered, for example, that his brother Patrick
(Packie) has become Rich Daley's corporation counsel (with apologies
to Kelly Welch and his successors as the corporation counsel in God's
world as opposed to my world). I am not engaging in exaggeration when
I say I discovered this fact (just as I discovered a number of years ago
that his sister Eileen Ryan Kane had become a federal judge, a role in
which she has subsequently appeared in a couple of stories). I didn't make
it up, I didn't decide that we needed to know more about Packie. I
merely stumbled over the fact of his new job (his wife's name is Tracy,
but I haven't met her yet).

Now since Blackie and his family exist only in the world of my imagination, it does not seem accurate to say that I didn't make up the details
about his family. If I didn't make them up who did?

Obviously a part of me did create them, but that part is something
quite different from my conscious self, from my ordinary consciousness,
from the reality principle which reads the books about character creation
and presides over the writing of this essay. My preconscious, my creative
imagination, my agent intellect (as Aquinas calls it), has created the Ryan
family and continues to create them. Periodically it informs my ordinary
consciousness—usually when the latter has the time to listen—what's

happening to the Ryan clan. Creation for me seems like discovering rather than constructing. If the storyteller is a metaphor for God—and I believe that to be the case—than it is precisely the preconscious self of the storyteller that is most godlike.

Does God create preconsciously? Does She hardly know what She's doing when She makes us?

I would rather not answer, not even think about that question.

The point is not how God operates but how we operate. I suggest that one way we might operate is to permit our preconscious or our poetic self or our creative intuition or whatever we want to call it to do the creating for us and then to listen to what it has to say and to observe what it shows us.

The preconscious is constantly creating fantasy people, spinning them together from the bits and pieces of memory that are lying about in the disorderly but fertile garden of the imagination. When we need characters for our stories we dip into the preconscious and bring to the surface some of the people who live there. Once we make them conscious they are, as it were, frozen into existence: the preconscious from then on is forbidden to spin them apart just as it has spun them together. Rather now it is deputed to explore them further and to report periodically to the conscious self about them.

I am asked often whether Father Blackie is a conscious imitation of G. K. Chesterton's Father Brown. Obviously, it is said, there are some similarities. Both have colors in their names (dull colors in both instances), both are short and pudgy, both seem innocent and innocuous, both *see* differently from ordinary people. Even Blackie himself, as we have seen, acknowledges the similarity.

However, there are important differences. Father Brown's parish activity and role in the Church are obscure to nonexistent. Nothing is known about his family. He does not seem to have any clout. He is not part of a geographic community. Blackie on the other hand is rector of the cathedral, confidant to the cardinal, a member of a colorful and contentious family, clout-laden in both Church and State, and very much part both of Chicago and Grand Beach, Michigan.

In passing I must deny the charges that Blackie neglects his parish work. He preaches; he hears confessions; he greets congregants in back of church after Mass (in various Chicago sports jackets); he counsels; he keeps records; he officiates at weddings, funerals, and baptisms; he visits hospitals and goes to cemeteries. He hangs around with teenagers and little kids, both groups think he is cute; he tolerates the oddities of his curates. He prays regularly in such an appealing fashion that one suspects that even God may think he is cute.

Thus whatever else may be said about Blackie he is a good and hard-working priest of the sort the Church does not have nearly enough. The charge that he is not, I suspect, is aimed rather at his creator in the mistaken notion that I am Blackie.

Blackie has lived in my imagination for a long time. I brought him to the surface in *Virgin and Martyr* because I needed someone to play chorus and part-time narrator in the love story of Nicholas and Catherine, those two namesakes of the late autumn saints—who, while they probably never existed, are nonetheless the most popular nonbiblical saints in Catholic history.

I did not originally intend that Blackie be a detective in the story or that he and his noisy family would return in subsequent stories. In fact, his mystery-solving role was originally quite minor in that story. However, like many other characters, Blackie, once he was permitted to surface, would not go away. He wrestled a much more important role in the book away from me and began to act like a detective, now not so much companion and confidant of Nick Curran as a Holmes to Nick's Watson or, let us be candid, a Brown to Nick's Flambeau.

Blackie was a shadowy figure lurking in my preconscious long before I began to write stories—though not before I began to imagine writing stories, an imagination I cannot remember not having. In those days, while I knew he had loads of political clout through his father, I thought he lived in a western suburb of Chicago. Only when I got to know him better did I realize that in fact he lived in Beverly, which is at the southwest corner of the city. I was a bit taken aback by this discovery because Blackie seemed to be a little too civilized to be a South Sider. However, I was reassured to understand that he is less a South Sider than any of his siblings, that is to say less noisy and clannish!

Once you let a character out of your deep fantasy and onto a printed page, however, you have only limited control over what happens as you get to know him better.

Note the difference between this approach and the one we are taught by the textbooks. The latter describe the process of imagining in full detail (and on paper) what a character is like before you write about him/her. I argue that you begin to write about a character and get to know her/him in the process of writing.

In favor of the latter approach, I can only say that it is the way we come to know people in God's world. Why should it not be the way we come to know them in the world of our imagination.

I am not making this up to amuse or entertain. This is precisely the way I perceived it happening. Most authors, I think, would report the same thing—a character once created takes on a life of his own which is sometimes at odds with what the author has in mind.

The most notable experience of that phenomenon which I have had involves Blackie, though this time as a victim. In *Rite of Spring*, the protagonist is Blackie's distant cousin Brendan Ryan (one of the "quiet" Ryans from the other side of the neighborhood). I had planned to send Blackie to Ireland with his cousin in search of the illusive (and arguably nonexistent) Ciara Kelly. It seemed to me that a confrontation between Blackie and Old Country would be interesting and illuminating, especially as the little monsignor (this was long before he became a bishop) would be at great pains to assure everyone that he was not an Irish priest but an Irish American priest.

Unfortunately for that plan, a minor character, one Jeanne Ryan, Brendan's daughter, got out of hand. She was originally intended to be a very unpleasant young woman in her late teens, one more of the many crosses poor Brendan had to carry. But she changed, as many young women do at that age, and became a loyal, if pushy, ally of her father. There was no way that she could be kept from going to Ireland with him. Hence Blackie appears only on the last page, in the distance amid the morning winds off Dingle Bay on the strand at Inch.

Jeanne Ryan represents another character, appearing under many different names in my stories, the teenage woman becoming young adult. As inexperienced in life as her male counterpart, she does not attack it with a headlong rush, but considers it with the sensitivity and perceptiveness that frequently characterizes members of the superior gender and faces the rest of her life with wonder and hope and a vision of grace which God grant she may not lose—Noele, the Ilel in *God Game*, Candibeth Cain in *Happy Are the Poor in Spirit*.

Later, Blackie did return to Ireland in *Happy Are the Peacemakers* with a niece and half sister in tow to act his "minders."

However, like all the rest of his family he is not very enthusiastic about any travel longer than the ride from Chicago to Grand Beach, Michigan, so I may not be able to persuade him to return to Ireland again, even if I offer him a ride on the *QE2* as I propose to do.

He is, by the way, one of the Tipperary Ryans, as in the Irish saying, "In the County Tipperary all the Ryans are rogues, but not all the rogues are Ryans." While the County Cook Ryans are all respectable and exemplary members of the professional class (albeit noisy, but they are from the South Side of Chicago are they not?), they are not that far removed from their County Tipperary roots. "Our family past," said Ned Ryan, Blackie's late father, "does not bear too close scrutiny."

The most recent disgrace in the family, one that is enormously embarrassing to the various teenage nieces and nephews of Blackie, is his elevation to the sacred purple. Things were bad enough without them having a bishop in their family. Barf city, I mean really!

How did this come to be, especially since the Holy See has a policy these days of appointing as bishops only men whose IQ and administrative abilities are at least half a standard deviation below the mean? Blackie at the annual meeting of the American hierarchy would create serious problems because it would be obvious that he could both read and write, skills many of his colleagues do not seem to possess.

It happened this way: Sean Cronin wanted Blackie as an auxiliary bishop precisely because he could read and write (not a requirement in the Archdiocese of Chicago in God's world I might add). He knew that if he asked for him, the mafioso who is the papal nuncio would have certainly rejected him because the Vatican does not believe in giving major American archbishops the men they want as auxiliary bishops. So Cardinal Cronin did not put Blackie's name on the list. In fact, he did not put the names of any of his real choices on the list.

So the nuncio said to himself, as the cardinal knew he would, "Aha, Cronin does not ask for the little monsignor from the cathedral. They must have fallen out. So, we will then make the little monsignor a bishop, thus causing trouble for both of them."

Naturally Blackie couldn't turn down the appointment under those circumstances, since it would spoil the joke. His family reluctantly agreed.

I insist again that none of this is a story I made up. It is something that actually happened, if only in my imagination. I listened and watched while it went on and corrected my Blackie story in preparation (*Happy Are the Peacemakers*) to take into account his elevation to sacred purple. Fortunately the Search and Replace utility enabled me to take into account this change with little difficulty.

Character creation is a matter, I submit, for listening and watching rather than for conscious and propositional activity.

Blackie and his family and neighborhoods and friends (including his North Wabash Avenue Irregulars) are a source of endless amusement, entertainment, and enjoyment to me. It is fun to watch them and write about them. When it stops being fun, I'll have to retire the lot of them, but I don't anticipate that happening.

Thus you have yet to encounter his sister Mary Anne, called Nancy, who writes science fiction stories for children and whose husband teaches statistics at the University of Chicago. But the two of them are there, with a house at Grand Beach (not a place where one normally expects to encounter an academic, though it is a place where one can easily

encounter a mayor, especially on Saturday morning in the summertime)
and a fairly strong determination to push their way into one of my stories.
The professor I can resist, but I'm not so sure whether I can hold off
one of the Ryan women.

As I reflect on Blackie and his clan and their antics, I realize that they
are a metaphor for the Church at its best. When the Ryans decide that
you need help, you are helped, effectively and totally, whether you want
to be helped or not. They are not accustomed to losing.

And Blackie represents the priesthood at its best, in all its classic wisdom and concern, its wit and determination, its learning and its openness,
its insight and its kindness. Not all priests are as clever or as gifted, but
if there were more priests as sensitive and as sympathetic as Blackie, the
Church would be in much better shape than it currently is, no matter
how many semiliterates are in leadership positions and how much slime
oozes out of the Papal Nunciature on Massachusetts Avenue in Washington.

Consider Blackie on Michigan Avenue at the beginning of *Wages of
Sin*:

> *My worthy parishioner, the near-sighted little priest thought to him-
> self, is entering 30 North Michigan for one of two reasons—either
> to see a dentist or to see a psychiatrist, those being the only professions
> that occupy the building. Judging by the fact that he seems confused
> rather than frightened, it must be the latter.*
>
> *Unless I am mistaken, my sibling, the exemplary Mary Kathleen,
> has an office in that building. Poor dear man. Surrounded by Ryans
> and all of us rogues of one sort or another.*
>
> *He has been troubled for many months. Nor do I think the cause
> is the departure of his wife from bed and board.*
>
> *The little priest was the Most Reverend John Blackwood Ryan,
> Ph.D, D.D. (honoris causa), titular bishop of Hellipolis in par-
> tibus infidelium, and by the grace of God and the mistaken strategy
> of the Apostolic See, auxiliary bishop of Chicago.*
>
> *There is something in the man's past, he mused, which has
> haunted him for as long as I've known him, some mystery, some
> puzzle that he has never resolved. He must make peace with his past
> and thus with himself.*
>
> *What might there be in the past which required peace and perhaps
> peacemakers, arguably in substantial numbers?*
>
> *A crime, perhaps?*
>
> *Bishop Ryan was in physical appearance so nondescript as to be*

practically unnoticeable. One could ride up an elevator with him and not be aware that he was on the car.

Hence no one on Michigan Avenue noticed that the little priest had come to a complete halt and turned to glance back at the 30 North Michigan building.

And certainly no one would have noticed that his pale blue eyes, blinking rapidly behind thick and rimless glasses, glowed with anticipation.

Then there's Nuala Anne, a young woman whom I slated for a minor role in a single book. She took over the book and created a series for herself. Now she seems to have taken over every story in which she appears and finishes it up for me. Which is very good of her.

Irish Gold was to be a story about the death of the great Irish revolutionary leader Michael Collins. When I was in Christ the King, Jack Casey was one of the most active men in the parish. He left Ireland after the troubles with, it was alleged, a price on his head because he had been on Devalera's side in the Irish civil war. Should he return, the parish legend (which I never heard in any form from Jack) said he would be shot. Could he have been involved in the death of Collins? I had no way of knowing. So I decided to create a fictional character that might have been. I assigned the grandson of this refugee from the troubles to Ireland to try to ascertain whether his beloved grandfather might have been part of the ambush in West Cork where Collins died. Like the characters in Josephine Tey's *The Daughter of Time*, Dermot Michael Coyne would have to solve two mysteries, the death of Collins and attempts to prevent him from finding out more about his "Pa."

Since Dermot was a young man with two heartbreaks to his credit, it was necessary to find an Irish love interest for him, perhaps someone who would heal the pains of his own past. Moreover, one of the best ways to create a mystery inside a mystery is to have someone keep a diary from the past. Sure enough, his remarkable grandmother, one Nell Pa Malone (after whom patently Nelliecoyne is named), kept a diary, but in her native Irish language. Dermot needed a translator. In O'Neill's pub down the street from Trinity College, he found one. Here is how she first emerged from my preconscious:

"The Irish," I insisted to the black-haired young woman whose face might have belonged to a pre-Christian Celtic goddess, "are different. They look like some of the rest of us and they speak a language that's remotely like ours. Many of them even have the same names as we

do. But they're different—almost like aliens from another planet."

I've never met a pre-Christian Celtic goddess but the girl looked like the images I formed in my head when I read the ancient sagas.

"Pissantgobshite," she peered at me over her dark glass of Guinness, mildly offended but intrigued.

Not very goddesslike language, huh?

I had sworn off women, for excellent reasons I thought. But, as my brother George the priest had insisted, the hormones tend to be irresistible.

"Womanly charms," George had observed, "are not of enormous moment compared to intelligence and personality. However, especially for the tumescent young male, they must be reckoned as not completely trivial."

That's the way George talks.

I avoided the distraction of telling my Irish goddess that the words of her scatological response ran together like a phrase in the writings of her man Jimmy Joyce. I was homesick, baffled, and a little frightened. My body ached in a hundred places from the brawl on Baggot Street the day before. I was worried that Pa, my beloved grandfather, might have been a terrorist and a murderer when he was a young man. I wanted some sympathy.

Womanly sympathy.

Young womanly sympathy.

"That's an example of what I mean." I leaned forward so she could hear me over the noise of the student-filled pub—O'Neill's on Suffolk Street across from St. Andrew's Church (C. of I.—which means Anglican) ". . . What did you say your name is?"

"I didn't," she frowned, a warning signal that I had interrupted her pursuit of World Economics and that if I didn't mind me manners she would stalk away from the table.

"Mine's Dermot," I said brightly, "Dermot Coyne, Dermot Michael Coyne—son of the dark stranger as you probably know."

"FockingrichYank."

The child—she was twenty at the most—was strikingly beautiful. At least her cream-white face and breast-length black hair promised great beauty. The rest of her was encased in a gray sweatshirt with "Dublin Millennium" in dark blue letters, jeans, and a dark blue cloth jacket with a hood—not goddess clothes, exactly. Her face, slender and fine-boned, was the sort that stares at you from the covers of women's magazines—except that the cover women don't usually have a haunting hint in their deep blue eyes of bogs and druids and old Irish poetry. The bottom half of her face was a sweeping, elegant curve which almost demanded that male fingers caress it with reassurance and affection. However, the center of the curve was a solid chin which warned trespassing, or potentially trespassing, male fingers that they had better not offend this young woman or they would be in deep trouble.

I'm a romantic, you say?

Why else would I loiter in O'Neill's pub around the corner from Trinity College with nothing to do except look for beautiful faces, the kind whose image will cling to your memory for the rest of your life.

The mists swirling outside the darkened pub, which smelled like Guinness's brewery on a humid day, seemed to have slipped inside and soaked the walls and floors and tables and the coats of the noisy young people with permanent moisture. My friend across the table was an oasis of light and warmth in a desert of wet and gloomy darkness. Blue-eyed, druid maiden light.

All right I'm a terrible romantic. I'm worse than that as you will see when I have finished telling my story. I'm a dumb romantic.

"That established my point," I continued the argument, unable to look away from her suspicious but radiant blue druid eyes. "Do you speak Irish?"

"Better than you speak English," she snapped. "And I'm trying to study," she gestured with a slim elegant hand, "for my focking world economics quiz which is why no one is sitting with me at this table."

"Ah, but someone is, indeed one Dermot Coyne. . . . Now tell me, nameless one," I smiled my most charming dimpled smile, "what obscene and scatological words exist in your language?"

She tilted her head back, and her chin up, ready for a fight. " 'Tis a pure and gentle language."

"Ah, 'tis all of that," I leaned closer so that her inviting lips were only a foot from mine—and felt the pain in my ribs from last night's brawl, "I'm surprised that you didn't say it was a focking pure language."

Did I detect a hint of a smile? What would she look like if she took off her jacket?

Like George would say, a not completely trivial issue.

"Now," I continued reasonably, "let me tell you about an event which I observed when I was doing research on this alien race which claims some relation to my own harmless Irish American people. In pursuit of this project I am attending a cultural exercise in an artistic center with which, O lovely nameless one, I am sure you are familiar—Croke Park."

The ends of her lips turned up a little more. I was a big Yank, probably rich like all Yanks, probably preparing to make a pass like all rich Yank males, but I was also ever so faintly amusing. My heart, which ought to have known better after my earlier failures in love, picked up its beat.

I must add for the record that I was not preparing to make a pass. I had enough troubles in life as it was without becoming involved with a woman. All I wanted at that point was a little maternal sympathy because of my recent and unfortunate encounters with the Special Branch, a euphemism for the local secret police. Nonetheless at twenty-five an unattached male of our species will inevitably evaluate a young woman of the same species as a potential bed partner and perhaps even as a remote possibility for a mate—even if my mother is convinced that I am destined to be a typical Irish bachelor. Such an evaluation will be all the more intense if the young woman across the table from him in a smoke-filled Dublin pub possesses the most beautiful face he has ever seen, a face all the more wonderful because of its total innocence of makeup.

"Maybe you'll find a sweet little girl in Ireland and bring her home," Mom had said brightly during our last phone conversation.

"Like your mother?"

Mom laughed. "Well, she was little anyway."

I was beginning to fall in love, you say? Ah, friend, I begin to fall in love almost every day and, having been badly burned twice, rarely get beyond the beginning. When I begin to fall in love, the issue is infatuation and flirtation, not the kind of love out of which permanent union might be fashioned. I'd known that kind of love too and I didn't want any of it now, thank you very much.

This lass from the bogs was more appealing than most of the women who stir my heart, you say? And I had actually talked to her, which is a rare event when I begin to fall in love?

Too true.

The nameless one had already forced me to reevaluate my contention that all the beautiful female genes had migrated to America.

"You went to the All Ireland match at Croke Park, did you?" She tapped her notebook impatiently with a Bic pen. I didn't have much time to tell my story or her royal majesty would dismiss me to the nether regions of her empire.

Most Irish conversational dialogue, I had discovered, ends in question marks. I tried to adjust to the custom, with only modest success.

I will not try to write English the way the Irish speak it in this story. For that I strongly recommend the books of Roddy Doyle.

Thus when you see the letters "th" you must realize that their language has (sometimes) no sound to correspond to those consonants. Moreover the vowel "u" is often pronounced as though it were "oo," as in "Dooblin." For example, if the Gaelic womanly deity to whom I was talking should say, "The only thing to do is to tell the truth when you're thinking about it," you must imagine her as sounding as if she said, "De only ting to do is tell da troot when you're tinking about it."

"Didn't I now?" I continued my tale of Croke Park. "And didn't Cork beat Mayo? And wasn't I sitting next to a nice old Mayo lady who prayed her rosary beads before the game, uh, match began? And didn't she put away her beads and shout encouragement to the players? I now recite a typical expression which I had the foresight to jot down in my notebook," I removed a spiral pad from my Savile Row jacket pocket, "Jesus, Mary, and Joseph, Slattery, for the love of God will you get the load of shite out of your focking pants and kick the focking ball into the focking net, instead of standing there like a pissant amadon!"

I snapped the notebook shut, my case having been made. The nameless one laughed, a rich, generous, and devastating laugh. She probably had no idea how beautiful she was or that even she was beautiful—an innocent child from the bogs.

Time would prove that the first part of my estimate was accurate enough. The second remains even now problematic.

"At least for an alien race," she conceded, "aren't we colorful now?"

"About that, lovely nameless one, you will get no argument from me."

"A song, Nuala," some large oaf with a thick Cork accent demanded, " 'Tis time for one of your songs!"

"Can't you see I'm studying me World Economics?" my companion protested with notable lack of sincerity.

"You're not studying," a woman shouted, "you're chatting up the fockingrichYank. Sing us a song."

"A song from Nuala," a chorus joined in, emphasizing their demand by pounding their mugs on the shabby and unsteady tables.

"Holy Saint Brigid," Nuala—for that must be her name—sighed loudly.

She winked at me, stood up, doffed her jacket, and stretched for a guitar under our table.

In this exercise her torso came enchantingly close to my face. It exceeded my wildest, or should I say my most obscene, expectations.

A matter of trivial importance for a young male, no doubt, but nonetheless she was so elegantly lovely that a spasm of pleasure and pain raced through my nervous system and caused me to bite my lip.

Yet I almost stopped ogling when she began to sing—in Irish. It was surely a love song and just as surely, being Irish, a sad love song. Nuala's voice was sweet and precise, yet powerful. She filled the pub with her song and reduced the noise of her fellow students to a whisper—though the steady traffic back and forth to bar was not terminated. Just the same they walked softly.

Like I say, I did not suspend my astonishment at her wondrous breasts. Presumably no male in the pub did. The gentle, melancholy song made my astonishment all the more pleasant and poignant and frightening.

She glanced at me a couple of times while she was singing, nervously I thought.

Ah, if I brought this one home to Mother, there would be universal rejoicing in the family.

The rest of the kids in the pub cheered enthusiastically. I was so dazzled that I forgot to applaud. She noted my failure and favored me with a dirty look.

Ah, you don't mess with this one, not at all, at all.

They demanded another song. Feigning reluctance, which was calculated to fool no one, she sang a lullaby which made me want to be a baby again. I noticed that her mug of Guinness, like mine, was nearly empty and tiptoed over to the bar to refill them both. I felt two scorching blue eyes burn holes in my back.

Oh, oh. I think I made a mistake.

I made it back to the table just as the lullaby ended. Her eyes avoided mine. I was afraid she wouldn't come back to our table.

There was no chance of that happening. As Nuala later told poor Dermot, she fell in love with him that night. He would be her "fella," the first man with whom she would sleep. The matter was settled.

The two of them provide a solution for the death of Collins and unmask those who are picking on Dermot. In the process he becomes the Watson and she the Holmes, a development which angers Dermot. She knows too much, sometimes because of her psychic sensitivities and sometimes because she is so smart.

I thought that ending of *Irish Gold* patently (à la Blackie) said that Nuala Anne and Dermot Michael would renew their love affair and in due course marry at Holy Name Cathedral, with Sean Cronin presiding from the throne, the Eucharistic celebrant being Dermot's brother George, and the homilist, the insignificant little bishop who is the cathedral rector.

That was so obvious that I thought I had seen the last of Nuala Anne. But it wasn't obvious to many readers. And, even if it were, there was no way readers, editors, and publishers would permit me to forget about Nuala Anne. So she came back in *Irish Lace*. She meets the little bishop at Grand Beach. They treat each other with infinite respect, as befits professional colleagues. She comes to his Mass in white tennis shorts and a red T-shirt which announces GALWAY HOOKER. Ever-faithful Dermot records the scene:

Nuala was flaunting it at the Grand Beach pious who had come to the Mass that the little bishop (for whom George works at the cathedral) says on the dune in front of his sister's house. There were a few raised eyebrows, to put it mildly. I had introduced her to the bishop, anyway. She had lost her nerve at the last minute and decided she didn't want to meet the bishop after all. I didn't let her escape from her folly.

"Did you crew on one of those craft, Nuala Anne?" he had asked her.

To be fair to her, there were some lines on the shirt which could have hinted at a sail.

"I did, Milord," she had said shyly. "Last summer."

"And you won the race?"

"We did, Milord," she had said more confidently, "though, as the Duke of Wellington said, it was a near thing."

"And the name comes from the Dutch word hookuh *which means fishing boat or something of the sort?"*

"So they say, Milord."

The bishop and Nuala had decided that they liked one another.

"Those that don't know the meaning would find perhaps some grounds for consternation in the word."

"They might, Milord," she was now grinning broadly. "As my mother would say, however, to the pure all things are pure. Besides, isn't there a drawing of a boat on the shirt?"

"People might not notice that," I had said.

I did not add that they might notice the shape of the person beneath the shirt.

At the presentation of the gifts, the bishop asked herself and me to bring up the water and wine and bread. Herself beamed proudly.

Everyone seems to love this fragile child from the Irish-speaking area of Connemara. They want to learn more about her. Since I'm in love with her too, I too wanted to know her better as she pursues her careers in accounting and acting and singing—and pursues Dermot Michael.

She is certainly the most popular of my characters with my readers. And, I guess, besides her colleague Bishop Blackie, mine too. I didn't know what I was getting into when I created her in O'Neill's pub. Now she often takes over a story and finishes it for me. I have learned from writing her series that I can weave plots and subplots into complex narrative fabrics. One of the disadvantages of that skill is that toward the end of the story I have to pull together the various threads and make sense of the whole fabric. In the process of telling the story I get nervous about the ending—not what the ending will be but how I will get there. If Nuala Anne is in the story, she often takes over for me at the end and resourcefully finishes the fabric for me. Thus in *Irish Mist* there is a crucial scene toward the end at a parish house out on the Shannon Estuary in the County Limerick. Dermot Michael and Nuala Anne are interviewing the elderly parish priest about events in the town seventy years ago. Nuala takes over the conversation and deftly ties up all the subplots. For which I was very grateful.

Do things really happen that way in storytelling, do characters take over the plot and finish it themselves without telling the author to get out of the way or killing him as did the characters in Flann O'Brien's novel *At Swim Two Birds*? The answer is that the characters have a life of their own even if they emerge fully grown from my preconscious. I do not hallucinate. But I do hear them in my imaginary ears and see them in my imaginary eyes. If you know your characters, they will write the story for you. All you have to do is listen and observe.

Am I in love with Nuala Anne? Who isn't?

Some E-mail writers (a tiny minority) and some reviewers bitterly dislike her, which is their privilege. Nuala Anne is too attractive, too smart, too gifted. Well, she's a special woman, that's for sure. But they do not understand, as does my Tucson friend Jim Harkin, that Nuala is "broken by talent." She is a shy child, the youngest offspring of a delightfully laid-back Irish-speaking couple, with enormous talent and no clear idea what she should do with that talent—often not even sure that it's worth anything. If she had not been fortunate enough to meet Dermot in the pub on that foggy night, she would have wasted that talent. She is still trying to come to terms with the responsibilities that arise from it and to balance them with the other responsibilities which come from being a wife and mother. If a reader can't see that often she tries too hard, then the reader has a closed mind and a resentful heart.

Right now I'm waiting to find out who is or was on that black schooner and how she finesses the family stress that arises after the birth of Nelliecoyne.

And how she and the little bishop will continue to connive.

V
Times and Places

I'm the most local person I know, so solidly rooted in the neighborhoods of Chicago that I feel out of place elsewhere. Yet my pilgrimage on earth has led me to other places, some of which I have also fallen in love with. They are each in their own way part of the warp and woof of my life and I am grateful to Lady Wisdom for all of them.

Cities

"We know," Stan Lieberson said smoothly, "that we are not going to get you away from Chicago for a whole year. So we're willing to settle for a semester."

We were sitting on a patio in front of the student union in the spring of 1977 with Paul Rosenblatt, then the dean of arts and sciences (and the best academic administrator I have ever known), trying to work out the final details of a deal which would bring me to the University of Arizona. We were eating sweet rolls (Danish as my East Coast colleagues would say) and sipping coffee (tea in my case). We were all being very cagey as is proper for this phase of the recruiting process.

"When does the first semester begin?" I asked cautiously.

"Around August twentieth," Paul said softly.

"A sin against nature!" I exploded. "School should never begin till after Labor Day."

No way was I going to give up the last two weeks of August in Grand Beach. For all is faults, the University does not begin class till the first week in October.

"Especially in this climate," Stan agreed. "But you could come in the second semester?"

"I suppose so," I agreed.

And so it was determined. Lifelong Chicagoan that I was, I would spend several months each year away from home—teaching and doing research in the eighth-ranked sociology department in the country.

I did not even consider that spring morning in Tucson that my new job would mean that I would escape Chicago winters. I never minded Chicago winters, because they were *Chicago* winters.

I am an incorrigible local. I read the brief bios of some academics and wince—born in North Dakota, college in Minneapolis, graduate school in California, taught in Georgia and Texas, now on the faculty in Missouri. How can people live that way? I wonder. What happens to the human propensity to sink geographical roots? What happens to the need to have friends and neighbors you've known your whole life?

They can and do live that way and seem none the worse (more or less) for their experience. But I'm not sure that my way is not the better way. Stan Lieberson was right. They were not about to persuade me to give up Chicago completely. Given the chance to add Tucson to my Chicago base, I saw no reason not to take that chance. So I'd have two homes instead of one, so what?

I was ambivalent about it when I came to Tucson in January of 1979 and twenty years later I am still ambivalent, though the meaning of the word has changed. I am reluctant to leave Chicago and I'm also reluctant to leave Tucson when it is time to go home. The last word in the previous sentence is critical. Chicago is and always will be home. But Tucson is a home too and I miss it when I'm not there. Not as much as I miss Chicago, however.

As I strive in this exercise to understand myself I think that this persistent ambivalence is symbolic of my life. My sister Mary Jule once suggested (facetiously, I think and hope) that I was so involved in research on Ireland and went there so often as part of my research and wrote about it so much (in four novels so far), that I really needed a cottage somewhere in the West or an apartment in Dublin.

No way. As the French proverb (around which Eric Rohmer made a wonderful film *Full Moon in Paris*) wisely observes: he who has two wives will lose his soul; he who has two houses will lose his mind. As is I have three[92]—a phenomenon I cope with by simply forgetting Grand Beach when I'm in Tucson and vice versa. However, I am aware of the wisdom of the proverb. I suppose it refers only to a physical house (so the pipes at Grand Beach are leaking again, but it's fourteen hundred miles away so why worry?). The problem becomes more acute when one takes into account the human community of which the house is a setting.

Nonetheless, I've been to Dublin and Galway so often and enjoy my visits so much that Ireland has become a regular part of my life too. Why not add a third locale or a fourth, a third or a fourth community? Haven't I enough relationships in Ireland already that the community in fact exists? What would be wrong with a fourth base, so long as Chicago would be primary?

Absurd? You bet. But if, as my friend Jack Hotchkin suggested to me long ago, it is Catholic to say "both . . . and" instead of "either . . . or" then I have deeply Catholic propensities to say "and . . . and . . . and . . ." These propensities make life very interesting. They also make me inevitably a marginal being, even if I didn't write things that many people like greatly and others hate fiercely. It takes a whole year, I have

[92]A fact which profoundly offends many priests and other envious critics. Do they expect me to live in a tent in Tucson?

learned, to be reasonably faithful to any community in which one finds oneself.

I apparently have this character trait which wants to add rather than give up. I didn't stop being a parish priest when I became a sociologist. I didn't stop doing sociological analysis when I became a novelist. I believe in adding roles instead of subtracting them. But this "belief" is not a matter of thought-out principle. It is rather a natural reaction.

Does that make for more work? Sure it does. Does it make for more stress? I suppose so, but the stress hasn't been intolerable. Yet. Is there an upper limit to how many things you can be?[93] How many bases you can have? How many communities on whose margins you lurk?

I turned down a chance to act in The Mission. Jeremy Irons's part, I think it was. But only because they wanted me to go to the jungles of South America. When I read later about the struggles on location and the sickness that plagued the cast, I realized that I had made a wise choice. Mr. Irons was doubtless better in the role than I would have been. But if they had filmed it in Hollywood, I probably would have said yes.

Long ago I learned that it was useless to fight Lady Wisdom's designs. If it were not for the warm weather in Tucson and the somewhat more relaxed lifestyle, I might well be less healthy (and less relaxed) than I am. On the other hand, movement between two cities and two universities means that I am not fully part of either. So living in two cities increases the marginality which has been a hallmark of my life and which I claim not to like. Maybe I do like it or have come to like it. Yet as someone who grew up in a neighborhood, I miss the sense of being part of a community, either in the university or in the city.

A nasty reviewer writing in the National Catholic Reporter once complained that I ought to learn that Chicago is not the center of the universe. I replied, "But Chicago IS the center of the universe!" At least of my universe and of the universe about which my stories are written. I know the streets and the neighborhoods and the parishes and the people and the traditions and the stories.

What is Chicago for me? It's the thrill of excitement when Sir George used to stride on the symphony stage, the hush of expectation when the curtain is about to rise on opening night at the Lyric opera, the Impressionists at the Art Institute, the Bulls, the pastel skyline against the rising or the setting sun, the lake with its thousand moods from sweet and gentle to outraged fury, the sweeping lines of the Magnificent Mile, the milling crowds on Michigan Avenue at every hour of the day or night, the serried layers of airplane lights at night—like orderly choirs of an-

[93]I have also published books of photography and poetry.

gels—as they prepare to land at O'Hare, the Bears trotting onto Soldier Field, the curves of Lake Shore Drive with the skyline hovering above, the Bulls, kids coming out of school, talking with people in back of the church after Sunday (or Saturday afternoon) Mass, the trees (of which the present mayor is planting many more) turning green lace in our brief springs and then red and gold in our long autumns, the Bulls, the Christmas lights on the downtown streets and at the top of the tall buildings often filtered by gently falling snow, old women in the cathedral, fingering their beads and praying for all that has been lost, the window displays at Marshall Field's (even if the store is owned now by an out-of-town company), midnight Mass and the Mass for kids at 5:30, St. Patrick's Day (though I can do without the disgraceful drunks) with the great parade (led by the mayor and my friend Father Jack Wall) and the river dyed green, the Easter parade at Old St. Patrick's, the great Italian restaurants, the number of which God alone has counted, the Bulls, the smiles a Roman collar always produces, the kids that grin at a priest, the stories that the older politicians can tell, the neighborhoods which in the morning sunlight have as many moods as does the lake, my family and friends, the ethnic churches which, if they could speak, could tell wondrous stories about brave young immigrants who left everything behind to chance a better life in a new world, the Bulls, the sign as one leaves O'Hare welcoming me home and assuring me that Richard M. Daley is still mayor, the surrealism of the Kennedy Expressway at night, the glittering orange lights marking the city streets, the Bulls.

Even Wrigley Field, sad place that it is as the Cubs are in a rebuilding program that has gone on for fifty years.

Grand Beach, with its luminous summers and its bittersweet autumns, is certainly part of Chicago, the place in the world where I most feel at home and where good friends like the Brennans and the Goggins and their children and now their grandchildren help me to stay alive (and fight a losing battle to keep me looking chic).

Many readers have told me that Chicago has become a character in my stories, not merely a setting or an environment or an atmosphere, but almost a living reality which influences my stories. I am not surprised at this reaction because that is the way I feel about the city.

When Erika From was teaching me self-hypnotism, one of the exercises was to imagine that a team of angels took me off to heaven. I found myself dressed in Lincoln green, striding through a forest with a group of men, all of us singing at the top of our voices. If I am singing, I thought, it must be heaven because on earth I can't sing at all.

We came to the edge of the forest and there was stretched out in front of us a great city, the heavenly city—broad boulevards, vast park spaces, tall buildings, splendid homes, vehicles speeding back and forth in the air and on the ground and a broad, placid, and seemingly endless lake whose waters were sliced by rapidly moving boats. I took a closer look at the heavenly city and realized that despite the lack of signs proclaiming the name of the mayor, it was still Chicago, Chicago with all its problems healed, but still Chicago. Not, after all, a bad metaphor for heaven, which will truly be a city that works.

A beautiful city, a city with problems, a city with possibilities, a city with pragmatic and hardworking people, a city that is loved as much by most of its own as it is despised by some of its literary and journalistic elite.

Tucson is the windless quiet of a sunny afternoon; the Catalinas behind my house dusted with snow, their tops hidden by low clouds; wildflowers of every shade and color; the red blossoms of the strange saguaro cactus; a calm and serene night, temperature perfect under a full moon when I come out of El Charo, the best Mexican restaurant in all the world; the (real) coyote howls at night; McKale Center, everyone in red, during a Wildcat basketball game; young people swarming down the U's mall, dressed for summer though it is still February; the choirs at Our Mother of Sorrows Church; the peace which seems to seep into my muscles and bones when I walk out of the airport into the warmth of mid-January; the saucer rim of mountains all around us; the moon above, watching me as I swim at night; Our Lady of Guadeloupe everywhere; bird cries every morning; Gambel quail screeching for each other to report in.

In Chicago I resent, perhaps (but only perhaps) irrationally, the carpetbaggers who come from out of town to run our companies and our media and who settle in the suburbs with total ignorance of, if not contempt for, the city—to say nothing of the media hacks that drift in and out and become instant experts.

This is a provincial, not to say a parochial, attitude. A perspective of an unreconstructed Chicago chauvinist.

I resent especially the Chicago literary and journalistic establishment types and their "second city" mentality, their deep-seated conviction that because Chicago isn't New York or Los Angeles it is inferior to both of them. These folks have never been able to value the city for what it is—one of the most beautiful cities in the world—and can only find fault with it.

Why doesn't Mayor Daley do something about the terrible public schools? (It doesn't matter which Mayor Daley.) Chicago public schools are worse than the public schools in Los Angeles or New York? Gimme a break! All urban public education is a disaster and will be until the top-heavy, lethargic bureaucracies are forced to compete. Besides, after the mayor was able to control the school board, he introduced striking and successful reforms, for which he gets little credit from the media hacks.

Why doesn't he do something about the crime rate? Crime rates are higher in Chicago than in New York or Los Angeles? Again gimme a break!

Why doesn't he do something about the public housing mess? Public housing is not a problem all over the country? At least the mayor has a plan to improve public housing which he'll have to sell to a stingy congress.

Why doesn't he stop all the corruption? There's more corruption in Chicago than in New York? You gotta be kidding!

Why doesn't he end the racial polarization? Come on, we're not trying to put Korean shopkeepers out of business. We're not killing Jewish yeshiva students. We are not letting killers go free because they happen to be of a certain race. We don't have urban riots. We're even able to celebrate the Bulls' championships without anyone being killed. In fact, most blacks and whites live together in relative peace and amity. They may not like one another but there are few racial controversies that are not stirred up by "militants" or "activists" and Chicago's black leadership does not have anyone like the Reverend Al Sharpton.

The (often suburban) elite who make the complaints about the city that I have quoted do not seem to realize that the problems they blame on Mayor Daley (and it doesn't matter which one they're talking about) are typical of all American cities, and city government can do little about them because they are prisoners of hayseed down state or upstate legislators who win votes from their constituents by sticking it to the cities whenever they can—and ignoring the truth that the cities are the economic engines which run the state. Only in America are world-class cities like Chicago at the mercy of such fools. Only in America do world-class cities not control their own destinies. And the suburban critics are not part of the solution, they are part of the problem. Make them leave before sundown and don't let them into the Bulls games.

In Illinois at the present time, the State, led by a governor whose only achievement is kicking Chicago on every possible occasion (and breaking his word to the city whenever he gets a chance), is trying to wrest control of the airports which Chicago has built and maintained from the city. Such a theft would enable them to please suburban voters who object to the noise at O'Hare Airport—though they knew about the noise when they moved in and that the costs of their homes were discounted because of the noise. Choke O'Hare and you choke Chicago. Choke Chicago and you choke the economy of the state.

Yet these same suburban parasites enjoy as a matter of right Chicago sports, Chicago theater, Chicago music, Chicago opera, Chicago restaurants, and the Chicago lakefront. Charge them extra, says I. They fled the city to escape its problems and their personal responsibility for the problems. They vote for legislators who want to destroy Chicago, and yet they presume that they have every right to enjoy Chicago. Blame them, not the mayor.

A goof who writes for *Chicago* magazine explained that the mayor was more of a Republican than a Democrat and much more conservative than his father. The only proof he was able to offer was that the mayor wants to privatize some government services. Then George Will, who is also a goof, even if he is a Cubs fan, came to town and repeated the same nonsense for the national media.

A man who will win by a huge majority in a city where the majority of voters are blacks or Hispanics is a conservative? Once more and with feeling, gimme a break!

I am more tolerant of national media types who distort Chicago than I am of the locals who feed this contempt because of their own embarrassment that they work in Chicago.

You're just a spokesman for the Daleys, some of them reply.

Not so you'd notice it. They don't need spokesmen besides the very shrewd people they hire for the role. I am their neighbor, but that doesn't mean that I'm wrong when I fight the self-hatred of Chicago in our would-be elite. I damned the same thing in the interregnum between the two Daley administrations. My defense of Chicago and of politics Chicago style, however, has caused me trouble I would not have expected.

In my early days at the National Opinion Research Center I wrote a review for the old *Reporter* magazine of Max Ascoli about Studs Terkel's book *Division Street:America*. The review was 99 percent favorable (I had grown up only a block off Division Street but much farther west than Nelson Algren's Division Street with which Studs was in love in those days). I expressed some reservations only about his view of Chicago politics which I thought—along with the University of Chicago political scientists—was maybe the only way to run a city. I received a fierce letter from Studs denouncing me as a tool of the Daley machine.[94] Fair

---

[94]I admit it in whispers and no reader should tell anyone but I voted against the mayor in the 1955 primary. Of course I supported him in the general election because I was a Democrat. But I owed a favor to Mayor Kennelly who had been good to me. You do, as the Mayor (Daley) would have said, what you have to do.

enough, I guess, but years later I would have been happy with such a favorable review.

Not content with that letter, Studs wrote to Pete Rossi, then the director of the National Opinion Research Center, suggesting he fire me on the same grounds. Needless to say, Pete didn't fire me. Studs and I have become friendly since those days, though he won't have me on his radio program, but I learned from that incident that "liberals" come in very different varieties.

Back in the early seventies when I had been recommended by the faculty for an appointment at Northwestern University, the late Phil Hauser from the University of Chicago phoned Ray Mack, the provost at Northwestern, to block the appointment. I was, he told Mack (also a sociologist), the house intellectual of the Daley organization. Why this would have been enough to block the appointment, I don't know, but it did.

In fact, at that time I had not yet met the late mayor (though I had waved at him in a boat at Grand Beach!). Moreover, the Daley organization did not need then and does not need now a house intellectual. And should, heaven forfend, it ever decide it needed one, I would not apply. And I would not serve if elected. Friend, neighbor, and priest are much better roles.

Why Hauser would bother escapes me completely. Pete Rossi, my mentor and very close friend, told me that Phil was mad because I had remained a priest. Before I showed up on the Midway, several priests (not from Chicago) had come to the University, entered the demography program, and eventually left the priesthood. I had taken one look at the demography program, which was building a record for exploiting junior faculty and graduate students and then dumping them,[95] and decided that it was not for me. Instead, I drifted to the National Opinion Research Center and Rossi (who did not get along with Hauser and vice versa). I didn't, as the reader may have noticed, leave the priesthood.

Anyway, the family of the younger Richard Daley and I have been friends and neighbors for a long time, from even before the days when he was state's attorney. I knew him as a teenager who used to hang around the CK high club thirty-five years ago.

In *Confessions* I told the story of how we became close friends. I must tell it again. I was out walking one night at Grand Beach and encountered Rich and Maggie walking down the street. Come back for supper, herself

[95]A record left in the past, thank heaven.

insisted. Why not, says I. My mother always told me never to turn down a free meal. Jane Byrne was mayor of Chicago (so it must have been in the late seventies) and Rich was nothing more than a state senator whose political future was very much in doubt.

The proper thing to do was to invite them back. But I hesitated. I was persona non grata in the Archdiocese and with Cardinal Cody (and I had yet to publish *The Cardinal Sins*). I did not want to be an embarrassment to them. So I wrote a note inviting them to dinner. I added that if, given my position in the Church, they would find it politically embarrassing to be seen going into or coming out of my house, I would understand. Maggie called and said that of course they'd be there.

At the dinner Rich added that as far as they were concerned the only problem would be if they got me into trouble with Jane Byrne.

So we became close friends, though I continue to be hesitant about being a nuisance. Their two older kids, Nora and Patrick, and their cousin Beth and her sisters, Anne, Carolyn, and Katie, became regular water skiing colleagues. Nora and Beth learned to slalom in a week or two and put me to shame as have many previous generations of teens.

Nora, student body president at the University of Chicago Lab School (before she went to St. Ignatius for high school and Fairfield University for college), inherits much of the family political talent, but she wants to be a museum curator.[96] Beth, who has equal political instincts, wants to organize a national, nonpartisan civic league for young people. Hardly generation X. Katie was elected senior class president at St. Ignatius College Prep *unopposed*.

There are two characteristics of Rich Daley that are worth noting.

I have never seen a public figure enter a room where there is a large group of people so inconspicuously. There is no entourage, no fanfare, no early warnings of his advent. He just walks in either by himself or with Maggie and stands at the edge of the crowd carefully sizing it up. On several occasions I have been the only one who noticed his arrival and that only because I have come to be fascinated by how low-key it always is. Sometimes I walk over and shake hands and am so absorbed

---

[96]I stopped by their Grand Beach house on Saturday evening (yielding to an invitation after Mass to come to supper) and discovered Nora curled up with a biography of Jackson Pollack. "School's over," I observed. "Why are you reading that?" "*Because I want to*." Later, on the ski boat, she would favor me with lectures about current exhibits at the Art Institute—whether I needed them or not.

in his dazzling Irish grin. Usually I just watch to see how long it takes for others to see that the "mayor is here."

In part, this remarkable phenomenon is the result of a personality that likes to be low-key. But in part also it is the result of a decision that he and Maggie have made to play the game that way. It is a decision that is simultaneously wise and admirable.

He also never engages in the negative campaigning which has become so common in American political life and which has so disgusted the voters (even though they are influenced by it). As he said after the last primary when asked about the candidate he would face in the general election, "He's a fine man. I respect him. But I don't discuss my opponents. I only discuss my own record." This is smart politics but it is also a manifestation of character. Rich Daley is characterologically incapable of dirty politics.

At Mike Daley's fiftieth birthday party[97] it was required that most of the people present rise and say something about Mike (who is doing a marvelous job raising four young daughters after the tragic death of his wife). The party was becoming a bit raucous because, after all, the Daleys are South Side Irish. When it came my turn I said that people who know that I am friends with the clan often ask me what they're really like. I always answer, I said, by saying that they do great-grandchildren and no higher compliment can I pay.

If I didn't know the Daleys from Grand Beach I would not dream of intruding myself into their world. As is I am often afraid that I might make a nuisance of myself with them—though there is no reason to think they view me as a hanger-on. Quite the contrary, the invitations come from them before they come from me.[98] From them or from anyone else this is the way I want it to be. Thus columnist Steve Neal and I became friends at his invitation. He later told me that certain other people (coyote types) had tried to cultivate him and had implied nasty things about me. I often wonder how many other wells coyote types have tried to poison.

I suppose I should outline my political and social views, if only for the record.

I am a junk-yard dog Democrat, which means that I would vote for the Democratic candidate even if he were a junk-yard dog, and I'm

---

[97]Mike and Bill Daley live in the parish I work at in Chicago.

[98]I am not so shy, however, that I refrain from honking my horn in front of their Grand Beach houses to collect water skiers at a fairly early hour in the morning!

proud of it. I'm not one of your "New Left" Democrats who have turned the party into a permanent minority by their emphasis on quotas and on bias toward certain groups and against certain others. I'm a Franklin Roosevelt, Hubert Humphrey, Richard (J. or M.) Daley Democrat.

I have never voted for a Republican and never will. If the Democratic candidate is someone completely insufferable (like George McGovern) I simply won't vote. You mean you vote for the party, not the man, some people ask in shock. You betcha! The decline of party loyalty and party discipline is one of the major reasons (in addition to television) for the erosion of responsbile government in this country. The two parties stand for very different tendencies. The Republicans tend to be the party of the affluent, the self-righteous, the haters, the racists. The Democrats tend to be the party of the poor, the working people, the minorities, the oppressed. Obviously there are both Republicans and Democrats who depart from the respective tendencies, but the tendency of the party in power does make an enormous difference in the policy of government. Ticket splitters and "independents" think they are smart and sophisticated. In fact, their refusal to take a stand one way or another notably harms the political process in our country.

Besides, as far as I'm concerned, the Democrat is always the better man.

Is it a mortal sin to vote Republican? Probably, but most people who do so are excused because of invincible ignorance.

I particularly despise the New Left's contempt for the Labor Movement, which betrays their elitist upper-middle-class bias. Labor has been responsible for much of the social change which has made this country a better place in the last half century. The New Left doesn't like working people unless they are members of minorities. They are too arrogant and too bigoted to realize that Labor (especially the big industrial unions) has done far more for minorities than all the "affirmative action" programs combined.

I absolutely reject "Liberation Theology" as a foolish attempt to combine Marxism with Catholicism. Surely it is clear by now that Marxism does not help the poor. Surely it is also clear that in South America the people, when given a fair chance to vote, choose social democracy over communism. Moreover, those would-be fashionable priests and nuns who like to flirt with Marxism are totally ignorant of the Catholic social theory which endorses a society in which nothing is done by a bigger or higher organizational level which can be done just as well at a smaller and lower level. Nothing should be any bigger than it has to be, a notion which rejects both communist and capitalist social policies of concentrating power. In recent years the world has not heard a powerful Catholic voice which says no to both communism and capitalism. I believe that anything which can be done at the local level should not be done by the city, anything which can be done by the city should not be done by the state, anything which can be done by the state should not be done by the federal government. This Catholic conviction which the popes have taught for at least a century really does maximize the power of the people. All power, I say, to the people! And I mean the real people, not their self-anointed spokesmen or well-publicized "activists."

While the Archdiocese pretends that I don't exist, much to my surprise, the Jesuits have become good friends. My former grammar school student John Costello, S. J., invited me over to their provincial headquarters in 1992 to meet the new provincial, Brad Shaffer. During dinner, Brad asked, "Andy, what one thing should the Jesuits do for Chicago?"

"That's easy," I replied. "Build a third high school for Hispanics."

Brad put his fork down carefully. "How did you know we're thinking of doing that?"

"I didn't, but I'm delighted!"

On public occasions since then Brad gives me credit for the idea that produced their Christo Rey High School. I don't deserve it. They had thought of it before I suggested it, but I don't argue.

When John Piderit became president of Loyola, he sought me out because, as he said, anyone coming to Chicago should do that. He goes out of his way to praise me at the various public events to which he persuades me to come.

I can't quite figure it out. To paraphrase Virgil, *Timeo Jesuitos, et donna ferentes.* However, there doesn't seem to be strings attached. I welcome their friendship.

In Tucson things are different. When I gave my first public lecture at the U both the bishop and the president of the University (John Shafer at the time) came, a phenomenon which in Chicago would never happen. The last president of the U of A, Manuel Pacheco, and his wife Karen invited me to their house for dinner almost as soon as they arrived (they both had read and liked my novels) and we became close friends (again I am reluctant to intrude too much into their busy schedule). In 1998 the U gave me an honorary degree. The clergy are more friendly in Tucson and so are my faculty colleagues. I am treated like I am more at home in my second home than in my first, which is, I guess, the result of coming from "out of town."

A couple of years ago, mostly by accident, four of my sociology books were published at the same time, the department[99] at U of A had a party to celebrate. I doubt that anyone at Chicago even noticed. But then they wouldn't have noticed anyone else's books either.

One steps into the corridor at U of A and almost always encounters a group of faculty talking—Dave Snow, Kathleen Crowley Swartzman, Doug McAdam, Al Bergesen, Alfonso Morales, Woody Powell, Lynn Smith-Lovett, Paula England, Linda Moln, Mike Sobel, Sarah Soule. The conversations are both informative and seductive. One doesn't want to leave them.

That doesn't happen in Chicago, though the faculty is equally interesting—Andy Abbot, Rafe Stolzenberg, Charles Bidwell, Linda Waite, Terry Clark. But we don't bump into each other in corridors.

I must be careful about comparing two brilliant sociology departments. There is more community at U of A than at the University for everyone. We all have offices on the same floor and bump into each other constantly in the corridors. At the University we are spread out all over campus and see each other rarely. No one is unfriendly but we all go our separate ways. Everyone is like me, I guess.

Yet I have the impression, perhaps inaccurate, that at U of A I am considered an asset to the department and at the University an interesting (and perhaps, but only perhaps, talented), somewhat eccentric marginal figure.

Except at the National Opinion Research Center where our current president, Phil Depoy, treats me with enormous—and unearned— respect. Having spent much of his professional life at the Center for Naval Analysis, he is my house resource for navy lore. He arranged for the "overnight" on a carrier, which led to *The Bishop at Sea*.

I teach at both universities and enjoy the experience and the students immensely. Generally I do a sequence of courses—introductory, a graduate seminar, Sociology of the Religious Imagination, and Sociology and Popular Culture—God in the Movies. When I offer the last two courses at Chicago, David Tracy often joins in, which makes it an even more interesting experience. Judging by the class evaluation reports, the young people like me as a teacher and I certainly like them. I am exhausted after class and worn-out for the rest of the day. But it's like being back in the eighth-grade classroom at CK in 1955.

People say to me, "I suppose your students at Chicago are much better?" Well, the young people at Chicago are certainly among the brightest in the country, but my students at Arizona are articulate and

---

[99]Rated as a "gem" in its last outside review and certainly among the top ten in the country.

intelligent and write coherent papers. Moreover, they are much more lively. The University of Chicago kids, intimidated by their distinguished faculty, begin to argue halfway through the quarter—tentatively and carefully lest they offend me.[100]

If you don't learn from your students there is little reason to teach (other than to earn a living). One only learns from students when they are free to say what they think. My dialogic style probably wouldn't work in accounting or calculus or astronomy. But it works in sociology of religion.

Like I say, it wears you out. But I enjoy every minute.

New audience for jokes every year too.

Another aspect of my double life is that I have three parishes, St. Mary of the Woods and until recently Christ the King in Chicago and Our Mother of Sorrows in Tucson. People are happy when I show up (or so they tell me) but I'm not around any of them enough to become part of the scenery. All are fine, active parishes with hardworking and creative pastoral leadership[101] yet I am nothing more than an occasional visitor to any of them. They are not my parish the way Christ the King was thirty years ago.

This is not the way I would want things to be. It is rather the way things are and must be, given my life in two cities, each of which are home. Yet I wonder if I blame too much on my two cities. Even if I had never come to U of A, I'd still be on the fringes, partly because that's where people put me but also and mostly because the kinds of things I try to do and the multiplicity of those things make me a fringe person.

I'm not complaining, only reflecting. While I did not anticipate my fringe status when I began, it is certainly an inevitable price and I don't mind paying it. Settle down and do one thing well, nasty priests tell me. Why try to do so many things and all of them poorly?

To which I respond that I'd like proof of what I do poorly instead of a priori clerical assertions that I must be doing some of them poorly.

Recently I have been pondering the question of courses not taken. I am really not part of the sociological profession in the sense that most of my colleagues are. I pay my dues in research and publications but I don't know most of my colleagues around the country and in general they

---

[100]My nephew Sean, one of the least intimidating people in the world, said that when he was a teaching assistant at the University, the students were afraid of him!

[101]Leo has developed a parish renewal program which is enormously successful, Tom has twice a year a program for "Alienated Catholics Anonymous" which brings scores of people back into the Church, people who were waiting only for an opportunity and an invitation.

know neither me nor my work. I am not part of the world of religious scholarship and rarely appear at the annual meetings of either the American Academy of Religion or the Society for the Scientific Study of Religion, though for the last five years I have been asked to participate in or organize special sessions at the ASA meeting (I always accept). I am not part of the networks, the grapevines, the social structures of these professions. Though I write columns and even articles for *The New York Times*, I am not really a journalist and not considered to be one by most journalists. I write novels but I am not part of any group of writers and barely think of myself as a writer. I'm a priest, of course, but on the margins of the priesthood and cordially disliked by most of the leaders of the priesthood both in Chicago and in the whole country. Indeed, the images most priests have of me tell more about them than about me.

The review in the last paragraph suggests that there are many paths, some of them very attractive, which I have chosen not to walk down. I ask myself whether my marginality is merely accidental. Do I have no community roots because deep down I don't want any? Am I on the fringes of most communities because that's where I like to be? Am I an outsider because that's what I've chosen to be? Do my two cities prevent me from having a real home in either because that is the way I like to live?

I have plenty of friends, I would have almost said more than enough if such an expression would not have seemed to imply ingratitude. I am not cut off from humankind—of either gender. I like people. They like me. I am not, Lady Wisdom knows, lonely. Indeed, I'd like to be alone a little more, if that were possible.

But I don't really belong to anything. Sometimes, not always, not often, but sometimes, and more than just rarely, that bothers me, perhaps because neighborhoods were so important in my early life and my formative years in the priesthood.

How has all this come to be, I ask myself. One answer is that the Cardinal Cody years in Chicago forced me to the fringes of the Archdiocese from which I could never return unless I was willing to pay a price that I would not pay. Another answer is that in the minds of many people a person who tries to wear all the hats I try to wear (with whatever success or lack thereof) is just a little strange and you do not want to let him get too close. (Maybe he's possessed by a demon!)

The partial move to Tucson, which has meant so much in good health, new friends, new colleagues, a wider perspective on life, has made me more marginal. The major collective ritual at U of A sociology is the weekly brown bag lunch on Friday at noon. Since my class is on Friday and my office hours are just before that, I felt it would be easy to join in at the brown bag. Yet at the present writing, halfway through the semester, I have made only three. At most I will be at one more besides my own before the semester is over. That's somehow not right. And at the University, the most important ritual is the Becker[102] seminar on every other Tuesday evening. Last semester I resolved I would make every one. I made only two (and came at the wrong time for another). Open paths, inviting paths, paths down which I did not walk. Paths that indeed I am sad that I did not walk.

So many abandoned paths, so many missed opportunities. So much sadness.

I didn't realize that when I made the move to Tucson yet more paths would open up and there would be more sadness that for one reason or another (mostly the demands of time) I would have to ignore most of them.

So I try to do too much and too many different things and it is foolish for me to lament that I can't do everything I'd like to do. Who do I think I am? God? Only She can do everything and She is probably not amused at those of us who try to imitate Her.

I've made my choices and I do not regret them. Like all choices in life there were more costs than I had anticipated. I would not trade my two cities for either one separately. I would not trade the freedom of my outsider status for membership in any establishment. I don't regret my decisions. I regret, however, all the paths down which I might have walked, but for perfectly good reasons having to do with what I am and what I want to do, I did not walk. You can't walk north and walk south at the same time, even if two cities can be, each in their own way, home.

It can be both immature and mature to hunger for everything. I think I am somewhere between the two.

---

[102]Nobel prize winner Gary Becker wrote a foreword to my book *Religion as Poetry*. He is one of the most original and insightful thinkers I have ever known. I have heard him spin out brilliant speculations on the spur of the moment. He directed the dissertation of my nephew Sean and smiled benignly when I showed up at the hearing to exercise my faculty right of questioning the candidate. Sean found my presumption that I was capable of asking a question about economics highly amusing.

Countries

That I would fall in love with Ireland and the Irish was to be expected. That I would become fond of Germany, particularly the land along the Rhine, was utterly unexpected.

In 1987 I got the idea of doing an article which would test my theory of the religious imagination and David Tracy's theory of the difference between the Catholic (or "analogical") imagination and the Protestant (or "dialectical") imagination. There were now data from the European values study which might make it possible to do this as an international project.[103] I realized somewhat dimly that Tom Smith, my neighbor across the hall at the National Opinion Research Center, was involved in some kind of international version of the General Social Survey (a project which like the General Social Survey was also a creature of Jim Davis's[104] creative imagination). I wandered over to Tom's office and asked what kind of data he had. It turned out that the International Social Survey Program, begun in 1985, was already a rich resource for my project.

"Ireland isn't in the project?" I said to Tom.

"Not yet."

"Too bad."

I thought about it and before the day was over went back. "If someone wanted to use royalty money to fund Irish participation, I don't imagine there would be any objection would there?"

"I don't see why," he said with his typical elfin grin.

For ages I had wanted to get comparable data about the real Irish and the Irish Americans. This seemed a golden opportunity. I wrote to my

[103]The article subsequently appeared as the lead in the summer 1989 issue of the *American Sociological Review*. I will not burden the reader of this memoir with the details, except to say that Father Tracy's thesis was validated, much to his delight and, I gather, surprised relief. The substance of the article can be found by those who are desperately interested in *Religion as Poetry*.

[104]Jim, who was my dissertation mentor along with Pete Rossi, has since returned to the National Opinion Research Center and is also across the corridor. It is like the old days all over again. And neither of us has aged a bit.

Irish co-conspirator (Father)[105] Conor Ward, a professor at University College Dublin, and proposed that we join forces. After some hesitation the then small (six countries) International Social Survey Program admitted Ireland and myself as a member of the Irish team. It has been a fascinating and illuminating experience—and one more project for me that I really didn't need but which I wouldn't give up for anything.

The miracle about the International Social Survey Program is not that sometimes its surveys are less than perfect but that it exists at all: a consortium of survey centers now from twenty-five countries which tries to put together each year a fifteen-minute questionnaire on some commonly agreed subject and attach it to another survey. To do so the delegates (three permitted, but only two can talk at a given session) must overcome barriers of language, culture, social science background, and interests. Moreover, while some of the discussions can turn acrimonious, most of us have become good friends and are happy to see each other again. International meetings of social scientists are routine. International projects are less routine but do occur. But ongoing projects that try to tackle a different subject each year are rare. Indeed, the International Social Survey Program is the only one of which I know.[106]

We have studied, for example, attitudes toward the role of government, equality, family networks, new family roles, and, in 1991, religion. Since the "social transformations" in Eastern Europe, Poland, Slovenia, the Czech Republic, Bulgaria, Russia, Hungary, and East Germany have joined the International Social Survey Program. The 1991 religion study was the first nationwide study of religion in Russia. My Russian colleagues, of whom I am very fond, permitted me to analyze the state of religion in that newly free country. I discovered that far from being dead in Russia, God was alive and well and living in Moscow as well as everywhere else in that country and that, in the midst of all the other complexities of the "social transformation," Russia was experiencing what might well be the largest religious revival in all human history. Socialism had failed in its battle with religion. St. Vladimir had routed Karl Marx. The revival was especially strong among the young and the better educated. Moreover, as our Russian colleagues would subsequently tell us,

---

[105]Now Monsignor.

[106]We meet each year in a different country—London, Milan, Graz, Dublin, Chicago, Tel Aviv, for example. In Chicago the mayor proclaimed the first day of our meeting the International Social Survey Program Day and the cardinal visited a reception at my apartment and said some nice things about the importance of social research. I guess maybe I do have some clout, though I wouldn't consider either of these the equivalent of picking up markets.

the newly religious people are most unlikely to vote for the old anti-Semitic, pan Slavic, nationalist candidates in Russian elections.

The findings were at first greeted with skepticism and disbelief. Obviously you couldn't trust the findings of a priest on this subject. But, as is often the case in social research, the findings made a quick trip from what couldn't possibly be true to what everyone had known all along.

I also wrote a report, *Religion Around the World*, which cast serious doubt on the so-called secularization theory which argues that religion is declining because it can't stand up to the truths of science and rationality. In fact, religion was declining in some countries (the Netherlands, for example) and growing in other countries (Russia and Hungary) and remaining unchanged in yet other countries. Ireland, Poland, the United States, and the Philippines were the most religious countries; East Germany the least religious; Britain, Norway, and West Germany were somewhere in between. I summarized these findings in *Religion as Poetry* and commented that the "secularization" model served too many people's emotional needs (including I might have added, Catholic theologians) to be routed by mere empirical research. It was a dogma, not a testable model.

I added in *Religion as Poetry* that a reading of the newly emerging literature on the social history of religion in the Middle Ages[107] indicated that the *terminus a quo* of "secularization" theory—a time of great religious faith and devotion as we moderns would define such things—never existed. Medieval religion was essentially magical with an overlay of Christianity. Magic continues to flourish today according to our 1991 research in many countries with the highest levels of superstition in Britain and the lowest in Ireland and East Germany. There is little need for magic in countries where belief is either very high or very low. It is in the "in between" countries like Britain where magic survives (40 percent of the British believed in at least one form of magic).

I am now deeply involved with the International Social Survey Program, though I find it hard to cope with the continuing flood of data, because the ability to use country as one of the variables is very powerful indeed. Thus frequency of prayer correlates with opposition to the death penalty (quite the opposite of what the academic liberal would believe) not only in the United States but in most other countries too. Hence critics can no longer write off findings about religion in the United States as a form of "American Exceptionalism."

[107]Some of the best of which has been written by Michael Carroll of the University of Western Ontario.

But my original concern was with the so-called white ethnic groups in the United States. To what extent have they sustained the culture of the land of their origins in the immigration process? The general assumption in sociology is that all these ethnic differences have washed out through education and intermarriage. *Moreover, the assumption often is that they should have washed out.* Neither the Italians nor the Poles nor the Irish are politically correct ethnic groups. No one thinks their cultures are appropriate for multicultural studies.[108]

My findings, as always counter-intuitive[109] and easily dismissed, are that the family structures and family cultures of the Italians and the Irish have demonstrated remarkable durability.[110] Indeed, the tightly knit family of the Italians is not different in the slightest from that of the Italian Americans. In neither country, moreover, is it affected by educational attainment nor region of the country nor age. All those films about the Italian family that you've seen are true.

As for the Irish, they too preserve a distinctive family culture, one with heavy emphasis on verbal communication, i.e., talk. The talk goes on even when they cross the Atlantic, especially with the women in their families, a talk which is facilitated in this country by the greater prevalence of telephones. The Irish talk to their mothers and their sisters (and presumably their daughters) even more than the Italians. The talk goes on in both Europe and America. The Irish can't help themselves. For them talk is an addiction.

[108]I am completely in favor of multiculturalism. So long as we get ours. But the Irish have never gotten theirs, even though it was assumed that they could not succeed in America (and that they have not succeeded is also assumed by many academics like Thomas Sowell, a black political scientist). However, I suppose we can laugh all the way to our commodity brokers.

[109]I guess I have the knack of choosing for my research interests subjects that offend many of my sociological colleagues. I have not mentioned in this book my work on religious, psychic, and mystical experiences which is a surefire "no-no." The tools of sociology do not enable one to comment on the metaphysics of such experiences but they do make it possible to estimate their prevalence and the incidence and their impact on the lives of those who have them. Clearly there is something perverse about my character or I wouldn't wander into such murky swamps. Mike Hout reminds me that in my presentation when I was recruited at U of A I talked about my research on mystical experiences, as though I was defying them not to want me. "You read us right, however," he says. "We liked the talk." Yeah, and I'm glad that they did. But you have to wonder about someone who is that outrageous. It is probably too late in life to change even if I wanted to and, naturally, I don't want to.

[110]Since Poland has only recently joined the International Social Survey Program, there has not yet been an opportunity to compare the Polish Poles with the Polish Americans.

These are merely highlights of two as yet unpublished (and probably unpublishable)[111] papers that show the remarkable durability and persistence of "white ethnic" subcultures which everyone knows don't exist anymore. And shouldn't exist anymore either, as far as that goes.

For a supposedly antidogmatic discipline, sociology has a lot of its own dogmas. I seem to have selected subject matters—religion, ethnicity, Catholic schools, Catholic sexuality—that offend those dogmas.

Conor Ward and I have written a number of articles on the Irish which establish that they are the most tolerant of diversity of any of the English-speaking peoples and indeed more tolerant than anyone else but the Dutch. Everyone knows, including the Irish, that these findings can't be true.

But in work that Wolfgang Jagodjinski and I are doing on Catholic culture in three countries, it also turns out that the Irish tend to be the happiest, the most pro-feminist, and the most sympathetic with condemned criminals of any of the people on which we have data. Again everyone, including the Irish, know that none of these things can be true.[112] Work done by Chris Whelan of the Economic and Social Research Institute has also shown that despite notable cultural changes in Ireland (a return to more tolerant sexual attitudes and to higher rates of out-of-wedlock births) and despite a growing anticlericalism, the Irish are still the most Catholic people in the world.

A Ph.D. student from the University of Chicago on whose board I served studied Irish drinking behavior and compared the myths about that subject with the per capita alcohol consumption for various European countries. The Irish have the lowest per capita numbers, which of course seems to refute the myths about the drunken Irish. The only conclusion to which a social scientist can legitimately come is that the

---

[111]Because the findings will be so offensive to sociological referees.

[112]I once exploded to a group of Irish social scientists that I had had it with their "frigging Irish, frigging self, frigging hatred," using the kind of participles and sentence structure which the Irish seem to prefer. I didn't say "frigging" of course, though some of my fiction publishers object to my attempts at realism in Irish English. The reader who is interested in how the Irish really talk should read the novels of Roddy Doyle. As Blackie Ryan remarks at the beginning of *Happy Are the Peacemakers* they mean no harm by it. It's merely that in the last hundred and fifty years a word-drunk people have come upon four-letter English words for which there is no equivalent in their own language and have been constrained by their cultural values to push the use of these words to the ultimate. In *Irish Gold* Nuala Anne McGrail tells Dermot Michael Coyne that Irish is a "pure and holy language." The latter, scoring one of his rare points in contention with that matriarch in the making, replies that he is surprised that she didn't say that it was a frigging pure and holy language.

myths are false. Where do they come from? Where do all such myths about the Irish come from? Anti-Irish bigotry of which the Irish themselves are the strongest supporters.[113]

One of the major payoffs from the International Social Survey Program is that I now have an even better excuse to go to Ireland every year and revel in, among other things, their marvelous ability with words. They are, as I have said, drunk on words.[114]

A few examples of Irish expressions:

- "Ah, sure, s/he's not the worst of them." As in "Ah, sure, me wife (husband) (bishop) is not the worst of them." This is high praise indeed. If you ask who are the worst of them, you'll be told that there are plenty that are the worst of them.

- "They won't be all that wrong who say that (we're going to get a new bishop soon)." Not to be all that wrong means that one is a skilled prophet or analyst.

- "There are those who say that (someone) doesn't have any ambitions to move up at all, at all." The meaning is that those who say such a thing are blind fools.

- One asks where, for example, the post office is. One is asked in response, "Is it a stamp you want to buy?" It is not true that the Irish always answer a question by asking another one. But it is true that in the old culture formed by the Irish language such a response is considered to be almost necessarily courteous. I'm not sure why, but I'm told the language avoids all harsh or seemingly harsh vocabulary and structure. To the question of whether you will mail the envelope with the stamp on it when you go by the post office, the polite answer is not "yes" but "I will." (Or perhaps, "I will not because won't the post office be closed when I get there and besides don't I have to go to the tobacco shop first and buy the *Irish Times*?") It is also alleged that the language lacks any forms for "hello" or "good-bye." In the West one greets a neighbor with, for example, "Jesus and Mary be with you" and hears in response, "Jesus and Mary and Patrick be with you."

[113]Consider four of them sitting around a table at a pub for much of the evening. There's always a pint of Guinness in front of them. Patently they are heavy drinkers, right? Only the close observer notes that it is the same four pints all night long.

[114]I told an Irish bishop once (not my friend Eamon Casey) that in *Happy Are the Peacemakers* the heroine manages to use "frig" or its derivates four times in one sentence. 'Tis nothing at all to do that, he replied. Well, says I, what would be something at all? To use it twice in one word. For example? Says I, "Well, what about frigging arch frigging bishop!"

As general rules of thumb the Irish rarely say anything directly when they can get away with saying it indirectly and never say anything at all when a sigh, a wink, or a nod of the head can convey meaning at least as well as words. If you're not plugged in to the meanings of such gestures, it will take you a while to figure out what they're talking about.

And even then you might be wrong.

In his analysis of Irish religious culture David Tracy asserts that the typical Irish religious experience is straightforward nature mysticism. The Irish tend to see God lurking everywhere in creation. However, the experience, Tracy continues, is never described simply. Rather the Irish seek elaborate and circuitous styles for describing their interaction with the Ultimate. He cites the art of the Book of Kells, the theology of John Scotus Erigena,[115] and the fiction of James Joyce. Since the first two are from an era long before British imperialism's invasion of Ireland, it can hardly be that the Irish love of the indirect and the evasive is the result of a conscious strategy of hiding the truth from the invaders (though it certainly helped). Rather this style of communication may be the result of an archaic worldview (dating to pre-Christian times) which perceived reality to be fuzzy, problematic, and uncertain. You spoke cautiously and indirectly because that was the best way to describe the fascinating, mysterious, puzzling, and sometimes dangerous world in which you found yourself.

Or maybe just for the fun of it.

Mary Maher, an expatriate Chicagoan now living in Dublin and working as a journalist and editor at the *Irish Times*, described Irish culture in a fashion not unlike that of David Tracy. "The best one-word description of these people," she told me, "is 'playful.' They love to play with their children, play with words, play in their poetry and their stories, play in their conversations at the pub every night, play with nicknames— everyone has at least two or three. They love games. Don't they have the biggest sports sections of any papers in the world. Wasn't the front section of the *Irish Times* the sports pages until not so long ago? If you understand that this is a country in which most everyone loves to play, then you'll have gone a long way toward understanding them."

Or in the local parlance, you won't be all that wrong if you take into account the play factor.

Hence you'll understand the "Irish bull" which the British often thought proved the low level of Irish intelligence. Such as:

"Was it yourself I saw on Leeson Street yesterday?"

---

[115]An early medieval theologian about whom, I must confess, I know nothing except that his name means "John, the Irishman, born in Ireland."

"It was not."

"I didn't think it was, because by the time I caught up with you, were you not there?"

Or (standing a queue) waiting for a bus, "Ah, isn't this line so long that by the time we get on the bus, there won't be the room for the half of us?"

The complexities of the Irish game of politics are especially intricate and delicate. The government fell not because the minister lied and not even because the *taosach*[116] lied when he said that he did not know that the minister had lied but because the *taosach* lied when he named the day on which he said he learned for the first time that the minister had lied.

Got it? Don't worry, you're not expected to get it.

My colleague Mike Hout and his wife Eileen, after spending a year's sabbatical at University College Dublin, insisted that Ireland was the best country in the world to be a kid. The Irish didn't spoil their children: there were always limits beyond which a kid dared not go. A raised eyebrow or a shake of the head defined those limits. But the limits seemed usually to be invisible and within them the kids were free to play and, more importantly, parents were free to play with their kids.

At Bewlery's Cafe

The blond doll, curly hair and all,
Is in fact an imp, a grinning little leprechaun.
Her young parents, when not devouring each other
With eyes of love, have joined her giddy game.

They laugh merrily at their clowning child
As, with pretense of mature delicacy,
She digs her fingers into the delightful icing
Of an intriguing sticky bun.

Aware that she is putting on a show,
Entertaining Ma and Da, she sniggers,
Smears each finger with gooey white
And then, one by one, licks them clean.

She beams proudly as, next to empty teacups,
They lay their heads on the table,
And chortle helplessly at her wondrous act,
This shining partner in their fun.

[116]Prime minister.

Now it's time to go.
Ma extends the coat
The imp puts her arms in the sleeves,
Wrong way round of course, so the coat
Must be zipped up in back.

With much struggling laughter
As the kid plays contortionist
They twist and turn
To get the coat on right.

She sees me laughing, I smile and wave.
She toddles over and grins up at me.
"A little monkey," her ma says proudly.
"A gorgeous little monkey," I reply.

The parents beam, Da pats me on the back.
They leave Bewlery's serene,
Someone else agrees that their kid
Is a very special little monkey.

After she has waved her good-bye,
I buy another hot chocolate for the road
And ask myself if I were made
For such play and fun by God!

The plays and the short stories and the novels about the harshness of Irish family life are doubtless true but not typical. However, the image they created has become one more of the stereotypes that are grist for anti-Irish bigotry and for Irish self-hatred.[117] Harshness and cruelty and fanaticism and joylessness exist in Ireland just as in other countries. I hated Frank McCourt's book because he blamed the suffering in his family not on the fact that his mother had married a drunk, but on the country and the Church. Not everyone in the country is playful. Some are innocent of joy and playfulness. There is a somber dimension of Irish culture too, one which forms strange combinations with the culture's emphasis on playfulness. However, of all the countries the International Social Survey Program has studied

---

[117] A self-hatred which doubtless is the result of being an oppressed colony for seven centuries. You begin to believe the things the oppressors say about you.

(as well as those countries which the less professional World Values Study has surveyed) the Irish have the highest morale measures. The Irish are more likely to be (or claim to be) "very happy" than anyone else, mostly because there is an interaction between "closeness" to God and happiness in Ireland.

Despite stories of great poverty in "Catholic Ireland" the present economic condition of the country, as it surpasses Britain's standard of living (as measured by per capita gross national product), is almost an Irish bull. At the present writing the country has the lowest inflation rate, the best balance of payments rate, and the highest GNP growth rate of any of the European Economic Community countries. Galway is the fastest-growing city in Europe, Dublin the best educated.

The Catholic Church is in deep trouble in Ireland because its leadership did not know when to give up power. Through the penal and famine times up to the emergence of the Irish Free State in 1921, the clergy were often the only leaders a poor and hungry people could find. The Ireland of Eamon De Valera was a stodgy, often repressive state in which clerical power continued to be great even though it was no longer a political necessity that the Church have that kind of power. In the years after the Second World War, the Church, if it had read the handwriting on the wall, might have begun gracefully to yield power to the civil society. No one, however, gives up power easily. So the Church clung to its power too long and lost it anyway as younger generations strongly resented the influence of the bishops in Irish life. Finally the bishops have learned to be more discreet (not including Dr. Desmond Connell,[118] the archbishop of Dublin) only after it was too late.

Enda MacDonagh, professor of moral theology at Maynooth and chaplain to Mary Robinson, the president of Ireland,[119] remarked to me a couple of years ago that there are two major religious movements in Ireland at the present—the literary flourishing among Catholics and the volunteer movement—and that the Church did not know how to respond to either of them. In truth it seems to me that most people in Ireland are hardly aware of these developments. They are still caught in the stereotype that Ireland is a dull little place.

[118]The last three archbishops of Dublin have been, in order, a professor of Semitic languages, a high school teacher, and a professor of metaphysics. As an "old fella" said to me, "Poor old Ireland! It must be a terrible country altogether if those are the only priests that the Church can find for a city with a million and a half people."

[119]In a well-ordered Church Enda would have been archbishop of Dublin or at least of his native archdiocese (Tuam). But the Church has a horror of bishops who are able, intelligent, and open-minded.

However, this might well be *the* golden age of Irish literature and culture—playwrights like Brien Friel, poets like Seamus Heaney,[120] novelists like Roddy Doyle, musicians like the Chieftains' Paddy Maloney, choreographers like *Riverdance*'s Michael Flatley (and himself from Chicago!), popular bands like U2, and now more recently the Cranberries. All of them—and scores more like them—living on an island whose population (counting the North) is hardly more than that of the Chicago metropolitan area. All of the people listed in my penultimate sentence are Catholics of one variety or the other, so for the first time an Irish "revival" is almost all Catholic and not in great part Anglo-Irish.

The Church is quite incapable of grasping that such a development is a sign of the Presence of the Spirit. However, the Irish Church has no monopoly on this blindness to sacrament makers[121] among its people. In the United States (and most other countries too, for that matter) official Catholicism is deeply suspicious of its own creative members—when it doesn't ignore them altogether.

The young Irish are incredibly generous with their time and their money and even, on occasion, their lives. There is no troubled place in the world—Rwanda or Bosnia for example—where you won't find young Irish men and women risking their lives (and sometimes losing them) in service of the poor, the hungry, the unfortunate.[122] Moreover, whenever there is suffering anywhere, the Irish are willing to dig into their often near-empty pockets to help. This generosity is so much a part of Irish life that it is often barely noticed, save by perceptive observers like Father MacDonagh.

---

[120]I am happy to claim both Friel and Heaney as personal friends. Perhaps Eugene will take that as a challenge to co-opt them the way he co-opted Cardinal Bernardin. Lots of luck!

[121]For that is the role of the creative person—painter, musician, poet, storyteller—to point at the presence of grace in the world.

[122]Some of the more intellectual (or would-be intellectual) of the younger generation of Irish clergy are strong supporters of "liberation theology" and hence anti-American—a characteristic that is almost invisible among most of the Irish, especially outside of academia. It seems to me that this political posturing is cheap grace (radical words without the need for radical action) as well as being bad sociology and worse economics. Moreover if they are so interested in siding with the poor and the oppressed I wonder why they don't join the only "people's revolutionary movement" in Western Europe, the IRA. If they want a revolution, there's one going on in the northern six counties of their island. I don't approve of terrorist violence but the Marxism which is the essence of "Liberation Theology" certainly does. You can't have it both ways: you can't support revolutionary violence in South America (or El Salvador or Nicaragua) and not support it in Derry of Falls Road.

I hope it's clear by this point that I admire the Irish more than they admire themselves and have a higher opinion of them than they do of themselves. That kind of mystifies many of my Irish friends. They are accustomed to criticism and complaints of foreigners (especially from a certain kind of Irish American with a very loud mouth) but they don't quite know what to make of a foreigner who tells them that they really are much better as a people than they think they are. Some of them are not altogether sure they like such praise. And himself a Yank and a priest at that!

In 1996 I was asked to contribute a paper to a conference at Nuffield College at Oxford on *Ireland, North and South*. My charge was to compare religion in the North and the South to see if there was any "convergence." There was not. However, I did discover that there were three religions in Ireland. Southern Catholicism, Northern Protestantism, and Northern Catholicism. The last-named had more in common with Northern Protestantism than it did with Southern Catholicism. Indeed, Ireland was the last battle site in the ongoing conflict between the pessimism about human nature of St. Augustine and the optimism of the Irish monk Pelagius (a saint in the Orthodox Church). The dividing line between the strongest Augustinians in the world and the strongest Pelagians was not the boundary between the two churches but the boundary between the six counties of the North and the twenty-six (plus two new ones) counties of the South. No one is more optimistic about human nature in the world than are the Irish in the republic.

My work in Ireland and my friendship with many Irish colleagues and acquaintances has been one of the high points of my life, not merely because I enjoy Ireland and the Irish but even more because I have learned to recognize the importance of the Irish component of my own character and personality.

My trips to Ireland are voyages of self-discovery.

So Ireland has become one of the locales of my stories. The last half of *Rite of Spring* is set in Ireland as is all of *Happy Are the Peacemakers* and more recently *Irish Gold* and *Angel Light*, a modern version of the Tobias[123] story from the Bible in which the Irish American Tobin must seek the fair bride not in Ectbana in Syria but in Galway City, with the assistance of course of the angel Raphael who is in fact the angel (seraph actually) Rafaella, Rae for short. In *Irish Mist*, Nuala Anne and Dermot Michael must try to understand the conflicts in Ireland after the civil war

[123]To my astonishment most people have not only not read the Book of Tobit, they have not even heard of it and indeed express grave doubt when I

(and the murder of Irish strongman Kevin O'Higgins) which shaped modern Ireland. There are three kinds of mist in the story: the weather, the mystery over the past, and the mystery of who is trying to harm herself. As to the liquor, well both of the young detectives prefer Irish Cream to Irish Mist.

Ireland, then, has become a matrix for my stories, though, characteristically, I guess, I haven't abandoned Chicago. The characters in my Irish stories are for the most part Chicagoans who have come there for one reason or another, not altogether unconnected with a search for an Irish wife.[124]

I don't know how well these books will sell in Ireland, though earlier in my career when I had data about Irish sales there was a higher rate in Ireland than in this country. As far as I know, only *Rite of Spring* has been reviewed and that in an extremely friendly and favorable review in the *Irish Times*—which doesn't give many favorable reviews, especially to books by Yanks or by priests, to say nothing of books by someone who is both a Yank and a priest. To my joy the reviewer found only two errors in the story: I had my characters eating lunch at the (excellent) restaurant in the National Irish Art Museum which I said was in the basement. In fact it was on the ground floor (I only thought it was the basement because I saw no windows!). I also referred to a ferry coming into Dun Leary when in fact it should have come into the docks on the Liffey River.

He half admitted that it wasn't really so bad for a Yank to make only those mistakes!

In *Irish Gold* the attractive Bishop Edie Hayes is based on Eamon Casey, a fact that should be evident as soon as the bishop (of Galway) makes his appearance.

I had written him into the story before the scandal blew up about his (perhaps)[125] having fathered a child. I thought maybe for five seconds about writing him out of the book and decided that no way would I do that. Regardless of his love affair long ago, he is one of the best bishops in the world, zealous, sympathetic, open, dedicated. The anticlerical Irish media pretended to be deeply shocked about the rev-

---

tell them that is a love story, a quest for the fair bride and for magic gold—a kind of proto-grail quest.

[124]Are all Irish American and real Irish women as strong as your characters, I am often asked. Well, no, not all of them, I guess. Only the ones I know.

[125]A friend of the boy's mother when she gave birth has insisted that the mother named another man as father at that time. While there is no doubt that Bishop Casey had an affair with her, there are some reasons to suspect that he

elations and saw the scandal as a fierce blow to the sexual teaching of the Church. Fortunately Catholic ethics do not depend on the good example of bishops and never have. Moreover, anyone with even the slightest knowledge of Irish history knows that Bishop Casey was not the first Irish bishop to engage in a love affair.[126] The people of Galway, I am told by everyone I know there, would, if given a chance, reelect him.[127] At least he had fallen in love with a woman, not a little boy or, God save us all, another bishop!

The bishop is now working in a South American country. A friend of mine who is in the same mission reports that Eamon Casey is every bit the fine man that I say he is. He plans, according to a story in the Irish media, to retire in Ireland eventually. It would seem at this writing that he will be back soon. The summer before the scandal broke, Eamon called to say he was in the Chicago area and wanted to visit me at Grand Beach. I was a bit surprised because while I knew him reasonably well, I couldn't imagine why he would go out of his way to come to Grand Beach. It was the last night before Nora Daley was to go off for her first year in college. We had planned a Mass for her and her family and relatives on the dune. The bishop concelebrated with me and charmed all the Daleys. Maggie swept us all up and brought us back to their house where the bishop sang songs and told stories and won over everyone. Why aren't more bishops like him? they wondered.

Fair question.

Eamon phoned me the week after the "scandal" was revealed. "I wanted to tell you at Grand Beach last summer," he said. "But I just couldn't bring myself to do it."

"I'm solidly behind you, Eamon," I replied. "You're still one of the best bishops in the world."

"Thank you very much, Andy."

I would have thought that we were friends, even close friends, but

---

was the victim of a false charge of fathering the boy and indeed of none-too-subtle blackmail.

[126]At the Synod of Maynooth in 1540 one of the items on the agenda was the abolition of concubinage—the "right" of an Irish lord under the ancient Brehon laws to have four wives. (That many! I've always felt that one Irish woman around the house was enough, perhaps on occasion more than enough!) The item was never voted on because the lords, both temporal and spiritual, were practicing concubinage and had no intention of giving up this "right."

[127]A "chance" which in the early Church would have been considered a right.

hardly so close that my support would have made that much difference. Clearly it did. I had missed the point again.

Will I continue to set parts or even all of some novels in the future (if God gives me time to write them) in Ireland?

Who could say? But I am addicted to the country and its people. Those who say that I will continue to bring Ireland into my stories would not be far from being right!

My relationship with Germany is more recent and more surprising. In the autumn of 1993 I visited Mannheim, the location of the German version of the National Opinion Research Center (ZUMA), in search of data which I could use in trying to study religious change in Europe. ZUMA had just become the site of the International Social Survey Program secretariat. Peter Mohler, the director of ZUMA, and his wife Janet Harkness could not have been more cordial.

My only previous experience with German scholars was an unfortunate period I spent on the editorial board of the international Catholic journal *Concilium*. The German theologians were arrogant, mean-spirited, nasty, left-wing ideologues.[128] They said they wanted an American empiricist on the board but they either really didn't or didn't realize what a person of that species might be like. They made it clear that I was a "positivist" and that was not a good thing to be. The only "sociology" about which they cared was the "critical" (i.e., Marxist) "sociology" of the Frankfurt School—the sort of sociology in which one could find numbers only at the top of the page and for whose assertions evidence was neither provided nor, apparently, expected. I finally had enough of them when they acted like boors at a meeting I had foolishly tried to organize for the magazine at Notre Dame.

The Frankfurt School has disappeared from the face of the earth, by the way, and has been replaced in Germany by American empiricism. Or "positivism" as the panzer commanders would have called it.

Before I came to Mannheim, Michael Terwy of the Zentralarchiv (ZA) had invited me to come up to Cologne to make a presentation on my work in the sociology of religion. ZA archives all the International Social Survey Program data and makes the data files available to the world; so I knew some of their people already and liked them. (Without them all the other work of designing questionnaires and collecting data would have been a waste of time.) But I was hesitant about taking on another group of Germanic scholars. In fact the atmosphere I encoun-

---

[128]I except my friend Hans Küng from this charge. In fact, Hans, as he often insists, is not German but Swiss.

tered at ZA was just the opposite of that of *Concilium*. The people who came to hear me were polite, friendly, and interested. They even laughed at my jokes (of which the first was to apologize for the poor way I spoke English—that is, with an almost unintelligible Chicago accent). I was invited to come back the following spring to be a "visiting professor" for a time. Again their courtesy and friendliness were impeccable. Wolfgang Jagodjinski, the new director of ZA, proposed that we work on a project together. Rolf Huer and Irena Müller, whom I had met at the previous International Social Survey Program sessions, welcomed me as an old friend. Ekkehard Mochman, an executive of ZA (whom I'd met in Dublin), was especially courteous and took me for a ride to Bonn and to the wine-producing Ahr Valley and the town of Ahrweiller, where we dispatched huge amounts of ice cream and I explained to him that ice cream was a revelation of God's goodness. The ordinary people of Cologne were so friendly[129] and helpful that I almost thought I was in Dublin! Should Lady Wisdom be willing, I hope to return there often in years to come.

In *A Midwinter's Tale*, my protagonist is a soldier in the American Constabulary Regiment (state police) in Bamberg in Bavaria only forty kilometers from the Red Army.[130] As the saga shapes up, he will be involved with Germany for the next quarter century. I wonder now why I chose to focus on postwar Germany, even before my encounters with ZA and ZUMA. Perhaps as someone who grew up during the war, heard Hitler rant on the radio, and saw the horrors of the Holocaust in the papers and the newsreels, I had a profound distrust of Germany and the Germans and was fascinated by the question of how much the country had changed. I was bitterly opposed only a few years ago to reunification of East and West Germany.

On the other hand, I knew that there was a strong democratic tradition in Germany, especially along the Rhine, and that the Center Party under the leadership of Windthorst had been a bastion of democracy (and had been abolished by Hitler when he came to power). I also realized that the Nazis had never won a majority in a free election. I do

[129]From an elderly woman who helped me on with my raincoat while I was walking from my hotel to ZA to a teenager (young woman) who noticed me puzzling over a map on the bank of the Rhine. Cologne I would later learn has the reputation of being the friendliest city in Germany.

[130]When asked if he was worried about the Red Army, Chuck O'Malley, my protagonist, says that he assumes the Russians are at least as incompetent as were the Americans (in 1946) and that they would break down halfway to Bamberg.

not believe in collective guilt and I could not see how those born in Germany since the war could be held responsible for what their elders had done or at least tolerated. If I were Jewish, I wouldn't trust Germany again for hundreds of years. As an American with a memory I would hold the younger generation of Germans responsible only to see that it never happened again and be just a little uneasy about whether the culture of the country had changed sufficiently so that in fact a Hitler would never again appear.

So part of my concern in the saga, a part which became conscious only after I got into writing it, was to understand the German economic and perhaps political miracle. My experience with the *Concilium* theologians made me wonder.

But my association with colleagues in Cologne (which was virtually destroyed during the war) and Mannheim (bombed constantly and devastated) has persuaded me that the success of democratic experiment in the Bundesrepublik is real. The West Germans indeed have constructed a civil and democratic society. It is not perfect (as, heaven knows, our own democratic society is less than perfect). But fifty years ago one could not have imagined the possibility of a democratic and civil political entity. The achievement is impressive and this makes my challenge in the saga even greater. Perhaps as in Ireland, I now have a higher opinion of the West Germans than do their own intellectuals.

I have also fallen completely in love with Cologne, so much in love that Blackie must visit it in the story *The Bishop and the Three Kings* (along with his nephew Peter Murphy and a Coast Guard person named Cindasue McLeod who has figured in earlier stories). It begins, as all Blackie stories must, in his rooms in the cathedral:

> *"They've stolen the bodies of the three kings!" Sean Cardinal Cronin, by the grace of God and the strained patience of the Apostolic See, announced in his most dramatic tenor voice, pointing his finger at me accusingly, as if I personally was responsible for the theft.*
>
> *He had swept into my study like a crimson tornado, his usual style when he needed a favor from me. His tall, spare frame was clad in a cassock with crimson buttons, and a cummerbund, cape, and zucchetto of the same color. He wore an ostentatious bejeweled pectoral cross, a gift from his sister and sister-in-law Senator Nora Cronin. Some social event of considerable moment must have transpired earlier in the evening.*
>
> *"Blackwood," he had announced as he seized a full bottle of my treasured supply of Bushmill's Green from its hiding place, "we're in trouble."*

I had turned away from the Pentium computer and my long essay on "Russian Trinitarian Mysticism as a Love Affair"—a late evening amusement—to face him head-on: if Milord Cronin said we were in trouble, it usually meant that I was in trouble.

"Indeed?" I had said cautiously.

He had filled a Waterford tumbler for me and poured a much smaller amount for himself. Since he did not usually drink a nightcap at all, I had become all the more convinced that I was in trouble. I had glanced at the icons on my wall—I called them icons now that I was into Russian mysticism—and prayed for help. The only one I could count on was the medieval ivory Madonna which my old fella had given me because it reminded him of my mother. The Johns of my youth—pope, president, and Baltimore quarterback—would be of no use in the present situation. Neither would the newest addition—Clare Marie Raftery Boyle, a young woman who had helped me solve a mystery a hundred years old.

The cardinal had removed a pile of computer output from my easy chair—cathedral financial records in this instance, depressing as always—sank into the chair, sipped from his tumbler, stretched out in satisfaction, and announced the grave robbery.

"Deplorable . . ." I said with a loud sigh as I sipped cautiously from my Waterford. "Which three kings?"

"The three kings from the Orient, Caspar, Balthazar, and Melchior," he replied as his blue Celtic mercenary warrior eyes flared with indignation. "What other three kings are there?"

"I would remind you that the current translation of the readings of the Feast of the Epiphany, which you yourself have approved for use at Eucharistic celebrations in this Archdiocese, depict them as astrologers, which may be more accurate but lacks some narrative vigor."

"That's besides the point, Blackwood," he insisted, a frown creasing his handsome face. "The point is their bodies have been stolen."

"From the Archdiocesan Cemetery system?"

"No, of course not, from the Cathedral in Cologne! This is a very big deal, outside of Rome and Compestella, the kings were the object of the largest pilgrimages in the Middle Ages. They deserve credit for making Cologne one of the great cities of Europe. To lose them permanently would cause a grave crisis in the Church."

"It is the devout and plausible conviction of the Greeks and the Russians that there were twelve of these astrologers. They argue that since there are twelve apostles and twelve legions of angels and twelve tribes of Israel there must be twelve, uh, astrologers. In its own way

*that argument merits some credence, particularly if you happen to be
a Russian or a Greek. We on the other hand conclude to only three
because there were three gifts brought, gold, frankincense, and myrrh.
One gift, you see, one king. It is, I must concede, a typical manifestation of the Western empiricism which the Greeks and the Russians abhor.''*

*"How come then that there are only three bodies in the Cologne
Cathedral?'' he demanded, baffled by my little excursus into scriptural interpretation.*

*"Is one permitted to observe that it is very unlikely that the bones
entombed in that lovely city on the Rhine are in fact those of the wise
men, of whatever number, who came out of the east to Bethlehem?
. . . Moreover, as I remember, they were stolen from the Cathedral
in Milano by that exemplary Catholic king, Frederick of the Red
Beard. So this is not the first theft.''*

*"That, Blackwood,'' Milord Cronin informed me, "is totally
besides the point!''*

*I refrained from noting that this was the second time he had accused
me of missing the point. In fact, he was well aware that I was deliberately missing the point, because I didn't like what it obviously was.*

"The point is that it is close to Christmas.''

*"Ah,'' I said. "I had thought that it was the first week in Oc-
tober, fully eighty-five shopping days till Christmas.''*

*"If we don't get the three kings back before Christmas, the word
will leak out and all the world will be in Cologne to reveal yet another
Catholic scandal. In the days of Freddy Barbarossa, you didn't have
Christian Armanpour descending from a helicopter to tell in shocked
tones that the Catholic Church had spoiled Christmas.''*

"Beat the grinch to it,'' I said, trying to sound sympathetic.

*The leprechaun who haunts my quarters at Holy Name Cathedral
had stolen most of my aqua vitae as he usually does. I decided that
it would be pointless to refill the glass: I would not sleep much that
night at all. At all, at all.*

*"You Ryans like to travel,'' Milord continued, stating what he
knew was a total falsehood.*

*"Patently, we do not. Why leave Chicago, as my sister the federal
judge often says, when we have everything here.''*

*That dictum from the good Eileen is something of an exaggeration.
Various members of the clan have traveled to the far ends of the earth
for reasons of necessity—kicking, screaming, and complaining all the
way out and back.*

"Except the bodies of the three kings.''

"Arguably."

"Claus is a good friend, right?" he continued, circling around our trouble.

He was referring to Claus Maria Heinrich Rupert Eugen, Graf von Oberman, the cardinal archbishop of Cologne.

"Arguably," I said again, with the loudest of my West of Ireland sighs.

"We do him favors, he does us favors, right?"

"That is the Chicago political tradition."

I sighed again. What he meant was that if I did a favor for the genial Viking pirate who presided over Köln, to spell it properly, he, Cardinal Sean Cronin, would have a marker to pick up. Such is the nature of the responsibility of auxiliary bishops whose role is roughly analogous of the character played by the excellent Harvey Keitel in the film Pulp Fiction: *we sweep up the messes that real bishops make.*

"So if we can help him get the three kings back, he will owe us one very big favor."

"That is the way it works," I assented.

"Besides," he said, swirling around the remaining precious fluid in his glass, *"this little puzzle is not without certain interesting aspects."*

He had stolen the line from me, patently. I in my turn had stolen it from Sherlock Holmes.

"Indeed."

"Oh, yes. The casket with the remains of your three friends is the largest gilded monument in the occidental world."

"Impressive."

"It would take four, arguably six, men to move it."

"Indeed."

"It is protected by a large, transparent case which looks like glass but is in fact bulletproof plastic."

"If terrorists wanted to destroy the shrine with automatic weapons . . ."

"Or something like that . . . Needless to say the case is wired with an alarm."

"Naturally."

"Moreover, it is behind the high altar which they no longer use for Mass, ah, the Eucharist, because we have different ideas of where the altar should be than the Goths did."

"Franks in this case, though both were Germanic tribes."

"Whatever . . . The whole area around the high altar and the

shrine is protected by a wrought-iron fence which is also wired and is locked unless opened by one of the head vergers of the cathedral.''

"A reasonable precaution.''

"Finally, they lock the cathedral up at night, unlike this place . . .''

"No one has stolen anything from our cathedral,'' I pointed out.

I hold the odd position for a priest of our age that a church building belongs to the people who paid for it and that it should be open to them at all hours of the day and night. A ring of visible light encircles a section in the back of the nave and warnings are posted that anyone who violates that circle will call down upon himself the Chicago Police Department, the Cook County Sheriff's Police, the Illinois State Police, the Alcohol, Tobacco, and Firearms Agency, the Federal Bureau of Investigation, and possibly the Swiss Guard. The warnings exaggerate somewhat, but only somewhat. There are also various electronic wonders, not excluding TV monitors, which preclude the possibility of anyone doing harm to anyone else in our ring of light without the risk of unleashing sounds that would awaken not only the intrepid cathedral staff but most human beings living within the boundaries of the parish.

We have had only a few false alarms.

"They wire their place at night too. They should with all the treasures inside. I wouldn't think it is as elaborate, however, as your network of instruments from hell.''

"Undoubtedly it is not. No church in the world . . .''

"I'm sure,'' he held up his hand. "The point is that you have a locked shrine inside a locked fence within a locked cathedral, all of which are not only locked but armed.''

"Fascinating,'' I admitted grudgingly.

"Last week the priest who comes over to say the first Mass . . .''

"Doubtless the pastor as in this cathedral.''

". . . Notices that the shrine is missing. The transparent cage is locked, the fence is locked, the alarm system is still functioning, but the three kings have disappeared.''

"Most fascinating.''

"I knew you'd think so,'' he said, triumphantly bounding out of the easy chair.

"What did the good clergy of the Dom do about their loss?''

I discreetly replaced the financial output papers. One must have an orderly room.

"They replaced it with the fake before they let anyone inside the place.''

"Fake!"

"Sure, you gotta have a fake. When they take the real one down to the basement to fix it up, they put in a wooden one that's painted gold. From a distance you can't tell the difference."

"Ingenious . . . No one knows about this surrogate and presumably boneless shrine?"

"Be reasonable, Blackwood! Everyone knows about it. When they were doing major repairs back in the seventies, they had the fake in for six months. Didn't bother the pilgrims at all, even if they knew, which they probably didn't."

"All the Kölners knew, however."

"Sure . . . They've talked to the Ministry of Justice or whatever they call it over there. Everyone is keeping it a secret, however, for fear of publicity. I guess they're having some kind of election."

"The polizei don't know?"

"You got it."

He leaned against my doorjamb, relishing the approaching moment.

"No one claims credit, no one seeks ransom?" I asked.

"Not so far."

"Nor is there a market for gilded shrines with the purported bones of three astrologers."

"Precisely."

"Though there are always the rich private collectors who enjoy knowing that they have something no one else has."

"Creeps," Milord Cronin agreed. *"But super-rich creeps."*

"It is, as you say, a little puzzle that is not without some interest."

"So Claus remembers that you do locked rooms and wants you to come over and have a look around. Strictly private. He doesn't want to upset the Ministry of Interior or whatever by bringing in an Ausländer. That means foreigner."

"How can I be a foreigner," I asked, *"when patently I am an American?"*

"Spoken like a true offspring of the South Side Irish. . . . Anyway we've got to help Claus get it back."

"So I understand," I said with the loudest of all my sighs.

"One of the young guys can take care of this place. They have more energy anyway."

"Arguably."

"We have to recover the three kings to save Christmas! See to it, Blackwood!"

*Then like a carmine jet which had just turned on its afterburners,
he swept from my study, trailing, as he always does under such
circumstances, maniacal laughter.*

The Germans are still somewhat more formal than are either the
Americans or the Irish. Theirs is the most hyper-regulated society in the
world.[131] I do not argue that there should not still be some unease over
what Germany did a half century ago. But I do believe that this unease
ought not to cause us to underestimate just how deeply democracy has
rooted itself in West Germany in that half century.

The point is subtle, complex, and ambiguous—which makes it all the
more interesting for both a sociologist and a storyteller.

The Church in Germany has missed the boat even more completely
than has the Church in Ireland. Supported by the Church tax as government employees (cardinals are paid the salary of field marshals!), the
German clergy are financially independent of their people and often seem
not to give a hoot about them.[132] However, recently two important
German bishops, who certainly have (or had) good prospects for the red
hat and are hardly innocent of ambition[133] ("Sure, aren't there some who
say that neither one of them has any ambition at all, at all?"), have taken
on the Vatican and the pope, head to head, on the subject of the reception of Holy Communion for those who are divorced and remarried.

One might argue that relatively young men who want to be cardinals
might do well to prepare for a very different Church after the next
conclave. Indeed, that there is a willingness to take on the Vatican would
suggest that the Germans want and expect a different kind of Church.
Nonetheless, the willingness of some of the brightest men in the German
hierarchy to do battle with Rome on the subject of Communion for the
divorced[134] shows a sensitivity to pastoral problems which one would

[131]Eckhard Moesman says with a laugh, "It is wrong to think that Germans
believe that they can do some things that no one else can do. I'm afraid, however, that some of us think we can do it better."

[132]Someone has remarked that the German cardinals, when they stormed
down to Rome to make sure the pope did not back down on the Hans Küng
case, did so with all the efficiency with which they had fought the Second World
War.

[133]Casper and Lehmann. The former had been a student and protégé of Küng
and then turned against him when the Vatican wanted a repudiation from the
Catholic faculty at Tübingen, an unforgivable act of disloyalty to this Irish American from Chicago. However, confronting the pope may win him some forgiveness.

[134]An issue which was settled long since in this country by pastors in the
parishes.

not have expected from German bishops not so long ago. Perhaps even the German Church is becoming democratic. It has a long way to go.

But my idea for the saga, an Irish American from Chicago trying to comprehend the new Germany, now seems more complicated and more challenging as I come to know the two countries and their people better. And more interesting!

I now fly the Atlantic three times a year, a lot of miles for someone whom such trips wipe out. Anything that can go wrong with the human organism in an airplane goes wrong with mine. I've learned that exposure to intense light at midday on either end of the trip helps to reduce the "jet-lag" phenomenon. Yet I am still a wreck after a transatlantic crossing. However, the International Social Survey Program has expanded my horizons and I'm almost eager to make the crossings. It is ridiculous to increase international travel as you get older. However, it is also more fun than it ever was before.[135]

If more transatlantic flights are a condition for new wonder, then it's fine with me.

I'd even be willing to try another transpacific flight, though the last attempt almost ended in disaster—and proves that I am not totally reckless. I had been invited to an international Catholic mass media organization meeting in Bangkok as a commentator on the principal address which was to be given by Cardinal Martini of Milano. The cardinal, a Jesuit Scripture scholar and enormously popular with everyone in his city, was clearly one of the leaders of the "loyal opposition" to Pope John Paul II, though the opposition was always discreet and respectful. Nonetheless, the Vatican had marginalized him[136] as too "liberal." I thought it would be interesting to meet him. We exchanged our papers and promised that we would meet in Bangkok. I had been troubled by a small fever for a few days before I was to leave, apparently a low-grade upper-respiratory infection. Marty Phee, my doctor, had given me Cipro pills to protect me from something more serious in Thailand. I was to fly from Chicago to Los Angeles (ORD to LAX, as we frequent travelers say) and then change to Cathay Pacific for a nonstop flight to Bangkok. On the flight to Los Angeles I became sicker and sicker. While waiting to change planes I dug a thermometer out of my flight bag: 101. Not good.

[135]I have not the slightest idea why they want a sociologist to talk about the religious imagination of a poet. Moreover, my hosts, being Irish, have not given me a very clear idea of what I'm supposed to do.

[136]He was not even invited to the publication party in Milan for the pope's books.

If the CP plane had left on time, I would have gone off to Thailand with, as it turns out, a full-blown case of pneumonia. However, there was a delay after we boarded the plane while they shifted fuel around because of some technical problem. I tried the thermometer. A hundred and two and a half. Oh, oh!

Then they announced that because the flight crew had now been working too long, the plane would stop at Hong Kong to change crews. The eleven-hour flight would take at least fifteen hours.

I still don't understand what happened next. I found myself gathering together my things and heading for the door of the plane, which they had to open for me just before the ground crew removed the jetway. My leaving the plane was not a deliberate or conscious decision at all. It was as though another aspect of myself had taken over.

Whatever made you get off the plane, several people who know me pretty well would later ask. "My guardian angel. I never get off a plane at the last minute." In the LAX terminal I called Kate Phee (Marty's wife and my travel agent) and asked her to cancel everything. Genial and vigorous as always, she assured me that she would take care of everything. It was the last time I would ever talk to her. Then I called Marty and made an appointment to see him at Little Company of Mary Hospital the next morning. It was pneumonia all right.

"Do you want to come into the hospital?" he asked. Marty is an unusual South Side Irish physician. He reads philosophy and science fiction and listens to classical music.

"No way."

"Good idea. Hospitals are filled with sick people."

Two weeks later I preached at Kate's funeral Mass. She had died of chronic diabetes. There were lots of ironies in the fire.

The story was not finished, however. When the infection had cleared out of my lungs, a spot remained. The radiological team at Little Company was convinced I had cancer and would die from it. They wanted to do all the tests. Marty absolutely refused. "He doesn't have cancer."

"He can sue you."

"He won't sue me."

The next time I came back for an X ray, a technician informed me that they were going to do a CAT scan and a biopsy. "Not till I talk to Dr. Phee," I said and refused to go with him. Marty showed up a few minutes later and canceled the test which he had not scheduled in the first place.

The spot, perhaps caused by an Arizona fungus, soon disappeared. One of the radiologists said to me, "I hope you know, Father Greeley, what a good doctor you have."

"Indeed I do."

Later Marty said, "It was unlikely, but those tests might have killed you. There was no justification for taking them."

"How did you know?"

"I just knew. I've read as many X rays as those people have."

I've never been so sick in all my life. Moreover, the physical depression which lingers after pneumonia hung on for many more months. The whole episode now remains as a surrealistic memory.

"What would have happened if I had not got off the plane?" I asked Marty.

"I would not have wanted to bet on your chances."

Ugh.

Anyway, I continued to send selected pieces of my work to Cardinal Martini and ate lunch with him several times in Milano. I was deeply impressed with him, though I disgraced myself by having three helpings of the delicious pasta his cook served (and waving off the main course). The cardinal and his colleagues at the table thought this was very funny indeed. I didn't care. It was wonderful pasta.

The cardinal has paid me two compliments I value very much.

Most sociologists, he said, confirm what we already know. That is useful, of course. But you tell us things we do not know. That is very important.

And: I read your novels when I feel the need to laugh.

I happen to think there's a lot of comedy in my stories (which most reviewers miss completely). But that someone who reads them in a language which is not his own finds them amusing is high praise indeed.

I don't know whether he will be the next pope as some say he will. He is in fact not so much a liberal as a moderate who believes in a more pluralistic and decentralized Church (the kind of Church we have had for most of Catholic history) than the one we now have. It is argued that since he is "the winter book favorite," he will not be elected pope, since those who go into a conclave "papabile" come out as cardinals. This is superstitious nonsense. Both Pius XII and Paul VI were also early favorites.

I don't think he will be pope because he is too well qualified for the job.

If he does become pope (John XXIV?), he will be a very good one.

Finally, there is yet another part of the world to which I travel, reluctantly and suspiciously—the World Wide Web.

The Net is useful for E-mail, football scores, weather forecasts, reading newspapers from other countries (like the *Irish Times*), listening to radio programs (Chicago's WFMT while I'm in Tucson and RTE One), sending manuscripts to colleagues, and hunting down illustrations for books (like my *The Catholic Imagination*.) It is a useful tool. It is also a terrible temptation to waste time. I do not Net-surf and I do not enter any mailing lists or chat rooms. If such behavior contributes to the well-being of others, I don't criticize it. But, I'm sorry, I don't have time for it. Pray thee hold me excused. The Carnegie Mellon research project which found that loneliness increases with use of the Net does not surprise me. Humans are not cyborgs.

That being said, I decided in the summer of 1995 to set up a Web page for my fiction. I mentioned this at an outdoor supper in hot Washington D.C., at the ASA meeting to my friend and colleague Terry Sullivan, now a vice president at the University of Texas.

"Greels," she said, "you gotta put a two-paragraph homily for every Sunday of the year, one for background and the other for a story."

That seemed like a good idea. One more windmill. Like I had nothing else to do. I persuaded my sister to do one a month and I did the rest. We are now getting fourteen hundred hits a day on the site, some indeed for novels and articles and columns, but most for the homilies. I still can't quite believe it. Who uses our homilies? Clergy (Catholic and Protestant) and laity (Protestant and Catholic). I suspect that on any given Sunday more people hear one of my (or Mary Jule's) stories than have heard me in all the sermons I've given in all my life as a priest (www.agreeley.com, if you're interested).

We get feedback on the homilies, most very positive. Though there are some goofy notes—like why don't we cross-reference the homilies (why?) or organize them according to the liturgical year (we do!) or why are my stories so cynical ("ironic" is the word I would use, like the parables of Jesus). Generally I remind the complainers that the service is free.

I also put my E-mail address (agreel@aol.com) on my columns and my books to give readers a chance for feedback. Now I get between thirty and sixty E-mail messages a day, which I don't need. Some of them are from colleagues, some from family, a few about my column (about even between those who agree and those who disagree—the latter if they are conservatives in letters filled with hatred).[137] Many are from readers of the books, almost all of whom understand the religious message of God's forgiving love. I bind those up every year and send them off to various people, including the cardinal, in his case so he will have

---

[137] Is it a mortal sin to be a conservative Republican, especially if hate goes with it? Oh, I think so, but the people are generally excused from grave guilt because they are not responsible for what they feel, say, and do.

records of the reaction to my stories, should Cardinal Ratzinger ever think that emphasis on God's love is dangerous.

The only negative comment I can remember in recent months was from a woman who complained that the married lovers in *Contract with an Angel* made love too much. She missed the point that this was their second honeymoon. Anyway, from my perspective as an outsider, how can there be too much sex? Isn't the problem in so many marriages not enough?

There are also occasional complaints that I am leaving out certain groups—why no wives of married deacons, why no gays or lesbians (there are), why only blondes and no redheads or brunettes (huh?), why no overweight women?

Fiction is not about affirmative action, folks.

The letters from overweight women are especially poignant. I hear their cri de coeur. But I don't think such matters are appropriate for a storyteller. (Susan Howatch's heroine in her most recent novel is overweight at the beginning but loses weight in the course of the story. I don't think that would help the woman who writes to me that she's overweight and proud of it.) I do not understand why women hate women who are beautiful. Rather I do understand it, but I think it is terrible. But to hate fictional women because of their imaginary beauty . . .

At least half my mail comes from people who need to talk to a priest. How can I cut that off? Much of it is from people with marriage problems. Some are perfectly free to marry, but some idiot of a priest or a deacon or lay staff member has told them that they can't marry. Others need to find a priest who will help them through an internal forum solution. Yet others need an explanation of what an annulment is (not easy because the contract approach to marriage squeezed out sacramental understanding for those raised in the Confident Church). I do what I can for all those who want to become part of my E-mail parish, though I'm not sure how much help that is. I urge them to find a sympathetic local priest. Many say there aren't any.

The most difficult to answer are from those whose spouse or future spouse is not Catholic and have been told that they must still have a prior marriage annulled. How can the Church demand that of someone who is not Catholic? You figure out how to answer that one!

My personal (not doctrinal!) opinion is that the request of the German bishops to permit sacramental reception to those who are in technically invalid marriages would solve a lot of problems in the annulment process, which is a complex and legalistic approach to a serious pastoral problem. But the Church isn't much into forgiveness these days.

Incidentally, the difference in the Catholic divorce rate and that of other Americans is only a couple of percentage points, so the insistence on the indissolubility of marriage does not have much impact on Catholic life—probably because it is so legalistic.

My own (again personal) opinion is that a marriage becomes sacramental—a reflection of the union between Jesus and the Church, between God and Her people—only when it has become existentially indissoluble. Sacramental because indissoluble, not indissoluble because sacramental. But what do I know!

Anyway, it would seem that in that country called www I have found an E-mail parish as well as a mailbox parish (as my newsletter to readers is called—it's on the Web site too).

I find myself wondering how I got into all this extra work.

VI

The Search for an Explanation

Most Catholics, our data show, like the Confusing Church more. Some, however, especially the ideological conservatives, detest it. They blame the Second Vatican Council for destroying the Confident Church and weakening the traditional strengths of the Catholic heritage (about which they often seem to know precious little). Many Church leaders also blame the council and have tried for thirty years (unsuccessfully) to turn back the clock to the Church in which they had far more power to control people's lives than they do today.

What happened? And how has the Catholic heritage survived? In the next two chapters I will try to draw together my research and my personal experiences to explain both what happened in the years immediately after the Second Vatican Council and where the strengths of Catholicism are to be found today.

At a minimum, the Confident Church might well seem in retrospect to have been monumentally overconfident. If it could be swept away so quickly, it must have been built on very shaky foundations.

The End of the Confident Church

On a summer vacation in Lake Geneva back in the 1950s, a classmate and I engaged in an (inappropriately) fierce argument about the reason for being a priest. He argued that he had become a priest to save his immortal soul. I argued that one should become a priest to reveal more clearly God's love. The argument was never resolved. Move the clock up several decades. This same priest, now a successful and popular pastor of a suburban parish, announces his retirement and informs the people and the cardinal that he has been married for two years. His fulfillment as a human person, he explains, required that he marry.

Thus the Confident Church and the Confusing Church.

What happened? What happened to him? What happened to all of us? What has survived, if anything? Is the Confusing Church, for all its confusion, a better Church?

The Second Vatican Council was certainly the most important event in the life of the Catholic Church in the twentieth century. It was also the defining event in the lives of those of us who were priests before, during, and after the council. We will never forget the euphoria of the years during and immediately after the council. Then the enthusiasm disappeared to be replaced by bitterness. What happened? What went wrong? Is the Confusing Church worse than the Confident Church?

Many Church leaders think that it is. They are trying to turn back the clock to the situation as it was before the Second Vatican Council, a Church with which they felt much more comfortable and in which they would have much more power than they do now. They dislike the confusion and argue (without any data) that the laity are confused. They won't go so far as to say (on the public record) that the Second Vatican Council was a mistake. Still, they'd like to close Pope John II's open window about 90 percent. Can they do it?

Both as a priest and as a sociologist I have struggled in a search for an explanation for the last thirty years of Catholic history. It has been important for me to understand the change of confidence to confusion. Indeed, I cannot even explain to myself my own experience as a priest unless I understand what has happened. At various times I have blamed the Roman Curia which refuses to give up its old power, the mediocrity of the hierarchy, the inadequate education of the clergy and the religious which left them unprepared by the shocks the council engendered, two popes for their refusal to drastically modify the style of governance of the last century and a half.

I now understand that these explanations are inadequate. I think I now know what happened. I must use the tools, the skills, and the experiences of a professional sociologist to tease out the whole story of the council. I make no apologies for such a strategy. As a sociologist I have monitored the changes in the Church in the United States for three decades. In a memoir I must report on the conclusions that have resulted from my research. There are no simple stories which can be told about the last thirty years. As a professional sociologist I have no choice but to tell the stories in all their complexity. Those who want simple narratives should look elsewhere.

There are two major tendencies in interpretation of the Second Vatican Council. The first, which currently dominates the Vatican, is that the council was an *occurrence*, a meeting of the bishops of the world who enacted certain reforms and clarified certain doctrines. This response and clarification were necessary but they did not drastically change the nature of the Church. To find out what this occurrence meant, the "council rightly understood" of Cardinal Joseph Ratzinger, one must go to the conciliar documents. The second interpretation holds that the council was a momentous *event*, indeed one of the most dramatic and important events in the history of Catholicism, a structure-shattering event which one could almost call a revolution.

I began to ponder this debate after a conversation with a senior American prelate. He had remarked that the American bishops had made serious mistakes in their implementation of the council, but that they could not be blamed because they never had to implement a council before. I agreed, though I thought to myself I probably meant something different than he did. While I can't be sure because we didn't pursue the subject, I thought he might have meant that they should have proceeded more slowly and cautiously while I meant that they should not have tried to make so many changes in the Church while asserting all along that nothing was changing.[138]

Then I discovered in the work of my friend and colleague Professor William Sewell, Jr., a model of social historical analysis (see *American Journal of Sociology*, 98:1). It made me rethink the council and what it did and didn't do. The council was, in fact, *both* an occurrence and an event. It is folly to pretend that the event did not occur or that it can be undone.

---

[138]It turns out that, in fact, such was not his meaning.

To understand Catholicism today, one must recognize what has happened and work from there. I must note here that I wrote some time ago that with or without the council, the same changes would have occurred. Looking back on that statement, I must admit that it was not the most intelligent sentence I ever put on paper. No one knows what would have happened. But the fact is that there was a council (in Catholic doctrine presumably inspired by the Holy Spirit) and the Church did go through enormous change. One must therefore strive to describe what happened.

Sewell, who has a joint appointment at the University of Chicago in both history and political science, is concerned with structures and events, patterns of behavior and historical shifts which drastically reshape those patterns. He does not believe in "social laws," inexorable historical processes which direct the progress of human events. He writes:

> Sociology's epic quest for social laws is illusory, whether the search is for timeless truths about all societies, ineluctable trends of more limited historical epochs, or inductively derived laws of certain classes of social phenomena. Social processes are inherently contingent, discontinuous, and open-ended.

Sewell thus rejects the historical models of Weber, Durkheim, Marx, Comte, and all the others who find inexorable trends in human events, including implicitly those who babble today about postmodernism. His description of what actually happens in the "buzzing, blooming pluralism" of the human condition may seem like common sense, but it goes against what many sociologists and most pop sociologists believe. For the purposes of this essay it also goes against the vague intellectualism of many Catholic commentators who think they can discern the secrets of history and summarize them in a couple of clear and simple paragraphs.

"Adequate eventful accounts of social process will look more like well-made stories or narratives than like laws of physics," argues Sewell. He uses what Robert Merton calls "middle-range" theories to account for contingent phenomena to determine why contingent events (about which there was no inevitability) have such important and sometimes momentous impact on the structures of human existence.

Sewell is also concerned with the "structures" of human behavior, that is, the *routine* patterns of human action. A structure, according to Sewell, is "the tendency of patterns of relationships to be reproduced even when actors engaging in the relations are unaware of the patterns or do not desire their reproduction." In contrast, an "event" is a series of historical occurrences that result in the durable transformation of structures. There are two dimensions of a structure, the *schema*—pattern it-self—and *resources*—the motivations and constraints that reinforce the schema and are in turn reinforced by it. Think of Catholics and the obligation of Sunday Mass. Sewell, who is not Catholic, gives another illustration:

> *The priest's power to consecrate the host derives from schemas oper-ating at two rather different levels. First, a priest's training has given him mastery of a wide range of explicit and implicit techniques of knowledge and self-control that enable him to perform satisfactorily as a priest. And second, he has been raised to the dignity of the priesthood by an ordination ceremony that, through the laying on of hands by a bishop, has mobilized the power of apostolic succession and thereby made him capable of an apparently miraculous feat—transforming bread and wine into the body and blood of Christ.*

Established and reinforced behavior patterns tend to be stable and durable. However, they can also change, either because of external forces or internal inconsistencies within structures themselves. A wartime defeat and devastation can savage the structures of a people, though in fact in many Western European countries after 1945, it seemed that the pat-terned and reinforced relationships were all that remained. The "fit" between resources and schemas is not so tight that inconsistencies, un-certainties, doubts, and conflicts cannot arise, more so under some sets of circumstances than others. Ruptures may then occur in behavior pat-terns and motivations—a basketball team swarms off a court to protest a defeat or a referee's decision that seems unfair. Such rupture events be-come historical events when they "touch off a chain of occurrences that durably transforms previous structures and practices."

To paraphrase and rearrange Sewell's argument, even the accumula-tion of incremental changes often results in a buildup of pressures and a dramatic crisis of existing practices, rather than a gradual transition from one state of affairs to another. Lumpiness, rather than smoothness, is the normal texture of historical temporality. And while the events are some-times the culmination of processes long under way, they typically do more than simply carry out a rearrangement of practices made necessary by gradual and cumulative social change. Historical events tend to trans-form social relations in ways that could not be fully predicted from the gradual changes that may have made them possible. What makes histor-ical events so important is that they reshape history by imparting an unforeseen direction to social development.

Events, then, should be conceived of as sequences of occurrences that result in the transformation(s) of structures. Such sequences begin with a rupture of some kind—that is, a surprising break with routine practice. But whatever the nature of the initial rupture, an occurrence only becomes a historical event when it touches off a chain of occurrences that durably transforms previous structures and practices.

Sewell's example of such a structure-shattering event is the storming of the Bastille in Paris in July 1789. Paris was on the edge that summer. The Crown had run out of money. The Estates General had convened and proclaimed itself the National Assembly; King Louis XVI dismissed the liberal minister Necker, surrounded Paris with troops, and seemed ready to suppress the National Assembly. Underlying the growing tensions between the king and his supporters and the Enlightenment-influenced National Assembly was a sharp division on the nature of sovereignty. Prospects for the harvest seemed poor. Pamphlets and newspapers were flooding Paris with incendiary articles. Mobs ransacked the city.

On the morning of July 14, representatives of this government and a mob went to the Hotel des Invalides to demand the arms that were stored there so that they could create a militia to defend the city against a possible attack by royal troops. They seized more than thirty thousand muskets and then moved to the Bastille to find gunpowder. After a bitter fight in which more than a hundred of the attackers were killed, they captured the fort, released the seven prisoners (forgers and madmen), killed two government officials, and paraded their heads around Paris on pikes.

There had been urban riots in Paris before and the battle for the Bastille was not a militarily important one, but within three days the king recalled Necker, removed the troops around Paris, and came to Paris to submit, in effect, to the wishes of the National Assembly.

At first the Assembly condemned the violence at the Bastille and indeed all political violence. But within two weeks, Sewell writes, they had changed their mind:

> In the excitement, terror, and elation that characterized the taking of the Bastille, orators, journalists and the crowd itself seized on the political theory of popular sovereignty to explain to justify the popular violence. This act of epoch-making cultural creativity occurred in a moment of ecstatic discovery: the taking of the Bastille, which had begun as an act of defense against the king's aggression, revealed itself in the days that followed as a concrete, unmediated, and sublime instance of the people expressing its sovereign will. What happened at the Bastille became the establishing act of revolution in the modern

*sense. By their action at the Bastille, the people were understood to
have risen up, destroyed tyranny, and established liberty.*

Within a month other structure-shattering events followed: the abolition of feudal exactions, provincial and municipal privileges, exclusive
hunting rights, venality of office, tithes, and the confiscation and eventual
sale of the vast properties of the Church. The storming of the Bastille,
now a culturally defined event, led to the utter transformation of the
structures of French society in an outburst of exuberant creativity. The
Old Regime would linger on at least till 1830 in one fashion or another.
But the New Regime had in fact replaced it.

Would the political and social development of the (then) largest and
most powerful country of Europe have been different if that event had
not occurred? Did there have to be a revolution and then the bloody
wars which lasted till 1815? Was the development on balance good or
bad? Might a more peaceful evolutionary transformation of power have
been less traumatic for France? There are many different answers to such
questions, and indeed the politics of France for two centuries have been,
in part, a battle between those who accept the revolution and those who
in some sense do not. But the important point in Sewell's analysis is that
the storming of the Bastille, once interpreted as a revolutionary, momentous event, shattered and eventually replaced the social, political, and
religious structures of France.

As I read Bill's papers on the deck at Grand Beach on a sunny late
spring afternoon, I saw suddenly the implications of his theory and analyses for my concern to account for the context of my last thirty years in
the priesthood. It was an insight, an illumination, a burst of understanding. That was precisely what had happened. Some of the "structures"
which had shaped the life of the Church and the religious affiliation of
the Catholic people for a century and a half (at least) had been swept
away by the council fathers, perhaps intentionally, perhaps not. Or, more
precisely, they intended the changes, but they did not realize the "latent
consequences" of the changes. If they had, would their votes have
changed?

It is the nature of latent consequences that they cannot be foreseen.
My guess is that the votes of some of the council fathers would have
changed if they had a vision of the Confusing Church thirty years later.
Still, I think the atmosphere of the council was such that the changes
would still have received a majority of votes.

To pursue my sociological analysis, I now propose to apply Sewell's
model to Vatican II, and to argue that while the council's various documents, either singly or taken together, are not of themselves the cause

of the shattering of structures in the Catholic Church, the council, as (irrevocably) interpreted, was, in addition to and beyond its decisions, a historical *event* of enormous importance for the Church, perhaps the most momentous in its history.

Catholic historians and theologians like Joseph Komonchak, whom I follow in this chapter, have for many years argued that the shape of the Church we inherited in the middle of the present century—the "structures" in Sewell's terminology—were formed by the French Revolution. Contrary to the "secularist" sociologists, the rigid patterns of Church-State relations survived the Reformation. Philip Gorski, for example, points out that the state churches, whether Catholic or Protestant, dominated life in the various countries, just as Catholicism had during the Middle Ages. This meant a very tight connection between religious and civil life—religious unity was taken to be the foundation of political unity. Hence there would be discrimination and intolerance against other religious, canon law was to be decisive for civil law, the Church had a monopoly on education and welfare, "the secular arm" supported the Church. The faithful would be pressured to fulfill their religious duties. Generally this connection was as true in Protestant countries as in Catholic countries.

The French Revolution either swept away or endangered this situation. The "liberals" who came to political power after the revolution were by definition anticlerical because they saw the continuation of such links to be an obstacle. In great part the Church shaped itself to repel them.

Komonchak summarizes what happened: "For a model of its political and cultural project, the Church turned to its own history and found it, not in the state religion of the *ancien regime*, not in the Counter-Reformation but in an idealized Middle Ages. Throughout the last two centuries the offical teaching of the Church was dominated by a regret at 'Christendom lost' and an ideal of 'Christendom Regained.' The era is marked by a desire for Restoration and it is medieval Christendom, insofar as it is realized the proper relationship between the Church and civil society, whose restoration is desired."

In Pope John Paul II's nostalgia for "Catholic Europe" one sees a hint that this ideal still survives. Needless to say, the real Middle Ages as we know them from recent social history were very different from the ideal.

In the light of this model, the "modern world" of the nineteenth and twentieth centuries was evil. The Church's task was to isolate its people from it and prepare for the eventual restoration of Christendom. It did that by various strategies, emphasis on mystical spirituality which was a response to the pernicious ideologies of "liberalism" (devotion to the

Sacred Heart and to Christ the King, both of which were medieval in tone if not in origin), development of separate Catholic organizations (doctors, lawyers, even sociologists), centralization of authority in Rome (in 1870 the pope claimed the right to appoint some seventy bishops, now he claims the right to appoint all of them), and absolute control of Catholic intellectual life. All attempts and movements for internal reform in the Church were rigidly repressed. Finally the Church redoubled its efforts to control the sexual behavior of its laity.

The strategy worked better in some countries than in others, though not very well in any. Nonetheless, until the beginning of the Second World War it prevailed. Whether this was an appropriate reaction to the French Revolution may be open to debate. Moreover, its continuation into the twentieth century was even less successful. The Church had in effect cut itself off from the modern world and was not about to change its mind on the subject—hence the importance of the document *Gaudium et Spes* of the Second Council which signaled that the Church was about to change its mind on the modern world, a document in whose development Cardinal Wojtyla was deeply involved.

Nonetheless, the Church that turned its back on contemporary culture (something Catholicism had never done before in its history) was the one into which most of the top leadership were born and for which they still have some, perhaps not altogether conscious, affection. Certainly the behavior of Cardinal Ratzinger of the Holy Office in recent years suggests that he would like to restore as much of the culture of the "Christendom restored" model as he could. Moreover, Pope John Paul II in his later years certainly seems bitterly opposed to modernity.

How did this model affect American Catholicism, the culture and the structure of the Confident Church? American Catholics were immigrants in a hostile society. Moreover, their religious patterns were shaped by the Irish experience of being on the defense against the "liberalism" of Great Britain.

I will consider four structures of twentieth-century Catholicism which shaped the Catholic institution in the United States: the centralization of power in the Vatican; the post-Tridentine understanding of sin; the conviction that Catholicism had the answer and the only answer to all human problems, and the immutability of the Church. Prior to Vatican II, it was assumed that decision making flowed downward, and that those who disagreed with any higher Church leaders or the pope were no longer Catholic. It was further assumed that the primary goal for a good Catholic was the salvation of his or her soul, a goal that could be attained by avoiding sins or, once committed, by confessing them in species and number. It was taken for granted that the Church had the answers to all human problems and could learn nothing from the modern world. It was finally assumed that the Church could not change, had not changed, and would never change. These "schemas," reinforced by such "resources" as theories of the divine origin of the Church and papal infallibility, set the parameters of Catholicism inside the worldviews of the Counter-Reformation, the centralization of papal power at the First Vatican Council, and the condemnation of "modernism" at the beginning of the twentieth century.

It might have been true that pluralistic decisions about power had been characteristic of the Church for many centuries (for example, the internal governance of some religious orders). It might have been true that in its long history the Catholic Church had often changed (most recently on such issues as slavery and coeducation). It might have been true that at one time the Church rejoiced in learning from the Greek philosophers—as reported by Arab writers. It might have been true that one ceases to be a Catholic not when one disagrees with the pope but only when one is excommunicated or joins another church or formally and explicitly renounces the faith. It might finally have been true that the central truth of Christianity was God's forgiving love which Christians were to imitate. Nonetheless, in the minds of most of the laity and the clergy and those who were not Catholic, Catholicism before Vatican II was in fact a centralized, immutable, overconfident, and sin-obsessed heritage. Most of the bishops who attended the council came to Rome accepting those assumptions.

On the surface, the Catholic Church in 1962 was not nearly as "edgy" as the populace of Paris in 1789, although patently the "restoration of Christendom" model was less and less relevant to the American Catholic population which had caught up with the rest of the country in both education and income. Yet Pope Pius XII, the predecessor of Pope John XXIII who would convene the council, had instigated changes during his long administration that might, in retrospect, seem seditious. He approved changes in the liturgy of Holy Week, the modern critical study of the Bible, and, in effect, birth control, by accepting the rhythm method. A new emphasis on the Mystical Body of Christ, the teaching that the laity, as well as the pope and the bishops, was in some fashion the Church, suggested to small groups of laity that perhaps the Church ought to listen to them. Scholars, digging into the liturgical, theological, and organizational history of the Church, found a much more variegated Catholicism than the existing official structure of immutable centralization. Bishops, however, conservative, did not like the heavy-handed behavior of the curial dicasteries. An increasingly well-educated Catholic laity was uneasy with the rigidity of the Church. Married people found the birth control teaching difficult (a teaching which became a matter of heavy emphasis only after 1930). Parish priests were growing uneasy with the apparent insensitivity of the Church to the problems of the laity, and the "Catholic Action" movements were producing cadres of well-informed, dedicated laypeople. Finally, the disaster of World War II and the surprising rebirth of Europe following the war created an atmosphere in which many Catholics felt that some modifications in the Church's various stances might be appropriate. None of these events, either separately or in combination, seemed then to have constituted a "pre-revolutionary" situation. In retrospect, they can be seen as the raw material for drastic change; in Sewell's terms, the resources for new structures.

Nonetheless, there were signs of "slippage." By 1963, half of the Catholics in American did not think birth control was always wrong, and studies showed that most American Catholic women practiced some kind of contraception before the end of their fertility period. Still, many, if not most, probably confessed birth control. By 1974, the proportion accepting the teaching had sunk to 12 percent, and most did not confess it. Moreover, the Catholic hierarchy in the United States was already bringing pressure on Rome to obtain some sort of relief for divorced and remarried Catholics, this despite the official posture that the Catholic Church could not change its teachings on marriage. The impression of many who were at the council was that if Paul VI had permitted the birth control issue to come to a vote, the majority would have favored change. Only in retrospect, however, do these phenomena suggest that there was serious ferment in Catholicism in the United States or anywhere else when Pope John convened the council.

The council's preparatory commissions, dominated by the Roman Curia, had prepared draft documents for the first session of the council which would have turned it into a rubber stamp for the then existing ecclesiastical structures. Most bishops, it would seem, were prepared to vote for them and go home, still able to tell their people what they (in the bishops' minds) wanted to hear: nothing had changed.

The occurrence which played a role something like the storming of the Bastille was the sudden opposition of two leaders of the Western European Church, Cardinal Joseph Frings of Cologne and Cardinal Achille Liénart of Lille. Elderly men with enormous personal prestige who had suffered through the war, they demanded that the preparatory documents be scrapped and that the council fathers themselves shape the documents on which they would vote. The pope agreed. It was clear then to at least some of the bishops that it would be their council, not the Roman Curia's. The bishops, it turned out, had power in practice as well as in theory. The Vatican bureaucracy could be defied. There was indeed a pluralism of power in the Catholic Church.

This was a dangerous truth, as subsequent events would demonstrate. Very few Catholics, lay or clerical, realized what had happened. As the council went on, the bishops by overwhelming votes endorsed a broad range of changes into the Church. Joseph Komonchak has noted three overarching changes: the council proposed a far more nuanced evaluation of the modern world; it introduced the necessity of updating and reform into the Church; and it called for greater responsibility in the local churches. The press reported, with increasing fascination and exuberance, the alteration of the unalterable.

I note six crucial changes that transformed the structures of the preconciliar Church:

The Liturgy. On Septuagesima Sunday 1965, almost every altar in a Catholic church in the United States was turned around. For the first time in at least a thousand years, the priest said Mass facing the congregation and partially (soon totally) in English. If the Latin liturgy could be abandoned that easily after more than a millennium (and seven-eighths of American Catholics approved of the change), the Catholic Church could certainly change.

Religious Freedom. The "American Issue" at the council was a defense of Americans' freedom of religion. The document *Dignitatis Humanae*, drafted by the Jesuit John Courtney Murray (whom the Vatican had silenced only a few years before), was in many ways the most revolutionary of all the documents. One hundred one years to the day after Pope Pius IX in his encyclical *Quanta Cura* had taught that freedom of religion was "madness," the fathers of the council by overwhelming majority endorsed this "madness." Even Murray's long-time implacable enemy Cardinal Alfredo Ottoviani voted for *Dignitatis Humanae.* Who ever said that the Church could not change its mind and its teaching, even reverse an encyclical if it wanted to?

Ecumenism. The council was now willing to admit that Protestant denominations were indeed churches and that Catholics should strive for mutual understanding with them in friendly dialogue. The heretics, schismatics, Jews, and infidels down the street were now suddenly separated brothers and sisters. Overnight, Catholicism was willing to change when it wanted to.

Meat on Friday. This change resulted from a decision of the American bishops. It may have been the most unnecessary and the most devastating. Fish on Friday had been a symbol that most visibly distinguished American Catholics from other Americans.

Bishops continued to insist that nothing had *really* changed. None of these reforms touched on the essence of Catholic doctrine. But such distinctions were lost on the laity (and on many of the clergy too). The immutable had mutated, what would change next?

The centralization of authority was not yet in jeopardy, however. Change did not in itself mean that ordinary priests or laypersons could make their own decisions about the conditions on which they would be Catholic. Yet implicit in the newly discovered mutability of the Church (and in the bishops' revolt against the Curia) was the notion that if something *ought* to be changed and it *would* be changed eventually, then it was all right to anticipate such decisions and change on one's own authority. The gradual drift in this direction in the late 1960s put the centralized authority structure in grave jeopardy.

Could the bishops have been more cautious in implementing the council? They might have left Friday abstinence alone, but liturgical reform and ecumenism by themselves would have created a heady atmosphere in which the expectation (often eager) of more change would have swept the Church. Two further developments, however, called the authority structure of the Church into question.

Birth Control. In an attempt to preserve the authority structure of the Church, Pope Paul VI in fact weakened and eventually came close to destroying the credibility of the Church's sexual ethic when he rejected the recommendation of his own birth control commission. There was strong sentiment among the bishops at the council to address the question, but Pope Paul VI, not trusting his fellow bishops with the issue, removed it from conciliar debate. Still, he had a special commission to report to him on the subject, the existence of which became common knowledge. Laity and clergy alike assumed that if change was possible, it would occur, especially after learning that the commission had recommended change almost unanimously.

When the pope turned down the recommendations, the "lower orders" of the Church had already made up their minds. In terms of protecting the authority structure of the Church, it would have been better for the pope never to have established the commission, to have followed its recommendation, or to have left the matter alone. In the confusion, disappointment, and anger that followed Paul VI's *Humanae Vitae* (1968), laity and clergy embraced the principle of "follow your own conscience." It was this development, more than any other, that shattered the authority structure. (It is often argued that priests and laypeople cannot make such decisions for themselves. Perhaps they cannot, but in fact they do. It is further argued that they cannot be good Catholics if they make such decisions, but in fact they think they can. This is what happens when a historical event shatters a behavior pattern and the resources that support it.)

In the late 1960s and early 1970s, every age segment in Catholic America changed its convictions about the legitimacy of birth control, and, more ominously, about the *right* of the Church to lay down rules for sexual behavior. Authority was no longer centralized; it had become pluralistic. Similarly, acceptance of papal infallibility fell to 22 percent of Catholics in the United States. Catholic laity, with the support of the lower clergy, had decided that it was not wrong to be Catholic on their own terms. Such was the fruit of the Second Vatican Council, not as a series of documents, but as a phenomenon which transformed the behavior patterns of Catholics with regard to their Church. Catholics who decided that contraception was not wrong justified that decision by appealing from a pope who did not understand to a God who did. The point is not whether such a justification was proper, but that it helped to erode the "sin concern" structure of preconciliar Catholicism.

Priests and Nuns. A fourth critical change in the structures of the preconciliar Church was the dispensation of priests to leave the priesthood and enter ecclesiastically valid marriages, often with former nuns. This development confirmed not only the possibility of change, but the willingness of Church authorities to back down in the face of pressure.

In effect, the "lower orders" asked the following questions: If the Church could permit men who had left the priesthood to marry, why could it not permit them to marry while still active in the priesthood? If it could change the playing field on liturgy, ecumenism, and Friday abstinence, why not on birth control and the role of women in the Church? If so many "mortal" sins were no longer sinful, was it necessary to worry so much about sin? There are complex theological replies to these questions, but they don't seem credible to many Catholics who conclude, unfairly perhaps, that the Church can change whatever it wants, if only it wants to.

Currently, a large majority of both priests and laypeople reject the Church's official teachings on the ordination of women, birth control, premarital sex, *in utero* and *in vitro* fertilization, oral sex, and the legality of abortion under some circumstances. There is also strong movement in the direction of tolerance for homosexuality. Moreover, media surveys indicate that the laity believe that they can "disagree" with the pope on these issues and remain good Catholics. Central authority has lost its credibility (and on social issues like immigration too). Thus the vigorous efforts of John Paul II to impose his teaching about the ordination of women seem to have had little effect on the attitudes of either lower clergy or laity. The structures of assent, the patterns of motivation and behavior which would have worked smoothly thirty years ago in response to such papal rulings, are simply no longer available. Catholics believe that the Church can change and that they can disregard the pope when it comes to making decisions, especially about sex and gender. Many American Catholics diminish whatever dissonance they may feel by cheering the pope when he comes to this country but ignoring what he says.

The atmosphere of the Church in America turned sour by 1970. It has remained sour ever since. Men and women left the religious life in ever increasing numbers.[139] Church attendance declined. Contributions fell drastically. Laity and clergy stopped obeying Church laws.[140] People went to Confession much less often.[141] Priests and bishops took unto themselves lovers of either and on occasion both genders.[142] Half-baked ideologies flourished. Women celebrated the Eucharist. So did married priests and married laypeople. Political action (often of the Marxist variety) replaced the Gospel. Liberation theology, that bastard offspring of vulgar Marxism and pop Catholicism, dispatched (even the memory of) traditional Catholic social theory. Native liturgies in Africa skirted to the edges of syncretism and folk religion. Homosexuality not only became tolerable but fashionable, or so it seemed. No one seemed to respect Church authority anymore.

On the other hand, defection from the Church has not increased in the United States—among non-Latinos, it remains at 11 percent for every birth cohort in this century. Moreover, Catholic acceptance of such central truths as the existence of God, the divinity of Jesus, the resurrection of the dead, and the presence of Jesus in the Eucharist (however explained) has not changed. The majority of American Catholics still attend the Eucharist at least once a month and there has been no decline in attendance across birth cohorts since the middle 1970s.

Is a restoration possible? At one time many bishops hoped that the new *Catechism* would instruct Catholics on what they had to believe and

---

[139]Richard Schoenherr of the University of Wisconsin estimates that by the time of the silver jubilee in the priesthood one out of four men will have left the active ministry. My own research both in the study for the Catholic bishops back in the early seventies and more recently in analyzing the data from the *Los Angeles Times* study suggests that about 5 percentage points of that can be attributed to celibacy—men who would have stayed in the priesthood if they could be married priests.

[140]Many priests grant de facto annulments in rectory offices, for example.

[141]But received Communion much more often.

[142]Not the first time in Catholic history that happened.

do, and lead to a restoration. Such a hope was patently naive. The twenty years of the present papal administration have been devoted to the centralization of authority and resistance to further change. All the evidence suggests that these efforts have had little impact. The old structures no longer exist and new ones are in place. Thirty-five years after the Second Vatican Council, thirty of them devoted unsuccessfully to restoration, the elimination of the structures which emerged from that historic event seems most improbable.

What is the content of the new structures, the "resources" for the new schemas, to use Sewell's term? A recent research project of Catholic identity (see "A Faith Loosely Held," *Commonweal*, July 17, 1998) indicates that Catholics under thirty are less likely to emphasize authority and sin and more likely to emphasize the presence of Christ in the sacraments, the Real Presence, concern for the poor, and devotion to Mary the Mother of God—a thoroughly Catholic identity if very different from the preconciliar identity.

Can Catholicism live with these new structures? Should it? To the first question it must be said that it has often in the past lived with very similar structures, indeed for much of its history. To the second I must reply that that is beyond my skills as a sociologist to judge. However, the new structures are not likely to go away. Purely from the viewpoint of a sociologist, I would suggest that perhaps the time ahead might well be a period of reconsideration and readjustment to what has become the reality of the structures of contemporary Catholicism.

Did the Second Vatican Council, considered as a historic event, destroy the Church? If the question is rephrased to mean did the council destroy some of the major structures of the Confident Church, the answer must be that it did. Whether that is good or bad or a mixture of good and bad, readers must judge for themselves.

Could the American bishops, if they were more adroit, more credible as pastors, and possessed better theological resources and media skills, have directed the process more wisely? Perhaps, but in the long run, it probably would not have made much difference. It is self-deceiving to argue with Cardinal Ratzinger that there is nothing in the actual documents of Vatican II to legitimatize the collapse of the old structures. For the documents themselves—those on liturgy, Scripture, religious freedom, the modern world, other faiths, the Jews, ecumenism—contributed substantially to the weakening of preexisting structures.

I conclude that after the interventions by Fringes and Liénart and their acceptance by John XXIII, there was no way to prevent Vatican II from becoming a revolutionary event. Sociology, to repeat, has no means of measuring whether what the council fathers proposed was wise as well as well intentioned, or whether the consequences are, in the main, to be welcomed or condemned. Speaking not from within any academic discipline, but simply as a Catholic, I believe the Spirit was at work within the council on that day, and remains on call. Speaking as a priest who has lived through these traumatic times, I rejoice in the Confusing Church. Whatever the losses (and they have been dramatic and often tragic), the laity act as mature adults and those wise in the use of authority listen to what they say. The Church perforce listens to the modern world, dialogues with it, and learns from the dialogue. Once again, Catholics understand that, as St. Therese wrote, "God is nothing but mercy and love." All of these changes strike me as being from God.

Among the shifts that should take place, it seems to me after living through the turbulence of the last fifty years, is the belief that the pope and the bishops are sacred persons. Consider the foundational literature of a certain religious tradition. It presents a brutally harsh picture of the early leaders of the tradition. They are depicted as stupid, hard-hearted, self-righteous, loudmouthed, ambitious, envious poltroons. Why would those who wrote about the early days of a religious heritage be so unmerciful in their denunciations of the leaders of the previous generation? Perhaps they were wary of religious leadership which was permitted to define itself as sacred. Perhaps they saw all too clearly that it was a sacred leadership which had put to death their founder.

In case someone has missed the point, I have the four evangelists in mind. They established early in the game that the leadership of the Church ought to be subject to constant criticism. Obviously the leadership of the Catholic Church has improved enormously since the time of Peter and his bunch. No one who wants to be accepted as a good Catholic engages in sustained criticism of pope and bishops. I suppose Catholics should be grateful that the quality of our leadership has improved so much.

On the other hand, if the quality has not improved since the apostles, then the only other reason why criticism is repressed in the Catholic Church is that unlike Peter and the rest of the first generation of leaders, Catholic leaders have become sacred persons, criticism of whom has been equated with sacrilege.

This situation probably is the result of the Catholic hierarchy taking over responsibility for civil leadership during the Dark Ages after the collapse of the Roman Empire created a dangerous political vacuum. The pope became a king, almost a surrogate emperor, and the bishops became feudal nobility. However necessary in the circumstances such a development was, it has not served the Church well in subsequent years.

Can you imagine a latter-day St. Mark, for example, bashing the pope and the bishops of the present time in the same tone that the original Mark attacked Peter and the apostles? Like Hans Küng, whose criticisms of the pope were mild in comparison with what Mark said about Peter, a St. Mark of our time would be slapped down promptly.

Peter wasn't a sacred person. The popes of the twentieth century have become sacred persons. Is this an improvement?

I think not. Criticism is a good thing in any institution and of any leader. No one likes to be criticized, especially when one is the head of an institution with whose sacred goals one is constrained to identify one's own person. Criticism forces one to listen, it provides a channel for upward communication, it provides for a free flow of emotions and ideas. Some criticism is nonsense, but some of it is very wise. The smart leader is the one who knows how to distinguish between the two.

Do I think that the pope should be subject to the same level of criticism as the American president? The bishops to the same level as members of Congress? Let us say rather I think they should be subject to the same kind of criticism that St. Mark aimed at men whom they claim as predecessors. The Church would be a much healthier condition if its leaders existed in the same ambience of criticism that Peter and his colleagues had to face in their own day.

But doesn't the pope have special guidance from the Holy Spirit? Is not criticism of him criticism of the Spirit? Every leader has special guidance (including the president). Even if the pope's is qualitatively different, it does not follow that popes have not made terrible mistakes in the history of the Church, mistakes which might have been avoided if there was free flow of criticism.

Sacred persons don't admit mistakes. The early Church did not trust sacred persons and with good reason. In the future the Church will need popes who do not take themselves seriously as sacred persons. Men like Peter the Fisherman, a fisherman who was a married man and who spent much of his life apologizing for his mistakes. Having learned from his wife the need to apologize he was perhaps prepared to apologize to the Lord and everyone else.

I'm not advocating that popes should be married men.[143] Only that they should learn from someone to say that they made a mistake.

Authoritarianism, centralization, an unwillingness or an inability to listen, the concept of a sacred person, a propensity to take the word of

---

[143]In principle there is no reason why a married man could not be elected pope. It might be in interesting innovation. Many widowers have become popes. Many more popes had mistresses before they were elected, and in some cases after they were elected.

spies, perceptions shaped by a garrison mentality, distrust of Western culture (and particularly a dislike of the United States), a conviction that orders from on high will change people's behavior (especially when it is sexual behavior)—these have been, alas, the hallmarks of a papacy led by a brilliant and gifted and holy man who made some major errors in judgment from which the Church will need a long time to recover.

For those of us whose early lives in the priesthood were shaped by the hope of the Vatican Council, these have been harsh and difficult years. Many feel that they have lost, that all they stood for and hoped in has been destroyed. I am convinced that the energies released by the council, damned up and soured as they might now be, cannot be restrained permanently. Eventually there will come a pope who will see the need to release them. Whether any of my generation will live to see that happy event is problematic. But it will happen.

The Vatican has lost its credibility (though the papacy is still honored); the hierarchy is trapped in a Janus-faced condition since it must try to please both the lower clergy and the laity and the Vatican, the clergy do not try very hard to respond to the laity's demand for good preaching and good liturgy and sensitive counseling and respect for women. The laity are profoundly angry at the insensitivity of the Church from the pope on down to their pastor. Is the Catholic Church therefore in crisis, the TV anchorperson demands?

On the contrary, I reply. At the level of the parish—where it really counts—the Church is in excellent condition precisely for the reasons I discussed in a previous chapter. The laypeople won't leave no matter how hard the Vatican and the hierarchy and we clergy try to drive them out. They stay because they like being Catholic and they like being Catholic because they like the stories.

Take a typical American urban or suburban parish. Appoint as pastor a man who is reasonably open, reasonably secure, reasonably sensitive. Add a modest amount of administrative skill and talent at preaching and liturgy, a moderate delight in children and teenagers, and perceptive respect for women, and you will have a generous, charitable, dedicated Christian community the like of which the world has never known.

You're sick and you want to receive the Eucharist. It won't come every month or every week but every day. Tragedy hit your family? The parish's Committee on Caring is right there to help. An inner-city parish in need? There's a committee for that too. And for a special collection or an item in the parish budget. Alienated Catholics want to return? There's people to help them. Help needed in the Appalachians? A team of teenagers goes off to the mountains for a month in the summer. In such a parish the parking lot is filled with cars every night of the week.

It is a neighborhood parish from the immigrant-era reborn with even more vitality, more resources, more energy, and perhaps even more wisdom than the parish in the old neighborhoods. In such places—and there are many though not nearly enough—Catholicism in the United States is alive and well.

And even in parishes where there is not a priest like the one I have described (and it remains good questions why all priests are not of that sort and why those who are not are ever named pastors), the laypeople continue to receive the sacraments and continue to listen for the stories which are at the center of their faith and wait patiently for a new pastor or a new associate, just as they will tell you they are waiting patiently for a new pope.

Or they simply pull up religious stakes and migrate to another parish where their modest standards for an effective pastor are met.

Many of the problems in the Confusing Church would be resolved if the principle *ecclesia semper reformanda* was applied to the papacy. The pope—any, pope—is utterly cut off from the laity by the present structure and ideology that surrounds him. He is deprived of the information he needs to understand the context and the impact (or lack of impact) of his decisions.

Catholic fundamentalists cannot accept the need ever to reform the papacy. The pope is the successor of Peter. He is selected by the Holy Spirit. When he speaks God speaks through him. Such simple faith may be impressive but it won't stand the test of any serious consideration of the history of the papacy.

For example, from 904 to 1048 Rome and the papacy were dominated by five generations of the Theophylact family. The gates of hell did not quite prevail against the Church. But it was, as Wellington remarked of Waterloo, a "damn near thing." One cannot reflect theologically on the papacy and not face this century and a half of history. It presents acute problems for those who argue that the Holy Spirit chooses each pope deliberately and that the pope is immediately and intimately connected to Jesus for whom he speaks.

The Theophylacts were killers of popes, bribers of popes, sons of popes, mistresses of popes, mothers of popes. Five of them were popes, none of them prizes, and three of them—John XI, John XII, and Benedict IX—made Alexander VI, Rodrigo Borgia, look like a saint. Installed in their teens or early twenties, they were given to gambling, drinking, adultery, rape, and murder. They plundered the papal treasury and pilgrims who came to Rome. The Lateran Palace where they lived was reported to have become a brothel. They were alleged to have raped women pilgrims in St. Peter's. John XI is supposed to have died during an act of adultery. John XII was murdered, it is said, by an angry husband who caught him in adultery. Benedict IX sold the papacy to a man who wanted to succeed him.

The most deadly members of the family were the matriarch Theodora and her daughter Marozia, who ran both civil and ecclesiastical Rome for the first third of the tenth century. The former was the mistress of John X, whom she installed as pope, only later to decree his death. The latter was the mistress of Pope Sergius III (at the age of fifteen) and the mother of John XI (of whom Pope Sergius was the father). In tandem these two women dominated papal appointments for thirty years, naming popes, deposing them, and ordering their deaths. Marozia was called the senatrix of Rome from 931 to 936 while her son reigned as pope. Then another son Alberic overthrew and imprisoned her and treated his brother the pope like a slave. Nonetheless, Alberic and his sons (one of whom became John XII, a man as bad as his uncle John XI) and grandsons ran Rome for another hundred years with the same iron hands as their maternal ancestors, until the Emperor Conrad deposed Benedict IX, the great-great-grandson of Theodora and the great-grandson of Marozia, and reform finally came to Rome. The power to name the bishop of Rome was taken away from the priests, nobles, and people of Rome and given to the cardinals, a reform that was unquestionably necessary at the time.

These were dark times in Europe. The Danes were raiding northern Europe; the Saracens had invaded southern Italy and sacked Rome. Rome was a lawless jungle. The German emperors tried repeatedly to impose reform on the city, but the Roman populace, mostly an unruly mob, just as repeatedly revolted. The streets of Rome were dangerous both by day and night. Power came from the tips of swords and spears. Anyone of prominence rose to power by the use of private armies and stayed in power through the strength of the same armies. The Theophylacts were no more murderous or corrupt or vicious or rapacious than any of the other nobles who lived in this jungle. They were only more successful. Given the times, the remarkable fact is that the papacy survived and that visitors like Otto I and England's King Canute had enormous reverence for the office of the pope.

One can certainly argue with some reason that the Holy Spirit preserved the papacy through these terrible times, no small achievement. But to see God doing much else during the reign of the Theophylacts is an insult to the deity.

The promise of Jesus is not that there will be great popes all the time, not that popes will necessarily be good men, not that they will be the best available choice for the office, not that they will speak for the Holy Spirit every time they say something, not that they will always reflect the wishes of God, but only that they will not destroy the Church. That promise has been kept, if only just barely on occasion. The Theophylacts did not destroy the papacy or the Church, but they sure gave it a try.

It is hard to see how the image of the papacy would suffer if the pope (a) would return to the local churches the nomination of bishops, power that the local churches had till the beginning of the present century; (b) governed ordinarily together with the synod of bishops (to which the Curia would be subject), as Leo the Great governed together with the priests and people of Rome; (c) delegated power to national conferences of bishops as was the practice perforce in earlier days because of problems of transportation and communication (Gregory the Great could lay down only general principles for Augustine of Canterbury); or (d) adopted the reform which Paul VI considered for papal elections in which the presidents of the national conferences would vote as well as cardinals—or perhaps appoint presidents as temporary cardinals.

Only the last reform would be novel. Given the wide variety of methods for the election of popes through the centuries it would hardly be revolutionary.

None of these reforms, either separately or together, would hurt the sacramentality of the papal office. Indeed they would enhance it considerably. Moreover, having set aside in practice absolute power, the pope would have more rather than less real power because his governance would no longer be paralyzed by the pretense of absolute power.

The Confusing Church, then, results from the specific changes that the Vatican Council introduced and the destruction of many of the old structures of the Confident Church which resulted almost inevitably from those changes. There have been losses and gains as a result of the council. In my judgment the gains outweigh the losses by far, though some of the latter are tragic. In a word, the Church could control the sexual lives of the laity as long as the structure of mortal sin morality was operative. The council weakened that structure. The Birth Control Encyclical, despite its intent to preserve that structure, wiped it out and in the process notably diminished the power of papal authority. It does not follow that the Church, from its vast store of wisdom on sexual matters, does not have important things to say on the subject, things the world needs to hear. But it needs a new style of rhetoric to say them, a new moral structure which does not depend entirely on the threat of eternal damnation.

Thus far in this chapter I have described the post-Vatican destabilization from the outside, as though I were watching it as a detached observer. In fact, however, I was on the inside. The destabilization had an enormous impact on my life.

In the first decade, perhaps even the first two decades, after the council, there was a flight from Catholicism among many priests, religious and laity. By way of an example, a certain Catholic women's college in that turbulent era announced that it was no longer Catholic but now ecumenical. The school had a wondrous history of educating the first women from ethnic families to attend college. If it was no longer Catholic, why should parents pay the tuition for a Catholic college when an education which was also not Catholic came at a much lower cost at a state school?

The sentiment was part of the era. Pastors announced that their parishes were now ecumenical. The Christian Family Movement informed its members that it was now an ecumenical organization. Priests and nuns showing up on secular campuses wanted to be "like everyone else." Although most of the women college presidents in America were nuns (and in my experience of them in my research in those days very able administrators at that), the religious communities seemed to vie with one another in a race to find lay presidents, male presidents, presidents who were not Catholic. Rules, regulations, and requirements disappeared from Catholic campuses.

Gregorian chant was replaced by guitar music from the St. Louis Jesuits. The altars, as Eamon Duffy says in a title of a book about another era, were stripped—saints, stations of the cross, crucifixes, votive candles, and private devotions disappeared. New Catholic churches didn't "look" Catholic; indeed, they often looked like Quaker meetinghouses. The baby was thrown out with the bathwater and the baby's mother too. The baby's mother, you see, was not very ecumenical.

The genius of Catholicism is that it can say "both . . . and"—both faith and reason, both marriage and celibacy, both neighborhood and foreign mission. However that genius was not operative in the decade immediately after the council. Few could say both preconciliar and postconciliar, both May crownings and liturgy, both change and continuity.

Many members of religious communities, especially the younger ones, argued for the abandonment of their old missions and the discovery of new ones. The Religious of the Sacred Heart, for example, were the best in the world at the education of middle-class young women. They retreated from that mission to serve the "poor"—whatever that meant. Although the Jesuits ran excellent high schools, many of their younger members argued that they did not want to teach adolescents and "discerned" other vocations, some, for example, deciding in unconscious irony that they were called to be clowns. The spirituality traditions of the religious orders were swept away with a wave of the hand. What did Madeline Sophie Barat or Ignatius of Loyola or Vincent de Paul know about political relevance or social concern? (There was even a Center for Concern which, in the spirit of à Kempis, seemed to believe that concern about a problem substituted for a competent understanding of its dimensions.) Prophets, true and false, rose up to pronounce new party lines. Theologians (Küng, Rahner) became folk heroes to be misunderstood, misquoted, and quoted out of context. Self-admitted atheists and agnostics taught freshmen theology. A master's degree in counseling and guidance became a license to practice therapy, a summer workshop on the Scriptures made one an expert about the subject, a couple of courses at the Notre Dame liturgy program qualified one as an accomplished liturgist.

It was the silly season, a time of shallow, angry, ideological romanticism.

Many of the changes of the years after the council were surely both desirable and long overdue. I tried to argue that in all the enthusiasm over change, there was little effort to try to understand what "Catholic" really meant. The council as a revolutionary event had destabilized the structures of certainty which had shaped the lives of American Catholics and their culture. Once it was said that the Church could change, that it didn't have the answers to every question, and that other churches and denominations had a validity of their own, then nothing was left. Catholicism seemed empty of content. If you had to find new certainties—and both individuals and institutions in that era needed new certainties immediately—then where else would one look besides to ecumenism and being "just like everyone else."

The difficulty was—though few seemed to understand—that if you (or your institution) are Catholic, you cannot, no matter how hard you try, become just like everyone else. Catholicism is different (as David Tracy would later teach us). There was no time in those harried, hectic, exhausting days to consider that possibility, much less to explore it. Patently there was nothing in the decrees or the theology of the council that supported the stripping of the altars, the banning of the baby's mother, the dismissal of Gregorian chant, or the effort to be like everyone else. It ought to have been evident from the document on ecumenism that ecumenicity involves a long and difficult effort and cannot be achieved overnight by administrative fiat. Yet no one was to blame for the romantic enthusiasms of the era. The American Church was caught by surprise. Destabilization swept it like a hurricane that the forecasters had missed. The Church in this country (and maybe everywhere) did not have the maturity, the scholarship, the depth, the poise, and the taste to cope with destabilization. So everyone ran wild. You cannot open wide the window as Pope John did without, to deliberately mix the metaphor, cracking some eggshells.

The college which became "ecumenical" by executive fiat? It no longer exists. However, it was Catholic to the end. It hired a few Protestant theologians, but it was still Catholic. It couldn't help itself, you see. "Once Catholic always Catholic" applies to institutions as well as to persons. Ethos, atmosphere, tradition, and custom are sticky qualities. "Secularization" is an inadequate detergent to clean away dense sacramentality and pervasive community. Ownership by a "secular" board does not put, for example, Notre Dame on the road to becoming as Catholic as Northwestern is Methodist or Chicago is Northern Baptist. To suggest that it does ignores both the richness of Catholicism and the profound Catholicity of Notre Dame, a veritable "Catholic theme park" as a faculty member has called it.

I was a man born out of due season during those times. The priests to whom I have dedicated this book taught me the importance of professional competence. Now concern, not competence, was important. I believed in the Catholic social theory of decentralization and cooperation. Now Liberation Theology, a mix of Catholicism and Marxism, was fashionable. I believed that the Church was for everyone, now the "preferential option" for the poor was being proclaimed. While I supported the postcounciliar changes, I did not think that the Holy Spirit had been idle in the Church before 1965. I believed in the riches of the Catholic tradition. Now the tradition was either rejected or most likely ignored. I thought that anger was understandable (I had a lot of pent-up anger myself). Many seemed to feel (and still do) that it was quite appropriate to fixate in anger.

In my columns I won no friends by pointing out that those who were doing the most for the poor were the priests and nuns and laypeople who were teaching in the inner-city Catholic schools, that clergy and religious who became involved in revolutionary movements in other countries were engaged in a form of American imperialism, and that social democracy not Marxism was in fact the movement of the day in Latin America. (More recently I have added that there is only one Latin American country which did not have a democratically elected government—their [and the pope's] friend Castro's Cuba.) I criticized the romantic fads and fashions from Sensitivity Training to Rite of Christian Initiation for Adults. I ridiculed the fussy and often campy pretensions of liturgists. I noted that many of those who embraced the "preferential option for the poor" did so with an agenda of their own which they attempted to impose on the "poor"; when the poor rejected that agenda, they went somewhere else.

Adversary: And then you're surprised that them folk don't like you!

In an age of romantic ideology which later turned angry, I was neither a romantic nor an ideologue nor particularly angry. Nor would I leave the priesthood, which had become a fashionable thing to do. I learned to stay away from lectures to priests and nuns. The atmosphere was poisonous before I began to talk. After I was finished, they would attack me not for what I had said in the lecture but for what they thought I had said in my columns (misquoted usually or quoted out of context) or what they thought I *really* believed. I have learned to stay away from such gatherings, though in the last year I have as a favor addressed two such sessions with utterly predictable results.

Sample question, from a nun:

Sister: Why do you abuse women in your novels?

Me: Which novels do you mean?

Sister: I am too busy working with the poor to read trash. Women whose opinion I value tell me you abuse your women characters.

Me: A small proportion of my women characters are victims, smaller than in the actual population. They are victimized by evil men. They survive.

Sister: Priests shouldn't write stories in which women are abused.

She doubtless thought that she was a liberal. In fact, she was an authoritarian and a reactionary. Novels must edify.

Adversary: You should have known better. Never argue about your books with someone who won't read them. Ask them to come back after they've read one.

Those were not good times. No one was to blame. We simply weren't ready for the hurricane. Nor did many of us understand why ordinary Catholics weren't leaving the Church in protest, like we were leaving the priesthood or the religious life. We didn't realize that it was because of the stories.

Why They Stay—It's the Stories!

Jack Rosenthal, the affable and sophisticated editor of *The New York Times*, was on the phone.

"Can you write us an article, maybe thirty-five hundred words, about why, despite all the conflicts in the Catholic Church, intelligent and well-educated men and women remain in the Church?"

"Sure," I said. "They like being Catholics."

"Why do they like being Catholics?"

"It's the stories."[144]

So I wrote him the article and he published it as I wrote it (with the few copy-editor changes that are part of doing business with *The New York Times*). So here, modified and extended somewhat (because I have room for more than thirty-five hundred words), is my answer to the question of why Catholics stay in the Church and then practical conclusions I draw from it for the work of the Church.

"If you don't like the Catholic Church," a woman in the *Donahue* audience, by her own admission not Catholic, screamed at me, "why don't you stop being a priest and leave the Church?"

I had been criticizing what I took to be the insensitivity of some Catholic leaders to the importance of sex for healing the frictions and the wounds of the married life and perhaps renewing married love. I was taken aback by the intensity of her anger. Why did it matter so much to her that I had offered some relatively mild criticism? Why did such criticism seem to her to demand that I decamp from Catholicism and the priesthood?

I encounter such anger frequently: if the Church is not perfect, if I disagree with some of the things it does, why don't I get out? I can never quite figure out why the demand is made that the Church alone of all institutions must be perfect for one to remain attached to it. Perhaps such people want to apply to Catholics the same standard that a certain kind

---

[144]I didn't add "stupid." A senior editor at *The New York Times* did not need to be reminded of Jim Carville's statement about what the issue was in the 1992 presidential election.

of reactionary Catholicism wishes to apply: you accept everything the pope says or you are not a good Catholic, so why don't you leave?

You don't like the way the Church treats women? Then leave the Church, don't remain inside and strive for reform. Yet if one was to withdraw from every institution which is unfair to women, one would have to retreat to a desert island.

Find a perfect church and join it, only realize that then it won't be perfect.

"Why should I leave?" was the only reply I could manage. "I like being Catholic and I like being a priest." Later I remembered the response to a similar question by my friend Hans Küng: "Why leave? Luther tried that and it didn't work!"

Yet the question persists. In its most naked form it demands to know, "How can someone who is intelligent and well educated continue to be a Roman Catholic in these times?" The question is not a new one. It has been asked by anti-Catholic nativists for one hundred and fifty years. Often the latent subtext is, "How can anyone who is intelligent and well educated believe in any religion, especially Catholicism?"

It is also usually asked by a person who has no real notion either historically or religiously what Catholicism is. The question is based on ignorance and perhaps on bigotry, the good old-fashioned anti-Catholic nativism which is as American as apple pie.

However, the question is worth a response, if only to clarify what religion is and what there is about the Catholic religion that explains its enormous appeal even to men and women who think that the pope is out of touch and that the bishops and the priests are fools.

Catholics remain Catholic because of the Catholic religious sensibility, a congeries of metaphors that explain what human life means, with deep and powerful appeal to the total person. The argument is not whether Catholics should leave their tradition or whether they stay for the right reasons. The argument is that they do in fact stay because of the attractiveness of Catholic metaphors.

You can make a persuasive case against Catholicism if you want. The Church is resolutely authoritarian and often seems to be proud of the fact that it "is not a democracy." It discriminates against women and homosexuals. It tries to regulate the bedroom behavior of married men and women. It tries to impose the Catholic position regarding abortion on everyone. It represents dissent and even disagreement. The Vatican seems obsessed with sex. The pope preaches against birth control in countries with rapidly expanding populations. Catholics often cringe when the local bishop or cardinal pontificates on social policy issues.

Bishops and priests are authoritarian and insensitive. Laypeople have no control of how their contributions are spent. Priests are unhappy, and many of them leave the priesthood as soon as they can to marry. The Church has covered up sexual abuse by priests for decades. Now it is paying millions of dollars to do penance for the sexual pleasure of supposedly celibate priests while it seeks to minimize, if not eliminate altogether, the sexual pleasures of married laypeople.

One might contend with such arguments. Research indicates that priests are among the happiest men in America. The Church was organized in a democratic structure for the first thousand years and could be so organized again. The pope's pronouncements on birth control are not the cause of the population explosion, say, in Mexico. Sexual abuse is not just a problem of the Catholic clergy. But let the charges stand for the sake of the argument. They represent the way many of those who are not Catholic see the Catholic Church, and with some nuances and qualifications the way many of those inside the Church see the Catholic institution. Nonetheless this case against Catholicism simply does not compute for most Catholics when they decide whether to leave or stay.

Do they in fact remain? Are not Catholics leaving the Church in droves? Professor Michael Hout of the Survey Research Center at the University of California at Berkeley has demonstrated that the Catholic defection rate has remained constant over thirty years. It was 15 percent in 1960 and it is 15 percent today.[145] Half of those who leave the Church do so when they marry a non-Catholic with stronger religious commitment. The other half leave for reasons of anger, authority, and sex—the reasons cited above.

How can this be? the outsider wonders. How can 85 percent of those who are born Catholic remain, one way or another, in the Church? Has Catholicism so brainwashed them that they are unable to leave? Or is it possible that those who ask the question misunderstand what Catholicism is?

The answer to the question of why they stay in the Church is that Catholics like being Catholic. For the last thirty years the hierarchy and the clergy have done just about everything they could to drive the laity out of the Church and have not succeeded. It seems unlikely that they will ever drive the stubborn lay folk out of the Church because the lay folk like being Catholic.

But why do they like being Catholic?

First, it must be noted that Americans show remarkable loyalty to their religious heritages. As difficult as it is for members of the academic

[145]Eleven percent in every age cohort of this century for non-Latinos.

and media elites to comprehend the fact, religion is important to most Americans. There is no sign that this importance has declined in the last half century (as measured by survey data from the 1940s). Skepticism, agnosticism, and atheism are not increasing in America, as disturbing as this truth might be to the denizens of midtown Manhattan.

Moreover, while institutional authority, doctrinal propositions, and ethical norms are components of a religious heritage—and important components—they do not exhaust the heritage. Religion is experience, image, and story before it is anything else and after it is everything else. Catholics like their heritage because it has great stories.

If one considers that for much of Christian history the population was illiterate and the clergy semiliterate and that authority was far away, one begins to understand that the heritage for most people most of the time was almost entirely story, ritual, ceremony, and eventually art. So it has been for most of human history. So it is, I suggest (and my data back me up) even today.

Catholicism has great stories because at the center of its heritage is "sacramentalism," the conviction that God discloses Himself in the objects and events and persons of ordinary life. Hence Catholicism is willing to risk stories about angels and saints and souls in purgatory and Mary the Mother of Jesus and stained-glass windows and statues and stations of the cross and rosaries and medals and the whole panoply of images and devotions that were so offensive to the austere leaders of the Reformation. Moreover, the Catholic heritage also has the elaborate ceremonial rituals that mark the passing of the year—midnight Mass, the Easter Vigil, first Communion, May crowning, Lent, Advent, grammar school graduation, and the festivals of the saints.

Catholicism has also embraced the whole of the human life cycle in Sacraments (with a capital S), which provide rich ceremonial settings, even when indifferently administered for the critical landmarks of life. The Sacrament of Reconciliation (Confession that was) and the Sacrament of the Anointing of the Sick (Extreme Unction that was) embedded in ritual and mystery the deeply held Catholic story of second chances.

The "sacramentalism" of the Catholic heritage has also led it to absorb as much as it thinks it can from what it finds to be good, true, and beautiful in pagan religions: Brigid is converted from the pagan goddess to the Christian patron of spring, poetry, and new life in Ireland; Guadeloupe is first a pagan and then a Christian shrine in Spain and then our Lady of Guadeloupe becomes the patron of poor Mexicans. This "baptism" of pagan metaphors (sometimes done more wisely than at other times) adds yet another overlay of stories to the Catholic heritage.

The sometimes inaccurate dictum "once a Catholic, always a Catholic" is based on the fact that the religious images of Catholicism are acquired early in life and are tenacious. You may break with the institution, you may reject the propositions, but you cannot escape the images.

The Eucharist is a particularly powerful and appealing Catholic ritual, even when it is done badly (as it often is) and especially when it is done well (which it sometimes is). In the Mass we join a community meal of celebration with our neighbors, our family, our friends, those we love. Such an awareness may not be explicitly on the minds of Catholics when they go to Church on Saturday afternoon or Sunday morning, but is the nature of metaphor that those who are influenced by it need not be consciously aware of the influence. In a *New York Times*–CBS News Poll in April 1998, 69 percent of Catholics responding said they attend Mass for reasons of meaning rather than obligation.

When we were in the seminary we were told that Catholic theology insisted that the Mass was the center of Catholic life. It bound together everything that the Church did and stood for. I don't think we much believed it then because the argument was so abstract and theoretical. It turns out that we were wrong. Or at least we would be wrong if we tried to reject the profound importance of the Mass to Catholics. When they return to the Church, often after many years, alienated Catholics often say that it is wonderful to attend Mass again.

Another important Catholic story is that of the neighborhood parish. Because of the tradition of village parishes with which Catholics came to America, the dense concentration of Catholics in many cities and the small geographical size of the parish, parishes can and often do become intense communities for many Catholics. They actuate what University of Chicago sociologist James S. Coleman calls "social capital," the extra resources of energy, commitment, and intelligence that overlapping structures produce. This social capital, this story of a sacred place in the heart of urban America, becomes even stronger when the parish contains that brilliant American Catholic innovation—the parochial school.

Perhaps the Catholic religious sensibility all begins with the Christmas crib. A mother shows her child (perhaps age three) the crib scene. The child loves it (of course) because it has everything she likes—a mommy, a daddy, a baby, animals, shepherds, shepherd children, angels, and men in funny clothes—and with token integration! Who is the baby? the little girl asks. That's Jesus. Who's Jesus? The mother hesitates, not sure of exactly how you explain the communication of idioms to a three-year-old. Jesus is God. That doesn't bother the little girl at all. Everyone was a baby once. Why not God? Who's the lady holding Jesus? That's Mary. Oh! Who's Mary? The mother throws theological caution to the winds. She's God's mommy. Again the kid has no problem. Everyone has a mommy, why not God?

It's a hard story to beat. Later in life the little girl may come to understand that God loves us so much that He takes on human form to be able to walk with us even into the valley of death and that God also loves us the way a mother loves a newborn babe—which is the function of the Mary metaphor in the Catholic tradition.

It may seem that I am reducing religion to childishness—to stories and images and rituals and communities. In fact, it is in the poetic, the metaphorical, the experiential dimension of the personality that religion finds both its origins and raw power. Because we are reflective creatures we must also reflect on our religious experiences and stories; it is in the (lifelong) interlude of reflection that propositional religion and religious authority become important, indeed indispensable. But then the religiously mature person returns to the imagery, having criticized it, analyzed it, questioned it, to commit the self once more in sophisticated and reflective maturity to the story.

The Catholic imagination sees God and Her grace lurking everywhere and hence enjoys a more gracious and benign repertory of religious symbols than do most other religions. On measures of religious imagery I have developed for national surveys (and call the Grace scale), Catholics consistently have more "gracious" images of God: they are more likely than others to picture God as a Mother, a Lover, a Spouse, and a Friend (as opposed to a Father, a Judge, a Master, and a King). The story of the life, death, and resurrection of Jesus is the most "graceful" story of all—the story of a God who in some fashion took on human form so that He could show us how to live and how to die, a God who went down into the valley of death with us and promised that death would not be the end.

How do they reconcile such gracious imagery with the often apparently stern and punitive postures of their religious leadership? It must be understood that religious heritages contain many different strains and components, not all of them always in complete harmony with one another. However, in any apparent conflict between images of a gracious God and severe propositional teaching of the leaders of a heritage, the latter will surely lose.

A new school in the psychology of religion, which bases itself on the so-called attachment theory of psychological maturation, supports my perspective. A happy and playful attachment between mother and baby prepares the child for similar attachments later in life, especially to God, who is in some sense a surrogate mother—an all-powerful source of love and reassurance. Professor Lee A. Kirkpatrick of the College of William and Mary has suggested recently that Catholicism is an especially powerful religious heritage on the imaginative level precisely because it offers so many objects of potential attachment. It has been suggested that the most powerful of all the objects of attachment is the metaphor of Mary the Mother of Jesus representing the mother love of God.

I believe that is absolutely right, although some progressive Catholics have tried to play down the role of Mary in the Catholic tradition lest it offend our ecumenical dialogue partners. Research on Catholic young people reveals that the Mary image continues to be their most powerful religious image. Who would not find appealing a religion which suggests that God loves us like a mother loves a little child? Who would not be enchanted by a story which suggests that we are, as the Chicago theologian John Shea has argued, not just creatures, not just sinners but, more than anything, beloved children?

What I was in grammar school in the mid-1930s, the nuns told a story that sums up why people stay Catholic. One day Jesus went on a tour of the heavenly city and noted that there were certain new residents who ought not to be there, not until they had put in a long time in purgatory and some of them only on a last-minute appeal. He stormed out to the gate where Peter was checking the day's intake on his Compaq 486DX Deskpro computer (I have edited the nuns' story)—next to which, on his workstation, was a fishing pole and a papal crown.

"You've failed again, Simon Peter," said the Lord.

"What have I done now?"

"You let a lot of people in that don't belong."

"I didn't do it."

"Well, who did?"

"You won't like it."

"Tell me anyway."

"I turn them away from the front gate and then they go around to the back door and your mother lets them in!"

It is the religious sensibility behind that fanciful story that explains why Catholics remain Catholic. It might not be your religious sensibility. But if you want to understand Catholics—and if Catholics want to understand themselves—the starting point is to comprehend the enormous appeal of that sensibility. It's the stories.

What then are the conclusions I would draw for the Church (and indeed for all religions) from my theory of the religious imagination and from the stories in this chapter and the last chapter?

I do *not* conclude that religion does not need teaching authority, leadership, creeds, codes, and catechism. Quite the contrary, I insist that all of these functions are needed, though I would wish that my own denomination would exercise these functions better than it does now. Because I focus on the imaginative dimension of religion (which has been neglected for a long time, though it continues to flourish) it does not follow that I reject the intellectual dimensions of religion. Having criticized, perhaps ad nauseam, the anti-intellectualism of so many priests (who as far as serious reading goes are functionally illiterate) I will not slip into the same trap myself. Religion involves both imagination and intellect (to use a typology which is far from perfect but which is the only one we have). Because I want more regard for the former, one would be dead wrong to argue that I want less of the latter.

But I do insist that Catholicism, with the richest repertory of images and metaphors of any of the world's religions, is wasting a precious and indispensable spiritual resource when it ignores the religious imagination—and therefore when it ignores the religious experiences of its laypeople. The hierarchy and the clergy and the quasi-clergy (liturgists and "religious educators" in particular) are devoid (with some exceptions) of any sense of the importance of the religious imagination. In fact, they don't know what it is and their own imaginative creativity—with which everyone is born—has become little more than a vestigial organ.

They believe that art and stories of any kind are merely gimmicks to gain attention of the faithful so that they can then drive home a prosaic and ideological point. You never tell a story, they seem to think, without explaining its point and drawing conclusions from it. The liturgists, (most of them, anyway) innocent of both taste and creativity, replace religious imagery with cutesy gimmicks which turn the stomach of the ordinary lay folk—who are almost always too polite or too resigned to protest. Moreover, liturgists (with my usual bow to the exceptions) have never seen a liturgy which they don't think could be made better by making it longer and slower—in violation of the genius of the ancient Roman liturgy which has always worked on the principles that you say what you have to say and be done with it and that you let nothing interfere with flow, the brisk movement of the ceremony (as Dom Gregory Dix pointed out in his magisterial book *The Shape of the Liturgy*—a volume everyone should read before they are permitted to mess with the Eucharist).

Liturgists, moreover, have absolutely forbidden Gregorian chant in church, an ancient and glorious tradition, and replace it whenever possible with sickening guitar music.[146] Chant records meanwhile become international best-sellers because the music is so beautiful, so deeply re-

[146]I have nothing against guitars, but there are other musical instruments of some merit, like the organ for example.

ligious, and, in some cases, so easy to sing. Greeley's first law: when everyone else discovers something, the Catholic Church has just abandoned it.[147] I do not want plainsong to dominate the Church's worship (as it once did, though usually it was badly sung plainsong), but it think it is monstrous folly to exclude it completely.

Liturgical art and music are in serious disrepair in the contemporary Church, both because it takes a while to develop a tradition after it has been dormant for half a millennium and because Catholic leaders want everything both quick and cheap.

Church architects, for some reason which escapes me, seem to have concluded that a "modern" church is necessarily one that looks not like a Catholic church, but like a Quaker meeting hall. We must be brave, they say, even if it means offending the laity who have paid for the church (and for the previous one if the issue is a remodeling job). The laity, it would seem, have neither good taste nor religious sensibility. "Liturgy committees" are lectured about what a "liturgically correct" church is and, their minds filled with ideology, accept the architect's and the pastor's plans and approve the plans for a new church or a remodeling project. If the rest of the parish is given a chance to vote on the project (a rare enough event), they usually turn it down flat.

Many such "modern" churches assume that the exuberance of the older style of Catholic churches—dark stained-glass windows, a multitude of statues, a faint smell of incense, and votive candles everywhere—are tasteless and old-fashioned. A church is only in good taste when it looks like a Protestant church. But such an assumption is surely invalid. What's wrong with saints, the Mother of Jesus, stained glass, and votive candles? Why must the tradition be wiped out completely? Cannot one build a modern church that "looks like a Catholic church" (as many laity wonder)? By which they mean in effect, is it not possible to have a modern church that integrates the Catholic tradition of exuberant churches?

Why not indeed?

The new church which was being finished when I arrived at CK in

---

[147]Greeley's second law: when the Catholic Church discovers something, everyone else has just abandoned it. And the third law: the propensity of a religious institution to tell other institutions how to solve all problems is in inverse proportion to the religious institution's ability to deal with its own problems. Thus the American Catholic Church, in a terrible financial crisis (and paying food stamp wages to many of its own employees), does not hesitate to issue a solemn high pastoral in which it tells the rest of the country of its obligations to the poor and to practice economic justice. The third law would seem always to imply a certain amount (usually monumental) of hypocrisy.

1954 seemed to have accomplished just such a feat. While the building is far from perfect (the acoustics were bad, are still bad, and will always be bad), it is still the best blend of the new and the old that I've ever seen and far better than the zeppelin hangars and the concrete block-houses that have sprung up all over the world, including, God help us all, County Mayo.

When my friend Tom Cahalane built a new church in Tucson (the parish at which I work when I'm at the U of A), the result was in many ways quite successful. But, as I remarked to the congregation during a lecture, he had room for only two saints.

"Sure," I said to them, "if your man from West Cork understood the Catholic imaginative tradition, wouldn't he have a whole closet stuffed with saints and bring two of them out every month to be the saint of the month? And then couldn't parents bring their kids over to the church and tell the stories of God's love the saint represents?"

Much laughter from the people.

The monsignor, never one to be upstaged, replied that if Father Gree-ley wanted to donate two statues to the church, he'd be happy to accept them. So aren't there two hand-carved wood statues at the entrance of the church (carved by Robert McGovern[148] of Philadelphia) and doesn't Father Greeley explain to the kids who St. Brigid and St. Brendan are?

And doesn't the monsignor have a collection of icons, two of which appear in rotation next to the main altar? And hasn't he built a garden outside the church, a garden of saints that will be filled with statues? And aren't there votive candles all over the church now?

Ah, you win a few now and then. But only, I think, when the other priest agrees with you already.

A perfect example of what happens to Catholicism when it turns away from its imaginative past and does not develop new images and stories that continue the past are the POF,[149] prayers the priest says after the creed and before the gifts (bread and wine and often the money gathered in the offertory collection. Ugh!) are brought to the altar. The ceremony is an anachronism resurrected from the ancient Church, but not all anachronisms are bad. Unfortunately, the congregants rarely understand the purpose of the prayers (kind of like the blessing at the end of Mass). More unfortunately the prayers are usually terrible. I cringe whenever I

[148]The statues are representational, but I do not believe that all church art must be representational. Neither, however, do I believe that the representa-tional should be excluded completely.

[149]I've only recently learned that this stands for "Prayers Over the Faithful." Unless I am mistaken they used to be called the bidding prayers.

hear them (as I cringe at the introductory comments at the beginning of the Eucharist). There has to be a center for bland and boring ideology somewhere in the land where these atrocities are ground out week after week by creatively disadvantaged and/or senile liturgists. As Sheridan Witside said in *The Man Who Came to Dinner*, "I may vomit."

The ideology is usually a variant of the worn-out radicalism of the 1960s ("That we may come to realize that Americans are consuming most of the world's non-renewable energy, we pray to the Lord!"), liberalism perhaps, but the liberalism which disappeared from *The New York Times* op-ed page (the bible of all "with-it" liberals) at least a decade and a half ago. I would like to think that I am a liberal and not even a "moderate liberal"—like my teacher and good friend the late Bishop Ernest Primeau.[150] But I do not believe any total ideology and I think those who wish to impose any total ideology with all its questions and all its definitive answers on others are not in fact "liberals" at all but neo-authoritarians. They have no right to try to do this during the Eucharist, especially when they do it blandly, uncreatively, and make the POF in the favorite word of teens, *"Boring!"*

Like I say, their creativity has become vestigial. If it wasn't so retarded, perhaps they wouldn't need ideology, which is perfectly suited to fill the vacuum which occurs when the religious imagination atrophies.

I realize that as I write these words that I could do more with the POF at Grand Beach where I do it myself. But I have become so impatient with the long, drawn-out, and *Boring* Liturgy of the Word (formally called the Mass of the Catechumens), that I am eager to take the Eucharist away from the liturgists and get on with the Action (as the Eucharistic Prayer used to be called—*Infra Actionem in Latin*). I will have to change that. And I will have to be much better at a creative prayer at the end of the POF.

The religious imagination will flourish again in the Catholic tradition only when the Church resumes its traditional patronage of the fine and the lively arts.

It's been a long way from, let us say, the Sistine Chapel, the Stanza of Raphael, the Pietà, the baroque Jesuit churches, Fra Angelico, Palestrina, Notre Dame du Paris, and the Book of Kells (for example). And

[150]Ernie, God be good to him, was introduced before an intervention at Vatican II, as the bishop of Manchester in England. He began by saying, in Latin, that he was in fact the bishop of Manchester, New Hampshire, in the United States and that the bishop of Manchester in England was a "separated brother." General laughter. The late John Courtney Murray once exploded, "Ernie, you are a radical centrist!" To which Ernie replied, "No, I am an extreme moderate."

all that way has been downhill. Fine art is no longer an absolute necessity for a church with a sacramental imagination, it has become at best a luxury which we can ill afford and at worst a dangerous temptation to pride. Artists, musicians, storytellers, and poets are treated with contempt, paid poorly, and lied about. Rarely will a priest or a bishop or a pope trust fourth-rate surgeons when they must have an operation (well, maybe the pope does, given the poor quality of the medical care he receives). Yet they all want art (in the wide sense of the word) which is quick, cheap, and will not trouble the Vatican.

Catholic imagery is out there and flourishing but the institutional Church, to the extent it is aware of it, doesn't give a damn about it. Indeed, most priests have no idea what I'm talking about—so prosaic and so unimaginative and so uncreative has been their education and is the clerical culture in which they are entombed.

Priests also tend to disregard the religious experiences of the faithful. From the pope on down, the assumption seems to be that the laity are unspirited folk, materialist, secularist, consumerist, out of all contact with God and Her Spirit. In the *Los Angeles Times* study of American priests, the researchers found that the priests had little regard for their lay folk. In an open-ended question priests were asked what they thought the greatest problems of the Catholic laity were. None of the problems which the laity routinely describe, save economic difficulties, made it on the clerical agenda. Nor, except for being less likely to think of the laity as confused, did "liberal" priests dissent from the rather dyspeptic portrait of the Catholic laity: their family lives are breaking down, they are losing their faith, they are not generous, they are materialistic, permissive, apathetic, confused, prone to divorce, and devoid of principles.

All of these problems are almost by definition the result of failures inherent in the laity themselves and are not the result of any failures in priestly ministry. Corrupted by the materialism and permissiveness and secularism and moral breakdown of society, confused by the conflicting demands of secular life and of religion, and lacking in generosity and moral principles, the laity are threatened with divorce, breakdown of family life, and are selfish and apathetic.

Nothing about the lay hunger for good preaching, effective liturgy, democratic leadership, sensitive counseling, respect for women, financial responsibility—the things the laity want from their clergy. A laity with spiritual experience and aspirations, a laity which encounters God especially at birth, death, marriage, and sexual love—which is revealed in the surveys of the laity—simply does not exist as far as the clergy are concerned.

How can the clergy be expected to respond to those who are living in such an evil environment and have been so poisoned by it? How could anyone believe that the laity are not all bad and that for many of them the most serious religious problem is the absence of inspiring religious leadership and sympathetic pastoral support from their clergy?

The portrait of the laity is a portrait which justifies despair—and might seem to be a self-serving escape from responsibility.

On the only matter concerning which there is disagreement between liberal and conservative priests—the confusion of the laity—the two groups converge among the younger generation as the younger "liberals" are more likely to consider "confusion" a problem than their elders.

It is not unusual for professionals to have a low opinion of their clients—college and university faculties of their students, medical doctors of their patients. Yet the clerical view of the laity presented is so at odds with the needs of the laity as they perceive them (and report them in other surveys) that one must conclude that communication about religious matters between Catholic laity and clergy in the United States has broken down completely.

If you are dealing with people like that, men and women who are scarcely Christian, who need to be "evangelized," you must pound home doctrinal truth because, you assume, there is no religious imagination at all. If your people are pagans—and I fail to see any other interpretation of the *Times* data—of what use is the popular tradition of Catholicism? Indeed, is it not little more than an accretion of pagan superstitions? Why let them have votive lights when they can't recite the Ten Commandments? Why permit midnight Masses at Christmas when they are not raising their kids properly? Why worry about making the Baptism ceremony a rich and exciting experience when they come in off the street and expect you to baptize their child and they go to Mass only a couple of times a year?

I am firmly convinced that this view of the laity is wrong, not only because my data show that it is wrong, but because once one persuades a group of Catholic laity to discuss their prayer life and their experiences of grace and of God, the depths of their spiritual sensibilities and longings put me to shame and would put to shame most of the priests I know. We priests have no monopoly on the Holy Spirit. If our laity are afraid to talk about their encounters with God, the reason may be that they sense that we are not particularly interested in them.

Neither in art (fine or lively) nor in the life of the average parish is there much attention paid to the two greatest resources of Catholicism—the imaginative tradition and the spirituality of the lay folk that correlates with that tradition.

When I try to make this case to priests, they look at me like I'm crazy—or tell me that I'm merely trying to justify and promote my novels. They lack the taste, the training, the sensitivity, and the creativity even to listen to what I say. I usually do not accept invitations to speak to groups of priests anymore because they cannot or will not grasp what my theory of the religious imagination is about and wait eagerly for the opportunity to engage in personal attacks. The experience is always unpleasant both for me and for those who have been foolish enough to invite me.

Who needs it?

While personal attacks are responses of the ignorant and half educated, I can understand the confusion of many priests over what I'm trying to say, even those who are sympathetic to the notion that religious imagination may be a more important part of the Catholic tradition than they had hitherto realized. Their education has emphasized the exclusion of all propositional truth—creeds, catechisms, theology. The new and dreary *Catechism of the Catholic Church* is a perfect example of what they think religion is.[151] While I am not repudiating any of these religious realities, I am arguing that the popular tradition, the tradition of story and image and experience and ritual is even more important—though it is always subject to critique by propositional religion.

I am urging as a challenge that Catholicism be far more aware of its imaginative tradition and have much greater respect for it. In practice this means that a typical parish should be exuberant and celebratory in its rituals, all of its rituals from blessing a medal to the Mass. Its approach should be sensitive, compassionate, open, eager to listen to the experiences of the faithful. The Mass itself should have the highest quality homilies, readings, music, ceremonies. It should be the kind of *representation collectif* from which the congregants depart happy, smiling, exhilarated, renewed—instead of grim, angry, bored, and depressed. If one does not see many smiles on the faces of the faithful after Mass, something is profoundly wrong.

This kind of liturgy (and the parish ambience of which it is a part) is possible. Many parishes in the United States have it—including the three I know best, Our Mother of Sorrows in Tucson and St. Mary of the Woods and Old St. Patrick's[152] in Chicago. Neither Tom Cahalane nor Leo Mahon nor Jack Wall needed or need my theorizing to direct their work or achieve their success. Perhaps my theory has to some extent

---

[151]I am not denying the truths in the catechism, I am merely questioning the pastoral assumptions behind it.

[152]The "Old" refers to the parish and not to the saint. Its church is the oldest public building in Chicago.

reinforced their instincts, but men of strong instincts that they are, they didn't and don't need much reinforcing.

If they can create such parishes, so can many other priests. Yet the expanded Catholicism which I hope will develop in the next millennium will be a long time coming, if only because it will be hard for many priests and bishops to understand, much less accept, the religious power of the imagination. I don't expect to live to see the change, but I rejoice in the increased understanding of the importance of the religious imagination and the increased number of priests who know what it means—even if they are still a small minority.

I do not claim nor will I claim any contribution to such a change, other than perhaps reinforcing some instincts.

In a one-sentence summary, the good parish, as I see it, is one that charms people to religion instead of trying to force them.

In this respect, of course, it imitates a God who tends to achieve Her purposes by attracting and charming instead of pushing and forcing.

Two Guys Named Jack

I knew that Jack Durkin belonged in our family when my sister Mary Jule returned from her first date with him. In those days in our neighborhood, many young people rode the bus on their dates and did not find it either a burden or a humiliation. However, when my sister walked by the driver as though he were not there, Jack feigned astonishment. "You mean she didn't pay? You mean I have to pay for her? How come?"

He must have analyzed his date pretty well. She was the kind who would love such a scene—which had everyone on the bus laughing—and who would laugh at his comic act as loudly as anyone else in the bus. She would continue to laugh at this wondrously funny man for the rest of his life. Even at the worst times in his life, Jack Durkin was always the witty entertainer, the outrageous comedian, the laugh-maker.

Thirty-eight years later, the comedy was over. But the laughs continue because the memory of them persists in all who knew him.

Jack, plagued by various forms of cancer for twelve years, finally died during the Easter season of 1994. When I came home from Tucson on Palm Sunday and stopped at Columbus Hospital, he seemed in good spirits and reasonably good health. I was convinced that he would beat this latest bout of cancer as he had beaten all the others. The next Sunday after dinner at the apartment of Sean and his wife Miss Molly (so-called and properly so-called because of her Georgia roots) down the street from the hospital, I walked back to visit Jack again. During the week he had seemed to slip a little each day, but I was still an optimist. After I left that Easter evening, I knew the end could not be far off.

Jack thought he was going on a trip, one of the many he had taken as a United Airlines executive, only this one would be different. There were many people around him who would help him on the trip, including my mother who had been dead for thirty years. Such deathbed experiences are common enough. I don't know that they prove anything, but they might be a hint of something.

A week later Mary Jule called me early in the morning. Jack was slipping. Would I come up to the house and administer the Last Anointing? Still groggy from being awakened I raced up to Park Ridge in the rush-hour traffic and found the family gathered around the sickbed, everyone in tears. Jack was not only a wonderful husband but also a father who was adored by his children. He was at best only intermittently conscious while I administered the sacrament. Mary Jule did not think that death was likely to be immediate, so I went back to my apartment.

It would not be a good day. A festival was scheduled in honor of Jim Coleman who was sick with cancer and I was to give the "keynote" address after supper. Fair enough, but somehow my paper had been locked up in a backup disk to which I was not able to gain access. So I had to write it over in a hurry, with the scene in Park Ridge still haunting me. I had just finished the paper when Mary Jule called again. Jack had died.

Dear God, what do I do now?

"Do you want me to cancel the talk and come up?"

"No," she said. "Let the dead bury their dead. Give the talk that everyone expects you to give."

Brave lady.

So I gave the talk with a heavy heart, doubly heavy. It was well received, especially by Jim and his wife who were the only ones that mattered, and I got out of the faculty-club dining room as quickly as I could. Only Norman Nie (for whose software company Laura and Dan Durkin both work) and a few others knew what had happened in my family.

The wake was like all Irish wakes, a mix of laughter and tears, with more laughter this time in memory of a truly funny human being. The night before the funeral, Mary Jule said to me, "If I manage to hold myself together, I'll say a few words after Communion."

"I'll keep an eye on you and you can give me the signal."

Eileen and Julie organized the liturgy and the music. Dan read one of his poems, a dazzling reflection on fatherhood (and it was obvious for the first time that he was indeed a real poet). I glanced at Mary Jule. She walked out of the pew—*with a manuscript in her hand*! Tough bunch, all the Durkins. I don't remember what she said, but I know there was a lot of Jack's wit in it.

Everyone was crying on the way out of church. Norman and Carol Nie embraced me with tears pouring down their cheeks. "It was the most beautiful funeral I ever attended," Carol whispered.

"Me too," I replied.

It was a bright spring day at the cemetery the next morning. Jack Wall led the prayers. There were no tears, only a few sad sighs. I visited my parents' grave (where someday I too will be buried) for the first time ever. Somehow that was also a grace.

Life goes on. I miss Jack Durkin, not nearly as much as his family does. He was a good man. He knew how to live and how to die. And he died much too soon.

Yet for all of us it is always too soon to die.

There are some bad times perhaps to be a Catholic. But a death in the family is not one of those bad times. We always wonder what such a death must be like for those who do not believe as we do.

My sister has not had an easy life. She went to graduate school, one class a quarter, for nine years to get her degree from the divinity school at the University. When she applies at a college or a university for a job, the issue is never whether she's a woman (which is a good thing to be in theology departments these days) but whether she is really my sister (which is a very bad thing to be in theology departments these days). A distinguished and very "liberal" priest tried to get her fired from a department (at another university) where she was a visiting professor (on the grounds that she was as bad as I am), unaware that, as he was denouncing her to the department's chair, she was standing right next to him. He has never really apologized.

Jack and Mary Jule and their kids have always been active in the Church. The parents were chair of the Cana Conference of Chicago at the time of the Birth Control Encyclical—an event which sent Mary Jule to graduate school. They were members of Mary Set of Wisdom parish (Mary, Lady Wisdom, we might better call it today) at the time when it was one of the most active and vigorous parishes in America. Then Bill Clark, the pastor, retired, another pastor was appointed, and John Cussick, the Durkin family priest (as opposed to the priest in the family), was forced to leave. The new pastor could not accept the parish as *his* unless he destroyed everything his predecessor had done, including all the projects that had made it an exciting place. He is supposed to have remarked that he could afford to lose a third of the people in the parish so long as that was what was required to make it *his*. The parish has been in open conflict for the last decade, contributions have declined, many parishioners go elsewhere, but now it is certainly *his*.

It was made clear to the Durkins that they were not welcome. So they decamped to Old St. Pat's which was, in those days, aborning.

I have been told that I was the one responsible for them being eased out of the parish.

Events like those make me really hate priests, not all priests of course, but the clerical culture which legitimates such behavior. Even if you don't like me, why try to punish me through my family? Especially if—as in the case of the theologian—you had said only recently that the rights of women were the most important issue facing the Church? Rights of women indeed, unless she happens to be my sister. I saw him recently and was polite to him because of the other people in the room. He told others later that at last we had been reconciled. The hell we have. Forgiven maybe, but hardly friends.

Life goes on. Now there is another Jack Durkin, Sean and Miss Molly's firstborn—a picture-perfect little punk according to all who have seen him (I agree). He's not the same Jack Durkin but the continuation of the name is a salute, a tip of the hat, to our conviction that, as G. K. Chesterton put it, life is too important for it ever to be anything but life. Life and death are twain yet one and death is birth.

Conclusion (For the Time Being)

My family and friends threw a big party for my seventieth birthday. It made the papers. A few days later I received a call from a member of the priests' retirement board. It was the first official notice the Archdiocese had taken of me since 1965.

"I see by the papers that you're seventy years old. You have to retire."

From what? I don't have a regular parish assignment.

"Well, retire. Everyone has to when they're seventy."

Oh.

I knew what it was about—health insurance. The Archdiocese covers all its priests with a decent health insurance policy. Indeed it had covered me for years without bothering to tell me. The parish at which a priest works pays his premium. I learned that I had been covered for at least five years when a bill showed up on my desk. Since I did not have a regular assignment there was no parish to bill so I would be required to pay for the coverage henceforth myself. For coverage I hadn't asked for and didn't know I had. I checked with Lou Briody, my insurance agent. The Church's policy is actually better than the one you pay for, he said. So I canceled the other one and paid the bill to the Archdiocese every year. At seventy they wanted to switch me over to Medicare. I knew that.

"All right," I said to the caller, "I'll write a letter to your office saying that you can switch me over to Medicare and then you can bill me for the supplement."

"You gotta write to the cardinal."

"Fine, I'll write to the cardinal."

"You're entitled to a pension." His tone was grudging. How dare I claim a pension from the Archdiocese!

"I don't want a pension."

After all, neither I nor a parish had made any payments to the fund—if there were supposed to be payments, which I didn't know.

"Everyone gets a pension."

"I don't want one."

"You mean you'll waive the pension?"

Ah, that was the magic word.

"Right, I'll waive the pension."

Then, would you believe, he read me a little sermon about how sociology could not explain the work of the Holy Spirit—as if I had ever claimed it could.

"Well," I said, as a parting shot, "as St. Thomas said, grace builds on nature."

All right, the Archdiocese had acknowledged my existence, but only to tell me to retire.

So I wrote a letter to the cardinal-designate as he was then and informed him that I was "retiring" formally for health insurance purposes and waiving the pension. I added that nothing else would, God willing, change in my life.

What's the new cardinal like? I am often asked. Is he liberal or a conservative? He's intelligent, I reply, very, very intelligent. And we'll never be able to paste a label on him. In this brief description I will not quote anything he has said to me in personal conversations. Too many priests are running around with quotes out of context. I must note a possible conflict of interest. He apparently likes me and my work. He reads and understands my fiction and says so on the public record. If someone likes me and my work, then I like him!

In his letter of response to my retirement, Cardinal Frances Eugene George, O.M.I., who is 75 percent Irish and has 200 percent Irish wit and charm, replied that he was grateful for the contribution I had made not only to the local Church but across the country and around the world. I could hardly believe my eyes. Praise for what I had done from my own archbishop! There were no particular costs to the cardinal for such words, but Joe Bernardin would never have dared to say them, for fear he might be quoted and thus offend the other priests in Chicago.

Cardinal George is one of the most brilliant and erudite men I have ever met (in the same category as Senator Pat Moynihan, though with a different style). He is a very complicated and intricate person. He possesses (and is possessed by) enormous wit and personal and pastoral grace. His charm and grace make one forget for the moment how lame he is and how much pain he must endure (with occasional falls) because of the damage polio did to his right leg.

The cardinal loves to argue, indeed to stir up argument, and is beyond intimidation or even insecurity. In an interview for the *National Catholic Reporter*, he said about my novels:

> *Father Greeley has given great attention to the role of imagination in the life of faith. What he is doing is re-evangelizing the imagination, using fiction to express the faith and the mysteries of faith. That's an extraordinarily significant project. Pope John Paul talks*

about faith creating culture; using fictions is one way to do that.

I've read four or five of [this] earlier books of fiction and a recent Blackie Ryan novel. I caught what he was trying to do. How well he's doing it is for someone else to judge.

"Re-evangelizing the imagination!" Yes, indeed. I did not expect that an archbishop would ever say that about my novels, much less my own archbishop, and on the public record at that. I was delighted. A terrible dark cloud of suspicion and distrust lifted. It had taken a long time, but those two paragraphs were worth waiting for!

Then in the summer of 1999, when the American Sociological Association staged a special session "in appreciation" of my work in the sociology of religion, the Cardinal attended the entire session, took notes on what was said, and at dinner afterward praised me both as a priest and sociologist.

Whether Cardinal George will be able to administer the large, complex, and, since Cardinal Cody, disoriented Archdiocese remains to be seen. If he can't, then no one can. Whether he will be able to build a competent staff also remains to be seen, especially since like former Chicago Bears, coach Dave Wanstadt he doesn't have much of a bench. Finally it remains to be seen whether those priests of the Archdiocese who are intimidated by his brilliance and quickness will learn how to argue back, but that's their problem not his.

However, he likes my novels and likes to argue with me. What more can I ask? For the first time since the death of Albert Meyer I'm back on good paper.

Adversary: Sure, shouldn't you be ashamed of yourself?

Me: Why now?

Adversary: And yourself just finished writing this monumental book about your life, all 120,000 words of it, and you don't get the point at all, at all, do you now?

(The Adversary talks with a brogue, authentic unlike my phony one. So he says "pint" for the word I spell "point.")

Me: What's the point at all, at all?

Adversary: Isn't the point that you've had one hell of an exciting life so far?

Me: Oh.

Adversary: And aren't you after telling your poor readers that they have to figure out why you get yourself involved with so many windmills and become such a public nuisance?

Me: Well, yes. I'm trying to figure it out myself.

Adversary: Don't you do it because you like to do it, just like they stay in the Church because they like being Catholic?

Me: Oh.

Adversary: You should stop feeling sorry for yourself and thank the Good Lord that He's given you the grace to make a public nuisance out of yourself.

Me: Oh.

Adversary: As for the priests in Chicago that pretend you don't exist, well, fockemall!

Me: I like the sentiment but I disapprove of the language.

Adversary: Yeah, sure. You don't regret any of them windmills you've taken on. You don't regret working a mite too hard. You certainly don't regret writing all them novels.

Me: I guess not.

Adversary: You are what you are and that's the way God made you.

Me: I don't think so.

Adversary: I do. If you really disagree, reread this monster book and you'll see what I mean.

Me: Well, maybe.

Adversary: No "maybe" about it. Admit it, you've had a hell of a good time and even now you're looking for other ways to stir up the shite.

Me: Please, this is a family-oriented book.

Adversary: Yeah, sure.

I suppose he's right.

At the end of writing this book I look back and wonder.

I think of a toddler running toward the water at Twin Lakes, Wisconsin, of the little boy struggling through the three-block walk to St. Angela in the primary grades—three blocks was a long distance in those days—of the shy (arguably cute, but I remain skeptical about that) eighth-grader who wanted to be a priest more than anything else in the world, of the Quigley seminarian who went to Mass every morning, no mater how bad the weather, of the major seminarian who kept all the rules and read French theology books, of the young priest who again kept all the rules—was home before eleven o'clock and did not own a car for the first five years, of the same young priest who inwardly raged against the pastor's efforts to keep him from the people of the parish.

I wonder what ever happened to him.

You give a guy a little freedom and he changes completely. The structures collapse and he becomes a public nuisance.

But I have a hard time coping with the transformation. I suppose there were a number of things that happened.

1. One surely was the move from CK to the University where people were treated like adults.
2. The Second Vatican Council.

3. The translation of John Patrick Cody to Chicago. It's hard to take seriously the claim of an institution to be speaking for the Holy Spirit at all times and in everything it does when it sends a paranoid psychopath to a See as important as Chicago. As the joke puts it, "There are more horse's asses in the Church than there are horses because the horse's asses are in the saddle."

4. The Birth Control Encyclical. As Dan Herr said, "What good is infallibility when it doesn't prevent a mistake like that."

5. My discovery through sociology that much of what everyone knew to be true about Catholics (including the agnostic liberal elite and most bishops and priests) was not true.

6. My discovery that many of my fellow priests are bums, mean-spirited, envious, uneducated, insensitive, stupid timeservers who don't do well their most important work—preaching—and don't even try to improve.

7. My realization that the strength of the Church currently is not in the institutional leadership nor in the theologians but in the laity who will not leave no matter how hard they are pushed.

8. My realization that despite the "intellectuals" in the Church who over the years have urged us to abandon what we are doing and follow the example of the French or the Dutch or the German or the Latin American Church, the real strength of American Catholicism lies in the neighborhood parishes like the one I grew up in and the one in which I served as a young priest—modernized and updated perhaps, but still neighborhood parishes and the most effective religious structure which human ingenuity has ever produced.

9. My theory of the sociology of religion that religion is story before it's anything else and after it's everything else and my resulting realization that it is the stories which keep people in the Church, myself included: stories of Christmas, stories of Holy Week and Easter, stories of the Eucharist, stories of the local community, stories of a God of charm—not an authoritarian rule maker.

10. My growing realization that what happened to the Confident Church of the forties and fifties was that it lost its confidence because it lacked the depth and sophistication that the council/encyclical years would require. We were not all that wrong in what we did in those days. But we were not able to articulate it to ourselves in ways that would have enabled us to defend it and develop it with the tools the council provided. So the Confident Church has been replaced by the Confusing Church of shallow fads, like the RCIA and Liberation Theology. Someday in the future, the worth of the incomplete but insightful Confident Church will be appreciated, probably when it is

too late to do anything about it—though it will perhaps still be alive among the laypeople in the parishes where it currently flourishes (albeit on their own terms and subject to their own choices). As Bill McCready said, all the Church has left is the Blessed Mother and The Catholic schools. That may be enough.

11. My life on the margins of several institutions which I would have served with all the training and talent at my command if they had not rejected me.

12. My horror at the silence of priests in the pedophile crisis, a silence which is destroying the tattered image of the priesthood.

13. My realization that Catholic leaders are so obsessed by sexual issues that the image of repressive sexual attitudes (and anti-women attitudes) is the only one that they are capable of presenting to the world. The only story the world thinks it hears from them is one in which good people practically never make love.

Those things will change a guy, I guess.

But one thing has not changed since that grammar school kid walked down Menard Avenue and later Potomac Avenue. I still want to be a priest more than anything else in the world.

I am not disillusioned or bitter by the transformations in my view of the Church which I have described in the previous paragraphs. Quite the contrary, I think they are experiences which have enhanced my understanding of what life is about. I have lived through one of the great eras in the history of the Catholic Church and watched Church leaders from popes to parish priests foolishly destroy the possibilities of the era— mostly because they have lost their nerve.

Well, things like that happen—especially when you are dealing with human organizations and communities.

The above outburst does not contradict the apparent mellow attitude in the early chapters of this book. I did not say that I have mellowed (I hope I haven't). Nor did I say I wasn't angry anymore. Rather I said I no longer felt defensive and encircled by coyotes and I now realize how many people appreciate my work. This does not mean that I do not lament the terrible waste of possibility during the last thirty years.

However I now understand better than I did that most human enterprises, given half a chance, go badly—at least in the short run. Those of us who expected that the energies released by the council would smoothly restructure the Church forgot about such human weaknesses as stupidity, laziness, shallowness, ambition, stubbornness, envy, and lust for power.

The last factor may be the most important. For the conciliar reform to have been immediately successful, too many Churchmen would have had to share power on which they formerly had a monopoly. No ruling elite does that willingly. In fact, it will do so only when it cannot escape the truth that its devoutly protected power is worthless. Much of the old hierarchical power in the Church is worthless now, that no one takes it seriously anymore, but those who think they still have that power haven't realized that yet.[153]

When will they?

Not in my lifetime I fear. Perhaps not in the lifetime of any of us who are alive today.

I could be wrong. But I have learned not to be naive about the clammy, cold grip on power to which so many Church leaders fearfully cling, their heads firmly rooted in the sand. They are a long way from abandoning their conviction that they are the Church.

Would not I have much more influence in the institutional Church if I didn't say things like that? I doubt it.

Since my very early years in the priesthood I have been plagued by a sense of failure (which sends the Adversary into paroxysms of anger). I have had some success (greater or lesser) at some activities I would not have thought very important or very likely when I went off to the seminary and have failed miserably at some other activities that I thought very important when Cardinal Stritch ordained me. One does in life finally what Lady Wisdom wants one to do and forgets judgments about success and failure.

Adversary: What about your stories, you frigging idjid!

Me: All right, all right!

What next?

The actuarial tables give me maybe fifteen years more of life. My doctor says my health is excellent so I might live even longer and enjoy reasonably good health. That may or may not be a good thing and anyway it is in Her hands, not in mine.

I don't know what comes next. I hope that in the years ahead, however many or few they might be, I learn better how to love and how to let others other (Herself included) love me.

Grand Beach
August 1998

---

[153]The other day the pope went over to the Jesuits and told them that the most important virtue was obedience. What, I wonder, gave the pope the right to repeal St. Paul's teaching that the greatest virtue is charity. When we were in the seminary our Jesuit spiritual directors tried to tell us the same thing with, as far as I could see, no more warrant from the example of Jesus or the Scriptures or the tradition of the Church than the pope has today.